David Palumbo-Liu

The Deliverance of Others

Reading Literature in a Global Age

Duke University Press Durham and London 2012

Library of Congress Cataloging-in-Publication Data
Palumbo-Liu, David.
The deliverance of others : reading literature
in a global age / David Palumbo-Liu.
p. cm.
Includes bibliographical references and index.
ISBN 978-0-8223-5250-1 (cloth : alk. paper)
ISBN 978-0-8223-5269-3 (pbk. : alk. paper)
1. Literature and globalization. 2. Other (Philosophy) in
literature. 3. Intercultural communication in literature.
I. Title.
PN56.G55P35 2012
809.'93355—dc23 2012011575

Portions of this book have appeared previously: part
of chapter 1 appeared as "Rationality, Realism and the
Poetics of Otherness: Coetzee's *Elizabeth Costello*," in
Mary Gallagher, ed., *World Writing: Poetics, Ethics and
Globalization* (Toronto: University of Toronto Press,
2008, 190–206); the discussion of Jean-Luc Nancy in
chapter 3 is excerpted from "The Operative Heart: On
Jean-Luc Nancy's *L'intrus*," *New Centennial Review* 2.3 (fall
2002): 87–108; and part of the discussion of Ruth Ozeki's
novel in chapter 4 is taken from "Rational and Irrational:
Narrative in an Age of Globalization," in Françoise
Lionnet and Shu-mei Shih, eds., *Minor Transnationalisms*
(Durham: Duke University Press, 2005, 41–72).

Contents

Preface

Although I am sure she has no recollection of this, the initial idea for this book occurred during a conversation I had with Regenia Gagnier many years ago. At that time, I had the pleasure of having her as a colleague at Stanford. Maybe it was partially because we both had been trained at Berkeley and shared some sense of displacement in Silicon Valley, but for some reason Regenia started talking about rational choice theory. Not only was she speaking about it with regard to her research interests, but she was also commenting on how, after having been what she felt a long time at Stanford, she sensed that this way of accounting for human behavior had become pervasive on campus. Eventually I came to feel that along with rational choice theory came an implicit set of values, which I later dubbed "rational choice thinking." By that I meant the belief that not only could human decision-making be formalized in rational choice's parsimonious and elegant formula, but also that its various manifestations could be widely articulated as "common sense" —"people" act on the basis of common ways of reasoning, and, what is more, they should be treated according to that logic. This kind of thinking undergirds our sense of how we behave toward each other and think about the world. Two incidents, which occurred a decade apart, illustrated this in a particularly dramatic fashion.

The first was Larry Summers's infamous World Bank memo of 1991.[1] During his tenure as chief economist for the World Bank, Summers issued a memo suggesting that there was indeed a problem with pollution —the First World had too much of it, and the Third World too little. He proffered a number of rational-choice type arguments, among them the rationale that since the life expectancy of those living in the Third World was so far below that of those living in the First World, the human cost of breathing toxic fumes and consuming toxic food and water would be much greater in the First World than in the Third. After all, those living in the Third World couldn't expect to live as long as "we" do, so what would be wrong with reducing their lifetimes by a minuscule amount, when, on the other hand, if we ourselves were to breathe in the by-products of our First World lifestyle, it would decrease our lifetimes by a much greater proportion? As Summers puts it,

> "Dirty" Industries: Just between you and me, shouldn't the World Bank be encouraging MORE migration of the dirty industries to the LDCs [Less Developed Countries]? . . . The demand for a clean environment for aesthetic and health reasons is likely to have very high income elasticity. The concern over an agent that causes a one in a million change in the odds of prostrate cancer is obviously going to be much higher in a country where people survive to get prostrate cancer than in a country where under 5 mortality is 200 per thousand. Also, much of the concern over industrial atmosphere discharge is about visibility impairing particulates. These discharges may have very little direct health impact. Clearly trade in goods that embody aesthetic pollution concerns could be welfare enhancing. While production is mobile the consumption of pretty air is a non-tradable.[2]

The response of Jose Lutzenberger, the Brazilian minister of the environment, on reading this leaked memo seems to sum it up well:

> Your reasoning is perfectly logical but totally insane. . . . Your thoughts [provide] a concrete example of the unbelievable alienation, reductionist thinking, social ruthlessness and the arrogant ignorance of many conventional "economists" concerning the nature of the world we live in. . . . If the World Bank keeps you as vice president it will lose all credibility. To me it would confirm what I often said . . . the best thing that could happen would be for the Bank to disappear.[3]

While one might applaud such a sentiment, Lutzenberger appears to offer a contradiction: aren't logic and sanity deeply affiliated? What could be their possible point of separation? Glossing the terms helps untease the "rational" from the sociopathic, the "impeccable" ethics of business based on some utilitarian notion of "the greater good" (particularly construed, of course) from the notion of an ethical system based on some sense of global community and the goal of a more democratic, just, and equal modality of interdependence. What were the respective fates of Summers and Lutzenberger? Lutzenberger was fired after sending his riposte, while Summers became President Bill

Clinton's secretary of the Treasury, then president of Harvard University, and then a chief economic advisor to President Barack Obama.

The second example took place shortly after 9/11: the Pentagon's Defense Advanced Research Projects Agency (DARPA) proposed a "terrorism futures market." As one news article put it,

> It sounds jaw-droppingly callous, not to mention absurd: An Internet gambling parlor, sponsored by the U.S. government, on politics in the Middle East. Anyone, from Osama bin Laden to your grandmother, can bet over the Web on such questions as whether Yasser Arafat will be assassinated or Turkey's government will be overthrown.
>
> If the bettors are right, they'll win money; if they're wrong, they'll lose their wagers. The site itself will keep numerical tallies of the current "odds" for various events.
>
> Why not just ask the guys at the corner bar whether or not we should invade Jordan, or play SimCity to make foreign policy decisions? But experts say the DARPA-backed Policy Analysis Market . . . is based on a legitimate theory, the Efficient Market Hypothesis, that has a proven track record in predicting outcomes. Basically, the idea is that the collective consciousness is smarter than any single person. By forcing people to put their money where their mouth is, the wagers help weed out know-nothings and give more weight to the opinions of those in the know.
>
> "Markets are a great way of aggregating information that a lot of different people have," said Eric Zitzewitz, an assistant professor of economics at the Stanford Graduate School of Business. "One of the big issues with intelligence that was gathered before 9/11 was that information wasn't aggregated within the intelligence community. This is directly aimed at addressing that."[4]
>
> Although the idea sounds offensive to some, "to the extent this has even a small probability of using valuable information to help prevent tragedies, that's got to be the overriding ethical concern," he said.[5]

Nevertheless, what led to the scheme's downfall was not its sheer weirdness, but the fact that it was broadly publicized. Even Fox News commented,

> When the plan was disclosed Monday by Democratic Sens. Ron Wyden of Oregon and Byron Dorgan of North Dakota, the Pentagon defended it as a way to gain intelligence about potential terrorists' plans. Wyden

called it "a federal betting parlor on atrocities and terrorism." Dorgan described it as "unbelievably stupid."

Criticism mounted Tuesday. On the Senate floor, Democratic Leader Thomas Daschle of South Dakota denounced the program as "an incentive actually to commit acts of terrorism." "This is just wrong," declared Daschle, D-S.D. At an Armed Services Committee hearing, Sen. Hillary Rodham Clinton called it "a futures market in death." At the Foreign Relations hearing, [Deputy Defense Secretary Paul] Wolfowitz defended DARPA, saying "it is brilliantly imaginative in places where we want them to be imaginative. It sounds like maybe they got too imaginative," he said, smiling.[6]

While there is much here to comment on, I focus on two aspects that relate to the main concerns of this book. First, there were the rival metrics of the various cost-benefit analyses—moral, ethical, practical, and "aesthetic" (it just *sounded* wrong). *The Deliverance of Others* is intimately concerned with how literary aesthetics in particular help us meditate on the ways we are connected to, and act in relation to, others. Second, there was Wolfowitz's chilling suggestion that the notion of a terrorism futures market was perhaps just a case of too much imagination. Really? Where did DARPA cross the line? And do we really want to harness the imagination of the world in this way?[7] In this volume I tackle the problematic of what drives our imaginations, especially of others, and what limits our imagination, for both good and bad reasons. Indeed, I am interested in how literature helps us think through these judgments.

In these pages I look at the various modes of representing and analyzing how humans behave, make choices, express preferences, achieve goals, and assess their place in the world vis-à-vis their goals. However, *The Deliverance of Others* addresses not only rational choice theory, but also other modes of defining human commonality and interaction—the discourse of the human body and how bodies can interpenetrate in (even) nonsexual ways; the discourse of the emotions and sentiments, and how both are common properties of humans, yet flow between us as well. These questions form the building blocks of my reassessment of the role of contemporary narrative literature in imagining this "togetherness" in and with the other in a critical fashion that I believe should be central to any reading of and any teaching of what we now call "world literature." Let me provide another anecdote—a more generic one.

One of the first rites of being welcomed into a new community is often the cocktail party. I am sure what I am about to relate has happened, for example, to every teacher of literature. You are nibbling on your curried shrimp, swilling your chardonnay, and a nice person comes and asks what you do. You say, "I teach at X." You feel secure—you have a job, it's a good school, people like schools. But you don't feel that way for long. "Oh? What do you teach?" Here I would say, "Comparative literature." My new friend's eyes start scanning for an escape route—where is there a venture capitalist or engineer or, even better, both in the same body? I can see reeling through my soon-to-disappear friend's mind a flashback to the English A.P. exam: "Lord, he's going to ask me what I have been reading, and even worse, to *discuss my thoughts on it!*" OK, I feel the same way when I meet engineers. That's why we have cocktails, and lovely weather to point to here in the Valley.

For twenty-odd years now, I have been trying to see how certain powerful ways of describing how we are bound together have taken hold: we are the same because we all define, rationalize, and reach for our economic preferences and utilities in the same way; we all have a human body; we all have human emotions. These are baseline assumptions, and they help keep us talking to each other. But what has happened now, in this age of increased globalization, when more and more people—closer to us in real and virtual ways than before—need to be vetted on whether or not they are actually the same as us in these ways, precisely? Furthermore, what happens when we try to imagine the genesis and consequences of seeing others through the systems that deliver them to us? And how can the humanities, and literature in particular, aid us in understanding these new sets of problems of "deliverance" in this newly interconnected world?

I admit that the phrase "the deliverance of others" has a strong biblical air and tradition, as it refers to how others can be lead into "the light." While this volume does not emphasize that connotation of the phrase, because of the import of its clear ethical connotations, neither does it disavow it. What happens when we take on the call to embrace others and take responsibility for them? Put more precisely, this book seeks to delve into the shape, nature, and structure of systems that deliver otherness to us—taking people from "different" worlds and importing them into ours—and analyze those systems when even the most benign and seemingly neutral ones of them actually work to filter out "excessive" otherness for the sake of the functioning of the system. The questions then come to be about what "difference" gets siphoned off and where it goes, and, more important, what stays in to change the system, showing its limitations when it comes to actually presenting others to us and creating an *ethical* global community. I look to literature—specifically, modern and contemporary prose narratives—as a unique mode of understanding a world comprised of new peoples, new choices, new data, all seeking to interact in the best way possible. It would be my hope that, at the cocktail party, I would pull out a literary example and show how its treatment of some issue about which my interlocutor surely knows (economics, choice theory, healthcare, biomedicine, advertising, information, media) not only describes how those systems work (or don't), but also how the literary imagination and literary art sees, from a point outside the system, another way of conceiving of those relations between people in those delivery systems. In my most hopeful moments, and if my friend is still there, I would close with some discussion of what this experience has tried to teach us about living together ethically. This is a short book, meant to be almost a kind of primer. I hope you find it useful.

Acknowledgments

I want to express my gratitude to a number of people. I have had the great benefit of talking about the subjects treated in this study, in direct and indirect ways, with many wonderful colleagues and friends. Renato Rosaldo and Mary Pratt welcomed me to Stanford and their cultural studies reading group two decades ago, and I will never forget the intellectual buzz, the comradely good humor, and the sense of doing something important in the curriculum and in our writing that kept their house aglow. It was in that context that I first met Regenia Gagnier, to whom I owe the kernel of inspiration for this book. I also want to thank two people who, along with their intellectual brilliance, exemplify for me the warmth, humor, and humaneness one would want to aspire to: Linda Hutcheon and Roland Greene. I also want to thank Heather Houser, whose work in a graduate seminar and in the fine dissertation that followed opened my eyes to so much, and whose work is now doing the same for all its readers. Gayatri Chakravorty Spivak has been a core inspiration for many years, and nothing has delighted me more than now working with her in various venues. Her notion of literature's "unverifiability" has always stayed with me, along with the need to actually read, and read, and read, and to think first, before anything else, ethically.

Lastly, there are some people without whom in all honesty this book really would not have been written. I thank Karen Kuo for patiently working out so many issues and sharing so much with me. Ruth Ozeki was kind enough not only to share her films and fiction with me, but also, over the course of a term here at Stanford, to discuss at length and with humor and insight her creative process. I owe a huge debt to Shumei Shih, Rob Wilson, Wai Chee Dimock, Bruce Robbins, Nirvana Tanoukhi, and Françoise Lionnet for their wonderful and inspiring enthusiasm, support, and friendship in many venues and encounters—much of what you find in these pages is in fact as much their thinking as mine. Each of these people has immensely broadened my sense of literature, helped me make my ideas as clear and compelling as possible, and lifted my spirits when I really wondered what in the world I thought I was doing. Finally, I owe a debt to Ken Wissoker, of Duke University Press, whose enthusiasm for and appreciation of the idea for this book did much to make it more than just an idea. I was also fortunate in the two press readers that Ken enlisted—their engaged, serious, and rigorous comments helped immeasurably in guiding revision of the manuscript.

As always, my greatest debt is to my wife, Sylvie, and to our son, Fabrice. Sylvie, with her deep love of the intellect and especially of literature, showed me, in conversation and action over these decades, how life and art are not separate, and that strolling down any avenue or oceanside can animate conversation about what, for instance, we had debated at a recent graduate seminar, or lectured about in class, or tried to prove to our son, and how what we experience in life can enhance our understanding of the lessons we try to teach our students (and ourselves) as we pick up a work of literature and open a page. My one wish is that the world becomes more aware of this truth about life and art, and ethics and pleasure, for our son's tremendous talent, creativity, and love of the arts deserves a home, too.

Introduction

One of the chief aims of this study is to help us arrive at a sense of responsibility toward others by learning to read contemporary literature in a way that includes a critical reappraisal of systems and discourses of "sameness" that deliver others to us. Specifically, I look to ideas of rationality, of the family, of the body, and of affect—each of these notions holds within it some sign of human commonality and communicability, or "deliverance." I show how these discursive "delivery systems" imply commensurate relations between selves and others, and yet how these relatively simple systems become less and less stable as they interact with, and try to accommodate, a more radical type of otherness produced in contemporary historical contexts. Each of the novels treated in this book rigorously tests the faith these systems place in commonality and commensurateness; each text offers a vivid and often troubling view of the disruption of such a belief in our contemporary age. Nonetheless, there is in each of these novels also a redemptive moment that, while certainly not unproblematic, gives a different view of each "delivery system," and this vision resides precisely in the deliverance available through the literary aesthetic. However, and critically, I update the idea of the aesthetic to include the specific problems literary aesthetics face in this age of increased "otherness" and virtual proximity.

I begin, in this introduction, by showing how the notion of empathy has defined the relation between self and other in rhetorical, social-philosophical, and finally literary discourses. The first two of these argue that similarity and identification are necessary between orator and listener, or between social actors. I juxtapose this to modern literature's valorization of difference—the aim of literature is precisely to deliver to us "others" with lives unlike our own. This makes literature qualitatively different in aim and scope. However, this also presents a historical problem today. The notion that literature should mobilize (or even instantiate) empathy for others and enhance our ethical capabilities is rooted in the early modern period, wherein "otherness," while certainly increasingly present, was not nearly as immediately, insistently, and intensely pressing itself into the here and now of everyday social, cultural, and political life. This voluminous influx, quantitatively and qualitatively new, is a distinct feature of the late-twentieth- and early-twenty-first-century age of globalization. We now have to deal with this question: if we still adhere to the modern valorization of literature as bringing the lives of others to us in a vivid way, once we admit "others" into "our" world and place value in the difference they bring into our lives, where do we set the limit of *how much* otherness is required, as opposed to how much is excessive, disruptive, disturbing, in ways that damage us, rather than enhance our lives? This forces us into taking an ethical position, and calls on us to address another kind of "selfishness": we take so much and then leave the rest, but at what cost? How have we learned anything more about "us" and the situation in which we find ourselves? Contemporary literary narratives generate worlds in which we must puzzle out these questions in particular manners.

Previously, people were thought to be able to identify with each other according to the fact they could "feel" as if they too could be in "the situation" of the other depicted in the orator's speech, in the social imaginary, or the narrator's text. In the present study I update that understanding. Aren't we all living in the same global "situation"? Don't we all perform rationally as economic subjects in the global economy that transfers goods, materials, bodies, images to all of us across real time and huge distances? Don't we now all ingest materials that we find from the same sources, transported laterally across the world without absolute regard to borders? Not only food, but also drugs and medical practices have become nearly universal. In the most intense form of sharing human experience, organ transplants disclose the new commonness, as elements from one body can be inserted into another. And haven't global media fed on and produced similar human affect? Don't people share a common register and repertoire in the realm of feelings, feelings that are touched and produced by worldwide representations of contemporary lives? Finally, hasn't the political world incorporated all sorts of previously disenfranchised people? "Our" situation now cannot so easily bracket off more distant parts of the planet or deny the participation of those close to us, even though separated by race, gender, sexual preference, religion.

Globalization has delivered to us far more distant spaces and peoples than ever before, with greater regularity and integration on multiple fronts—economic, political, social, cultural, ecological, epidemiological, and so on. "Otherness" is thus not only increasingly in contact with the "same," but the points of contact and contagion with otherness are far more numerous. Therefore, the degree to which we are the same as or different from others is discernible only in very specific manners that demand to be carefully and critically scrutinized. I am thus interested in otherness as both a "thing," manifested in various forms, and as a relation.

Essentially, the problems of otherness press up against the mainstays of Western liberal thought. The primacy of the individual, the safeguarding of her prerogatives to act freely in the world so as to manifest in the fullest way possible her distinctive humanity, is negotiated against the recognition of our being together as social creatures. The problematics of otherness, as taken up in the course of this study, are therefore played out in the realms of rationality and choice-making, the integrity of the body, the freedom to feel. And yet "sameness" (and "equality"), though declared, is not guaranteed, and calling attention not only to inequality, but also to its sources, is as old as liberalism. However, events of the postwar era set the stage for ever more potent insistence on "otherness," which paralleled the emergence of new structures that drew people together.

The seeds of enfranchisement sown in the eighteenth century were more fully manifested in the postwar era of decolonization and eventually in the anti-apartheid era, bringing forth widespread tension over the distribution of wealth and resources not only in terms of the "Third World," but also according to the different mappings of hemispheres and peripheries. Widespread liberatory movements called up issues of race, gender, and sexuality. One example of the crisis of expanding and disruptive otherness was evident in the seventies, as described in a report by the Trilateral Commission, *The Crisis of Democracy: Report on the Governability of Democracies to the Trilateral Commission* (1975). In it, Samuel Huntington remarks, "The essence of the democratic surge of the 1960s was a general challenge to existing systems of authority, public and private. In one form or another, the challenge manifested itself in the family, the university, business, public and private institutions, politics, the government bureaucracy, and the military service. People no longer felt the same obligation to obey those whom they had previously considered superior to themselves in age, rank, status, expertise, character, or talents. . . . Each group claimed its right to participate equally—in the decision which affected itself."[1] In short, while lauding the active participation of an increasing number of diverse populations on the one hand, Huntington is concerned that there may be *too much* of a good thing (or, in the language of this volume, too much otherness): "The vitality of democracy in the 1960s raised questions about the governability of democracy in the 1970s."[2] This increase in political participation is "primarily the result of the increased salience which citizens perceive politics to have for their own immediate concerns."[3]

So what's wrong with that? Isn't this precisely the picture of a robust democratic society? Not exactly, for this vigor is largely made up of minority voices and viewpoints demanding attention to their particular needs, and acted on the basis of other kinds of rationality. This puts pressure on the political institutions of the state: "In the United States, the strength of democracy poses a problem for the governability of democracy. . . . We have come to recognize that there are potentially desirable limits to the indefinite extension of political democracy. Democracy will have a longer life if it has a more balanced existence."[4] This ominous phrase is indeed Huntington's concluding statement, and is emblematic of the kind of swelling up of anti-authoritarian "otherness" that shows the tipping point of liberalism that occurred not only in the United States, but globally. Where were those limits to be drawn? How was "balance" going to be achieved? Liberal values, seen both in the ethos of modern literature's role in diversifying our frames of reference and in liberal democratic rule, become challenged by others who insist on entering the system as full participants, with their otherness fully intact. Hence the crisis of governability. This hugely revealing statement from the mid-seventies signals the historical instantiation of a problematic of otherness that spreads into other realms as well, and has only intensified as new technologies have created both the promise of new kinds of commonality and new ethical dilemmas. In today's world, the hierarchical recognition of some rationalities as existing below the threshold of the rational, of some bodies as harvestable and commodifiable, and of some affects as dangerous to the psychic and somatic health of the self occur precisely within global delivery systems that owe their existence to contemporary politics and technologies.

Today we find new political economies of organs, tissues, genetic materials that build on and indeed reinforce preexisting structures of inequality, affluence, need. The value placed on "the body" is now negotiated in ways once unheard of; now what is up for sale is not only a cadaver, but parts of living beings. The very psychic equilibrium of the "self" is put into greater and greater affect of contact, virtually and in face-to-face encounters with others who now appear on our everyday communications apparatuses. The sale and transfer of goods and commodities is premised on continually produced affect in a global market. Given these imperatives, which are facilitated by the logic of neoliberalism, how do we regulate the influx of otherness so as not to destabilize the system? How much of this goes beyond the pale of what liberal ideology, so protective of the self, can allow? How much variance in the exercise of rational acts can we tolerate? How do we both facilitate the transfer and mobilization of bodies and body parts across borders (to satisfy our needs for labor and bodily rejuvenation, even survival), and create walls and barriers to stop autonomous flows of bodies across borders? How do we hope to tap into an "oceanic feeling," so as to instantiate need and desire for the products we wish to sell, yet stem the influx of affect that emanates from disruptive others and circulates back to us?

This study shows how contemporary literary texts register this new historical "situation" differently and asks us to reexamine more closely the grounds for those claims of commonness and to see the still vital resistance of otherness to it. Not only do the texts I have selected for this study vividly illustrate the precise ways that globalization today differs from that of the past, but reading them in the ways I undertake to do helps us to critically reflect on how we negotiate this new being with otherness.

That others occupy the "system" differently is not hard to recognize. Despite the celebratory gestures of "globalization," this occupation discloses the fissures and residual differences that remain beneath the surface of systems of sameness. Literary aesthetics today thus involve a recombinatory poetics that would not have been possible without the friction, resistance, autonomy that otherness still insinuates into the "same." In this study I show how the selected novels each reveal the effort to deliver others to us within the contingencies of our historical condition. I start by examining closely how "sameness" has been a linchpin in social thought, variously evident in rhetorical treatises and social philosophical writings, and then consider the premium modern literature has placed on "difference." I then move to a discussion of the relation between the notion of "situation" that englobes self and other in classical rhetoric and in Adam Smith's social philosophy, and adapt that notion to my idea of contemporary "delivery systems."

The Sameness Requirement

"Stepping into the other guy's shoes works best when you resemble him.... If you are structurally analogous to the empathee, then accurate inputs generate accurate outputs—The greater the isomorphism, the more dependable and precise the results." Or so says Ray Sorensen, writing on what he calls "Self-Strengthening Empathy" in the journal *Philosophy and Phenomenological Research*. Thank goodness, then, that Sorensen believes "Mother Nature has made your mind isomorphic to mine," because this isomorphism aids in the perpetuation of the species.[5] To put it another way: we empathize, therefore we survive. The pragmatic aspect of empathy has not been lost to thinkers from the classical age on. Empathy—feeling the pain or joy or fear experienced by others—is *useful*, whether it be to convince one's audience of the rightness of one's position, or as a key element in fostering moral sentiment and social equilibrium, or, indeed, in propagating human kind.

In *The Rhetoric* we find Aristotle claiming that effective acts of rhetoric rely on the listener feeling that he could find himself in the very situation being described in the speech of the orator. Chapters 1 through 10 of the Second Book of *The Rhetoric* are devoted to discussing the emotions and the way they may be enlisted in rhetorical argumentation. The eighth chapter takes as its subject Pity, and Aristotle's discussion seems to touch on familiar ground: "We pity those who are like us in age, character, disposition, social standing, or birth; for in all these cases it appears more likely that the same misfortune might befall us also" (114). Self-interest and indeed self-empathy is not slightly a part of this receptivity.

In their discussion of *The Rhetoric*, William K. Wimsatt and Cleanth

Brooks raise three useful points. First, they say, one should regard the text as "an approach to knowledge."[6] I will argue that a large part of this knowledge is eminently social; Aristotle's meditation on language and discourse has everything to do with how members of a social group present themselves—their ideas, desires, needs, fears—to others, and how that presentation can be best effected. This notion is supported by another claim Wimsatt and Brooks make, that *The Rhetoric* can be regarded as an offshoot of dialectic and also of ethical studies.[7] In that respect the logic attending *The Rhetoric* is embedded in both dialectical thinking—reasoning out the exchanges of assertions and responses—and a consideration of the ethical and moral bases and implications of taking certain positions vis-à-vis the orator's discourse. Finally, Wimsatt and Brooks point out that *The Rhetoric* "presents alternatives, things that might have been."[8] In that sense the epistemological and ethical realms are enriched by a set of data that exceeds the empirical. So we might raise the question anew—the imagination of "things that might have been" seems in *The Rhetoric* tightly bonded to a realist logic—as to whether "things that might be" are contained within the scope of experiences we might plausibly imagine happening to us. Simply put, if we cannot "relate" to it, the situation the speaker puts before us falls flat. We might well react to it, but Aristotle says that our response and our receptivity will be less than if it were something we could imagine happening to us. Now what kind of moral does that teach, what kind of *action* can take place, given this new requirement for identification?

Aristotle's basic premise regarding rhetorical effect and the emotions in the classical age—that we feel most strongly about and are most receptive to the stories or topoi that we could imagine inhabiting—is found as well in Adam Smith's *Theory of Moral Sentiments*. Indeed, Smith's text likewise connects this topic to the issue of social exchange and norms—feeling "the same" is a powerful force in social interaction. And Smith also turns his attention to the imagination and the kinds of imaginings made possible solely by feeling that one could be affected in similar ways that others are. Critically, in the course of his disquisition, the "original" situation that prompts our identification with the sufferer recedes into the background as our imaginations latch onto that event in order to launch a separate set of sensations in our own bodies. We can never actually feel the pain of others, but we can *imagine* what it *must* feel like. Smith even goes so far as to say that since we can never empirically verify what the other is feeling, it really doesn't matter what he or she feels. We dwell instead in our own imagined sense of what we, in the situation of the other, would feel. Indeed, in the following passage, "we" are channeled into the imagined body of the other person.

> As we have no immediate experience of what other men feel, we can form no idea of the manner in which they are affected, but by conceiving what we ourselves should feel in the like situation. Though our brother is upon the rack, as long as we ourselves are at our ease, our senses will never inform us of what he suffers. They never did, and never can, carry us beyond our own person, and it is by the imagination only that we can form any conception of what are his sensations. Neither can that faculty help us to this any other way, than by representing to us what would be our own, if we were in his case. It is the impressions of our own senses only, not those of his, which our imaginations copy. By the imagination we place ourselves in his situation, we conceive ourselves enduring all the same torments, we enter as it were into his body, and become in some measure the same person with him, and thence form some idea of his sensations, and even feel something which, though weaker in degree, is not altogether unlike them. His agonies, when they are thus brought home to ourselves, when we have adopted and made them our own, begin at last to affect us, and we then tremble and shudder at the thought of what he feels.[9]

One notes how this passage ends in sketching out the grey areas of this merging of self and other. This points to a key element in the problematic examined in this study and which achieves full force in this concise statement from Smith's text: "Sympathy, therefore, does not arise so much from the view of the passion, as from that of the situation which excites it. We sometimes feel for another; because, when we put ourselves in his case, that passion arises in our breast from the imagination, though it does not in his from the reality."[10] We cannot be the other, but we can try to imagine what her or his situation would make *us* feel like. However, we then need to ask, on what basis do we assume to be able to feel anything like they are feeling? What norms, assumptions, presumptions, what notions of mimesis, what norms of "human behavior" do we intuitively draw on to make sense of our bold statement that "we feel your pain"? Let me be clear—I am not suggesting that we should or that we even could avoid such attempts at sympathy and empathy. My point, rather, is to examine closely the ethical and political nature of those acts of empathy, and conversely, those moments when we assume we cannot "relate."

These concerns are evident as well (though not expressed in that fashion) in the social pragmatic of Smith's treatise, which is made clear in the title of section 1: "Of the Sense of Propriety." The key use to which these insights into sympathy are put is not unlike the one found in *The Rhetoric*: emotions, intersubjective feeling, identification are all considered in light of what kinds of social norms need to be maintained among individual emotions. Smith describes in detail how individual emotions are to be contained and disciplined by social norms—without this moderation, emotions can run amok in their excessive difference. And it is precisely through a complex process of imagining what *others* might think of *our* emotions that social emotional norms are installed in individuals. The following passage from *The Theory of Moral Sentiments* reminds us not a little of Sartre's notion of the "gaze": it is not that we actually believe someone is looking at us and hence we adjust our behavior, but rather that as social beings we have internalized the gaze of others and act *as if* someone were always watching us, as through a keyhole. Smith's subject finds himself watching himself and "abating" the power of his emotions, abashedly, under the gaze of others.

> As they are constantly considering what they themselves would feel, if they actually were the sufferers, so he is constantly led to imagine in what manner he would be affected if he was only one of the spectators of his own situation. As their sympathy makes them look at it in some measure with his eyes, so his sympathy makes him look at it, in some measure, with theirs, especially when in their presence, and acting under their observation: and, as the reflected passion which he thus conceives is much weaker than the original one, it necessarily abates the violence of what he felt before he came into their presence, before he began to recollect in what manner they would be affected by it, and to view his situation in this candid and impartial light.[11]

All this is to enable the individual to ascertain the correct level at which to express his emotions. As with Aristotle, this has a pragmatic purpose—too much or too little will result in the individual not gaining the empathy of his audience: "He can only hope to obtain this by lowering his passion to that pitch, in which the spectators are capable of going along with him. He must flatten, if I may be allowed to say so, the sharpness of its natural tone, in order to reduce it to harmony and concord with the emotions of those who are about him."[12]

Smith expresses the desired outcome of all this as being therapeutic for the individual, emanating from a Freudian super-ego: "Society and conversation, therefore, are the most powerful remedies for restoring the mind to its tranquility."[13] And yet the barely concealed complement to this curative imagined negotiation is also social tranquility. Individual emotions circulate dynamically and also smoothly; encounters, real or imagined, with an other's pain, suffering, joy, happiness are, after an initial expansion, ultimately contracted, drawn back into the "proper" register. In the terms of this book, we find here a "delivery system": a social discourse—that set of conventions for both communication and behavior—creates and maintains norms that convert otherness to sameness. Extreme behavior on the part of the individual is tamped down and readjusted to the system of behaviors and emotional expression proper to society.

The Difference Requirement

The valuing of sameness in Aristotle and Smith contrasts sharply with literature's privileging of difference, which gives the literary work of art an opposite role to play. Rather than holding to the values of rhetoric, which relies on sameness to realize its persuasive force, or those of Smith's moral sentiments, which rely on sameness to understand and facilitate practical moral action, or even those of Sorenson's "preservation of the species" theory, in which sameness is required for the empathy that will continue, precisely, "us," literature is supposed to deliver us out of our "comfort zone." Literature has another purpose—to become something else, something better: "The sole advantage in possessing great works of literature lies in what they can help us become."[14]

The tradition of regarding literature as a particularly powerful vehicle for conveying a sense of another's life, and of believing that being put in touch with that dissimilar life is important for one's moral growth, is well established and specifically attached to realist narrative. One of the most famous statements on the matter comes from George Eliot's review essay on *The Natural History of German Life* (1895).

The greatest benefit we owe to the artist, whether painter, poet, or novelist, is the extension of our sympathies. Appeals founded upon generalizations and statistics require a sympathy ready-made, a moral sentiment already in activity; but a picture of human life such as a great artist can give, surprises even the trivial and the selfish into that attention to what is apart from themselves, which may be called the nearest thing to life; it is a mode of amplifying experience and extending our contact with our fellow-men beyond the bounds of our personal lot.[15]

What is noteworthy here is the manner in which Eliot uses this distinction in tandem with another distinction, this time between two different kinds of sympathy. Generalizations and statistics seem to belong to the conventional, learned forms of moral sentiment—they produce predictable results.[16] Indeed, one almost gets the sense that they tap into a universal affective register: when presented with this or that statistic, one will likely react in this or that fashion, manifesting an already existing and eminently shared feeling. This is not so far from what we find in *Theory of Moral Sentiments*, where Smith very plainly states the need to "abate" excessive and potentially damaging emotional expression in order to adjust one's emotional register to the social norm. However, the picture shifts with Eliot's discussion of "great" art.

In the case of great art, there is nothing ready-made, already existing, part of a sentimental consensus, so to speak. Instead, we are presented with something outside ourselves and outside our conventional behavior. This is a potent force, affecting "even the trivial," even "the selfish." What are we presented with in great art, and why is this good? What we obtain through reading is a life not like our own and a life specifically beyond "our lot." Not only does it not seem like what we have experienced, it also comes from experiences that are not likely ever to be ours at all. And that is the point of great art—it stirs in us a sense of difference, and this difference, if delivered well, in turn prompts us to reach beyond the ordinary sphere of our proper existence. This transcendence leads to a deeper and broader sort of empathy. And at that moment, we "become" something different, something inflected with otherness.

One of the most notable contemporary proponents of this view is of course Martha Nussbaum, who writes, "Literary works typically invite their readers to put themselves in the place of people of many different kinds."[17] Literature can help us appreciate "what is it like to live the life of another person who might, given changes in circumstance, be one-self."[18] While there is an unmistakable liberal tone to all this—literature puts us in touch with a wider range of experience, which causes us to be more tolerant because we now understand the lives of others as being imaginable as ours—there is also and no less a sense of acquisition and agglomeration. We are getting *more* out of this encounter.

Indeed, these sentiments reach a crescendo in a passage from Wayne Booth that sounds like nothing so much as the Twenty-third Psalm.

> To dwell with you is to share the improvements you have managed to make in your "self" by perfecting your narrative world. You lead me first to practice ways of living that are more profound, more sensitive, more intense, and in a curious way more fully generous than I am likely to meet anywhere else in the world. You correct my faults, rebuke my insensitivities. You mold me into patterns of longing and fulfillment that make my ordinary dreams seem petty and absurd.[19]

In each of these pronouncements we are led to the same conclusion—great works of literature deliver difference, otherness, that which is nonsimilar to us, all with the effect of making us better, richer, more moral, more tolerant, more sensitive to the world and the lives it contains. Critically, there seems to be a convergence of two different sorts of otherness: literature presents the worlds of others to us, leading us to inhabit those worlds and live those lives; concomitantly, the representation of this otherness is itself of a nature entirely different from the world of experience, and while it brings us closer to others, it cannot or does not reach complete deliverance, so to speak. It stands alongside, or apart from, life. As Eliot puts it, it is "the nearest thing to life." In that sense, literature itself is otherness.

The Problem of Otherness

Even the most ardent proponents of the school that would have us read the lives of others radically different from ourselves are confronted by an essential problem: how much otherness is required? How much confounds us, rather than enriches us? How "different" can their "lot" be from ours before it recedes into unintelligibility? We become caught in a oscillating movement, identifying and de-identifying, weighing what we can, and cannot, learn from. The encounter provided by literary texts involves both sameness and difference in an unpredictable relation. We cannot know in advance what this "other" actually is, or the circumstances in which they find themselves. Both similarity and difference may be deceptive, and in the working out of this ratio, we extend generosity, empathy, pity, but also perhaps distain, even contempt. This is not only, as Nussbaum says, "the political promise" of literature, but also the political *problematic* of literature. When she says, "It is the political promise of literature that it can transport us while remaining ourselves, into the life of another, revealing similarities but also profound differences between the life and thought of that other and myself and making them comprehensible or at least more nearly comprehensible," the question I want to ask is, *how* are "they" comprehensible?[20] If so, how so? How much? These are precisely political problems, and they just grow larger when we take it to the next level—that of the effect that this literary encounter is supposed to have on how we sense ourselves anew in the world and how we act given this new sensibility.

The adjudication of how much otherness we need to encounter and grapple with in order to be better people and how much will prove to be our undoing is, again, both a logistical one and a political problem. Booth himself finds a tension between otherness of a degree sufficient to present the occasion for learning, growth, and revaluing the world, and *too much* otherness. On the one hand, he openly acknowledges that "surely no beast [that] will prove genuinely *other* will fail to bite, and the otherness that bites, the otherness that changes us, must have sufficient definition, sufficient identity, to threaten us where we live."[21] Yet, on the other hand, that threat has to be tamed. Four hundred pages later in his stunning book, Booth admits, "I have had to play both sides of this street throughout these chapters: we must both open ourselves to 'others' that look initially dangerous or worthless, and yet prepare ourselves to cast them off whenever, after keeping company with them, we conclude that they are potentially harmful."[22] Indeed, as Booth says, we are playing both sides—of similarity of "situation" and lives beyond our lot. The line between the requirements of, on the one hand, similarity (rhetoric and Smith's social theory) and, on the other hand, difference (modern literature) is not at all as clear as I have initially drawn it, for literature, it seems, demands both identification and difference at once. We find a vacillating dynamic between empathy and critique, sameness and difference, that creates in the texts I examine a particular image of what it is to live with others in the contemporary world.

Let me sum up what we've learned thus far and then offer another possibility. First, there is the notion that we read to open ourselves to experiences that are not ours and will most likely never be ours, but by acknowledging that otherness as otherness, we both see its difference from us and are thereby enriched, and we also appreciate the complexity of the world. Second, there is the belief that we also may be presented with an otherness that, as true and formidable otherness, knocks us off our feet, sweeps away what Ricoeur calls "the stability of the same," and leaves us on the canvas. How to know when to keep reading and when to close the book? The literary text will not tell us. It is itself of another world and is not constrained to make sense in the ways we are used to expecting of communicative objects. So why read?

Perhaps the search to find the "right" or necessary balance for the encounter with otherness, along with the related issue of transparency of meaning ("Once I have established the necessary and tolerable balance point of sameness/otherness, how do I know that I am actually under-standing what is going on?"), is indeed an abysmal task and a question impossible to resolve. How does one codify and set conventions for encounters with others? What protocols can anticipate every kind of meeting between such vaguely defined entities as "same" and "other"? I suggest that rather than focusing entirely on meaning-making, and whether we get it or not, we should think of how literature engenders a space for imagining *our relation to others* and thinking through why and how that relation exists, historically, politically, ideologically. This in turn creates *new forms of narration and representation*, which I will put forward in analyses of four novels. Reading with this in mind would attempt to ascertain how and why our relationship to others is not natural or immutable, but rather the result of a number of complex and often contradictory forces, some that draw us closer, others that drive us apart. Notions of radical alterity are herein considered just as tentative as notions of universalism and unproblematic commonality. Ethically and politically we can imagine—indeed, we must imagine—that the les-sening of otherness can be and is often not only desirable but also necessary—in fact, it happens all the time (and is often called coalition politics, or politics in general)—and that encountering difficult things can be crippling, again, not only spiritually but politically as well.

Put concisely, there is no way to say in advance what the proper response to alterity should be or what would be the grounds on which to judge the proper or complete deciphering of meaning. Rather, it is important to turn our attention to the purchase we make in the names of sameness, otherness, commonality, radical incommensurability, and so on. This gesture might well be called deconstructive. And it is in a careful attention to a newly invented, contemporary literary form that such imaginings and meditations are made possible, as the literary text, in refusing or at least deferring meaning, gives us pause to see more precisely our relationship to others—what enables or disables certain modes of connection and meaning-making. We should better attend to the historicity and contingency of social and collective identities as precisely intersections of both proximate and distant identities. The task is not only to measure the distance, but also to try to account for it. Literature, and more specifically *reading* literature, helps us fess up to our standards of measurement, our yardsticks, because the text takes us outside our usual habitations of meaning, sense-making, self-assurance. In this process, the way literature comes to be written in different, difficult ways shows its elastic powers, but also its breaking points. Sometimes the system is overwhelmed by the task of delivering too much otherness, of reconciling radically disparate actions that cannot be made into sense. We then are forced to ask why and how we set those limits.

For example, I regularly teach a course titled "Comparative Fictions of Ethnicity," in which we read a number of different narratives, many autobiographical; we discuss how the authors articulate the idea of ethnic identity. We consider things like the difference genre makes when we read John Wideman's *Brothers and Keepers*, which vacillates between the voice of the award-winning novelist John and his attempts to represent the voice of his convict brother, Robby, who is serving a life sentence for murder. We talk about how this attempt to convey otherness challenges the author to both convey it and let it remain a place of incommensurable difference. Having the class accept that doubleness was hard enough. But then we turned to read an autobiography titled *Restavec*, by a Haitian man named Jean-Robert Cadet. Cadet was born the bastard child of a Haitian prostitute and one of her white French clients. The narrative is harrowing, dwelling in poverty and disgrace and loathing and illiteracy. It is crudely written, and while we might sympathize with the author, a real experiential distance is insisted on, making identification impossible. He comes to the United States, but no immigrant narrative of self-improvement takes place. After he enlists, he finds comradeship among African American servicemen, but he informs on them after they start smoking dope. How is this an admirable character? Many in the class simply hated the novel, despite all my attempts to get them to suspend their assumptions about what made a good piece of writing.

I could have insisted that the students read the story closely, and I did, but the usual way of reading for content left them unenthused. A different world was depicted in *Restavec*, and they didn't like it, and they were glad Cadet's lot was not theirs. I changed tack, asking them to consider what this dissonance could tell us about our relationship to otherness, to consider how that relationship was not inevitable, to consider what assumptions about narrative, about value, about ethics, about what a family is, about what an immigrant narrative was were overturned, or at least stymied, by Cadet's book, by both its form and content.

Yet the questions raised by this particular classroom experience—which, I think one has to admit, are often ours as well as we encounter particularly "difficult" texts—force us to revisit Aristotle, Smith, and others who place such emphasis on the notion that the *situation* of the character, speaker, audience, reader, and so on is the determining factor of the degree of empathy available and the launching point of the imagination as well, that is, that we must be able to imagine being in another's situation, and that imagining itself will then spur our imaginations in new directions. And literature ups the ante. In it, we are no longer seeking only common ground—situations we, too, might find ourselves in—but now also situations beyond our individual lots. This, again, is the oscillating dynamic engendered and problematized by literature. Furthermore, the degree to which these "situations" are similar or not is hard to discern these days, precisely because "globalization" seems to have "flattened" things out such that significant (in the minds of Friedman and his disciples) markers of difference no longer remain. More important, perhaps, the "situations" others find themselves in are often regarded by inhabitants of the First World, northern hemispheric regions as either indecipherable or negligible, that is to say, they are either beyond our ken, too saturated with difference, or that difference is not insurmountable under the logic of what I am calling our contemporary "delivery systems." These systems either finally relinquish the notion of commonality and consider these particularly obdurate others to be unassimilable to our logic and reason, or they winnow out difference and bring the other to us in some now recognizable form. My focus thus shifts from the enrichment literature is supposed to bring into our lives by presenting us with the lives of others, and the supposedly enhanced empathetic powers it gives us, to the grounds on which we strike that encounter—how are such terms as *same* and *different* secured?

Both Aristotle and Smith, in their respective domains, consider situations to be critical for self-other identifications, but both are vague as to what would qualify as a situation. Does it simply refer to a plot element, like the loss of a parent or a perceived injustice? If so, how much detail has to be omitted for the situation to be general enough to solicit identification? In the next section I connect this problem to the ways in which contemporary thinkers have revisited Smith and deployed the imagination as the faculty by which to see in another's life a "situation" that one might find oneself in, but in these cases that act of imagination is anchored in global material history, ethical action, and political practice. In the same spirit I examine closely the dynamic between the self and "others" (both in terms of characters and "other" situations) as read against and delivered through ready-made, already existing codified structures, discourses, and institutions. More specifically, I am interested in the ways certain assumptions about "all people" are embedded and manifested in institutional practices, and, critically, how literary narratives both comment on these assumptions and present variants, countermodels, critiques that thereby challenge "global" conceptualizations of "we humans." This has, of course, a powerful effect on how we perceive others and act toward and with them.

Rethinking "Situation," Delivering across Structures

Richard Sennett's study of respect, *Respect in a World of Inequality*, draws on the sociological work of C. Wright Mills and Hans Gerth in an important manner. Specifically, he notes how their idea of "character" is based on "a person's communication with others through shared 'social instruments'—laws, rituals, the media, codes of religious beliefs, political doctrines."[23] For Mills and Gerth, character "is a capacity to engage the larger world which defines a person's character; character can be thought of as the relational side of personality, and transcends the dictum that only face-to-face relations are emotionally gripping."[24] We might thus trace the formation of *literary* "characters" as developing from the mobilization and instrumentalization of these and other discourses and belief systems, not only as they interact with these structures and systems as individuals, but also as they interact with distant others in non-face-to-face encounters and imaginings, having these structures and discursive systems as mediating forms. We can thus have a clearer sense of not only how but also why others differ from us, or not, and when, precisely, we are to award "respect."

This question is especially difficult, and important, when it comes to globalization. Luc Boltanski's study of "distant others" makes this especially clear. He declares that in today's world "distance is a fundamental dimension of politics which has the specific task of a unification which overcomes dispersion."[25] This "dispersion" is precisely the disunified world, the nonequivalent material histories of those unlike (to one degree or another) ourselves. Politics must bring together particular (and particularly different) situations, conveying them across a distance. And yet while Boltanski is emphatic about the need for an "imaginary demonstration" of unfortunates, he is scrupulously wary of this process. He notes two contradictory requirements: "On the one hand there is a requirement of impartiality, detachment (no prior commitment) and a distinction between the moment of observation, that is to say, of knowledge, and the moment of action. This requirement points towards the possibility of generalisation. On the other hand there is a requirement of affective, sentimental or emotional investment which is needed to arouse political commitment."[26] In other words, the lives and situations of others have to be regarded impartially, lest the prejudices, desires, blind spots of the observer skew her reading and assessment and actions one way or the other. But at the same time, regarding the other at such a distance might well obviate any affect, affect that would be necessary to compel the observer to act. We need both—but how can we arrive at a noncontradictory formula? Once again we find the fluctuation between identification and disidentification.

In order to get out of this quandary, Boltanski marshals forward two concepts. The first is "aperspectival objectivity":

The relevance of the demand for public speech is due to the existence of a public sphere which is progressively constituted along with the conception of a politics of pity such that it is sometimes difficult to separate historically the two analytically distinct processes. The constitution of a public sphere and a definition of political legitimacy based on a conception of objectivity that emphasizes the possibility of an observation without any particular perspective are strictly interdependent. We know today that, among other possible conceptions of objectivity, this conception [aperspectival objectivity] which is often associated with the development of the sciences, and of the experimental sciences in particular, actually originates in the political and moral philosophy of the eighteenth century—from where science will take it fifty years later— and especially in Adam Smith's attempt to reconstruct morality, together with the foundations of a morally acceptable politics, around the double figure of an unfortunate and an impartial spectator who observes him from a distance. Thus we turn now to an examination of the relationship between public sphere, spectacle, and aperspectival objectivity. We will then take up again the position of the spectator and endeavour to understand how we might reduce the tension between the demand for public speech and the prohibition of a description without perspective.[27]

What Boltanski is seeking is a way to affect and leave open the possibility for public speech, a source of authorizing such an activity even as the constraint of objectivity remains. But if we are talking about "aperspectival" objectivity, then from where does the voice make its utterance, and, concomitantly, what kind of space is imagined in which that voice is heard? Boltanski remains within this spatial metaphor (of location, direction, perspective) to articulate his response to those contradictory demands.

Coupled with aperspectival objectivity we find something different, something deeply rooted to the subjective and now seen to enable an ethical intersubjectivity—it is the imagination, but the imagination tethered in a particular way.

> The obstacle this distance creates can be overcome by means of a faculty however: the imagination. In the original situation the spectator is not involved in the scene of suffering he observes. Like the spectator affected by the sentiment of the sublime in the account given by Burke . . . , he is sheltered and fears nothing for himself. It is by incor-

porating distance that the possibility of aesthetic sentiments and moral sentiments (still partially mixed up with each other in Hutcheson) must be understood. In Smith, as in Hume, distance is overcome by a deliberate act of imagination. The spectator represents to himself the sentiments and sensations of the suffering. He does not identify with him and does not imagine himself to be in the same situation. As Smith remarks in the chapter of *The Theory of Moral Sentiments* in which he criticizes Hobbes and Mandeville, the spectator imagines what the woman in child-bed may feel, but does not imagine himself actually in the process of giving birth, and this excludes a Hobbesian interpretation of pity which is based upon the possibility of experiencing the same reversals of fortune oneself and consequently on selfish interest. The mediation of the imagination is important because it supports the moral and social edifice without recourse to communal identification or to an Edenic fusion.[28]

What we find is not a focus on "fusion," the evaporation of the walls that separate self and others, but rather a meditation on the mediation of that relationship. That meditation is imaginative, but not fantastic. It takes into consideration the real, material circumstances in which the event is embedded and reflects back on the relation the sufferer and the observer have to it. This meditation takes place within an engagement— various forms of communication, among which is literature.

In order for imagination to play its role in the coordination of emotional commitments, different persons must be able to nourish their imagination from the same source. To illustrate this topic, Smith frequently refers to works of fiction and, in particular, to the feelings inspired in us by the heroes of tragedies and romances.[29] In an article devoted to the links between impartiality, imagination and compassion, Adrian Piper calls *modal imagination* that ability to imagine what is impossible and not only what actually exists (or what has been directly experienced), and he considers this ability indispensable to the formation and sharing of pity in the face of the suffering of someone else.[30] To understand this ability we must have recourse to the "forms of expression" of myths, tales, historical narratives, novels, autobiographies, songs, films, television reports or fictions, etc., in which in particular we find descriptions of the internal states of other people to which we can have no direct access and which by that fact *nourish the imagination* of spectators when faced with distant suffering.[31]

Once again it is precisely the imagination that fills the gap between self and other; specifically, the imagination seems to finesse the requirement that, on the one hand, the situation of the other be imaginable to the self for its own habitation, and, on the other hand, that the situation of the other be beyond our lot. Once again, literature tests the conditions of each side of the coin, and I once again maintain the political ramifications of this vacillation. I return to the mediation of the discursive and material systems that argue that they can "deliver" others to us in a less problematic fashion. Contemporary literature, read in the ways I will suggest and illustrate, says that it's not that easy, these days. I will specify a set of frames of reference, frames that seem to be neutral and natural, disclosing a common "form" of all *human* beings. I examine literary works of fiction to show how literature, read with specific ideas in mind, elaborates, extends, complicates, redefines, and sometimes even explodes these common forms as it discloses the poetics and politics of the vacillation between self and other across and in these delivery systems.

In what follows I show how discursive "delivery systems" precisely imagine relations between selves and others, and then how their relatively simple systems become less and less firm and stable as they interact with, and try to accommodate, a more radical sense of otherness produced in contemporary historical contexts. For example, I consider how, after all, one of the main things that is said to distinguish human beings from other living creatures is that we possess rationality, that is, that we can process the world and reflect on our place in it. Importantly, we can make choices informed by that rationality. So doesn't "reason" provide us with an empirically verifiable commonness, and aren't rational systems that work equally well for all people proof again of that common ground? If we can bracket all those minor differences that might complicate the system—like history, culture, gender, race—then we should have a powerfully efficient way of talking to each other and negotiating our preferences. But that pure formula for economic behavior, which I take as my example here, becomes sorely tested when different notions about rationality and reason start to compromise that model, and that splitting apart is evident in the very world of language saturated with the voices of newly enfranchised others.

I examine the notion that all human behavior can be understood according to notions of reason and rationality in chapter 1, "When Otherness Overcomes Reason." In it I counterpose the powerful formula of "economic behavior" that we find in rational choice theory to the history of literary realism, specifically as it has involved the incorporation of new, diverse, "other" peoples. How have both our ideas of rational choice and action and our modes of presenting them in literature been disrupted by new populations? After providing a short discussion of rationality, rational choice, and literary realism, I move to a discussion of how in his novel *Elizabeth Costello* J. M. Coetzee poses rationality and choice as the linchpins of the realist novel, then proceeds to methodically dismantle them, exposing them to ever increasing doses of otherness, the otherness of the anti-aesthetic, the otherness of the nonhuman, the otherness of race. The paradox here is how literature can both present radical otherness and simultaneously be disarmed by it. Following up on the questions "How much otherness is required for literature to have any traction at all, and how much pushes it over the edge?," in this novel the answers to both are presented. The response proffered by *Elizabeth Costello* puts into crisis not only literature, but also literature's ethical purpose (presenting the reader with otherness and thereby widening her or his moral scope). If in *Elizabeth Costello* the specifics of history and politics are muted, taking a back seat to a discussion of aesthetics and ethics, Coetzee's explicitly historical and political novel, *Disgrace*, echoes exactly these issues in its representation of and meditation on the new South Africa and the precise moment when the balance of power shifts toward newly enfranchised blacks.

In chapter 2, "Whose Story Is It?," I turn to the family, writ both at the local and national levels, and see what happens when strangers, particularly strangers of different races, enter and insinuate themselves into these domestic spaces, both forming a common bond and yet destabilizing as well those alliances built into family structures. In these microcommunal spaces we are formed and act as subjects; "family values" are persistently alluded to for both the consensus they seem to bring forward from national audiences that hear them every election year, and the assumed transparency they evoke between the two scales of social organization—what goes on in the family is a smaller version of our national sense of belonging. But what happens when that common ground of empathy and cohesion is shot through with otherness, and the family drawn into a destructive yet inevitable relation with the political world in the public domain? In chapter 2 I offer a reading of a second South African novel, Nadine Gordimer's *My Son's Story*, wherein the empathetic is split and fissured, demanded at multiple and contradictory levels, as the characters meditate on what holds new others to themselves, and how familiar people, so similar to themselves, have become alienated from them. Politics, gender, sexuality, and race all act in concert to problematize this thing called coalition politics. In the end, it is art that takes on, perhaps reluctantly, the task of reunifying and conveying to the outside the new political world after apartheid.

The irony of *My Son's Story* is that the story is told predominantly from the point of view of the son, not the father. So why isn't it titled, simply, *My Story*? Gordimer asks precisely these questions: how do stories circulate? Who takes ownership of them? How do they pass through this otherness, and to what effect? The protagonists of this novel are drawn together, despite differences of gender, class, age, and race, by three common interests, interests that are counterposed to each other: that of the family (and, by extension, the national collective), that of sexual desire, and that of the political (specifically, liberation politics). The suppression and resurgence of difference under the force of family loyalties, sexual desire, and liberation politics is presented via very precise literary structure, language, and emplotment. I look carefully at the ways Gordimer, in her public speeches, in her literary essays, and in this novel, outlines the hazards and necessity of crossing racial lines during this period of uncertain historical shift, what she calls, borrowing from Antonio Gramsci, "the interregnum." It is precisely the period with which Coetzee is concerned in *Disgrace*. But I argue that the resolutions of the two novels are different in very important ways. Whereas Coetzee seems to give up on realism, as the new historical context has eroded the foundations of such a concept, Gordimer's skepticism gives way to a bifurcation of art and political action, assigning each different roles.

My third example, Kazuo Ishiguro's *Never Let Me Go*, comes from the world of the body, and biotechnical and educational systems. Again, we all seem to have corporeal forms that are not radically different. There is enough commonness that medical students can use the same models to learn the basic ways to diagnose and treat human bodies. But what happens when the seemingly unbreachable "self" of the individual human body gets intruded on by another's body, part of which is inserted into one's own for the sake of one's very life? Here we are talking about organ transplants, as well as the delivery system that sets up that point of exchange—the industry for organ harvesting, and the biotechnological, pharmaceutical, and medical systems that deliver an organ to its new body.

In chapter 3, "Art: A Foreign Exchange," I critique *Never Let Me Go*, a sinister and morbid story of human cloning and unintended self-sacrifice. Parts of bodies are intermingled, organs harvested and re-planted in a radical and ethically problematic "encounter" with otherness. This particular delivery system has immediate connections to both life and death. I look at how historical changes in medical technologies have changed the barriers between discrete bodies, and how that technology opens up new understandings and imaginings of not only being with other bodies, but also sharing bodies. I draw on medical history and ethics, as well as the philosophy of Jean-Luc Nancy and his remarkable essay on his own heart transplant, and compare its handling of such concerns with that of Ishiguro's novel. Yet even as we may be seduced by the novel's wild and wrenching plotline, and its seeming artlessness (it is presented as simply the remembrances of a schoolgirl), it turns out that Art is everything. It is both the sign of humanness and a token of redemption.

Ishiguro himself makes this point, time and again, in his remarks on the novel; for him, the story he tells in the novel presents not an apocalyptic picture of an inhuman and dehumanizing brave new world, but rather an argument that art can save us from even the worst horror imaginable. I account for this discrepancy by bringing to the fore one key idea found in both the novel and in Ishiguro's pronouncements on its composition—the idea of the contingency of history, and the ways in which such contingency informs what we call "moral luck." Ishiguro's famous notion is that there are no bad people, only people born with an ethical system out of step with their historical age. I use *Never Let Me Go* to explore this notion and the moral conundrum it offers. And just as in Coetzee and Gordimer, the deliverance of others is contingent on history; where in the latter cases this involved the rupture in apartheid, in Ishiguro it involves biomedical breakthroughs. In each instance, interaction with others is radically altered, and ethical choices are put into crisis.

This focus on art becomes more complicated in chapter 4, "Pacific Oceanic Feeling: Affect, Otherness, Mediation." The source text for this chapter is the novel *My Year of Meats*, by the Japanese American author and filmmaker Ruth Ozeki. I tackle the issue of mass communication and advertising, tracing how their particular schematizations of literacy, desire, need, and behavior may be read in cross-cultural and gendered manners, seeing how emotions and affect are wielded trans-Pacifically. I show in particular how Ozeki's novel and her film, *Body of Correspondence*, share common concerns about affect and media. If we largely know the world via mass media, how do the various delivery systems of literature and television interact with the economic? In *My Year of Meats*, the economic is explicitly set forward in long disquisitions about the meat industry and pharmaceuticals, and I connect Ozeki's concern with the transnational Body that ingests these commonly circulating and affecting materials to Ishiguro's poetics and ethics of the body. I place the penultimate phrase of Ozeki's novel, "that is the modern thing to do," into strict scrutiny as a way to reflect back on all of the chapters of this study—what is the status of the modern, of the realist novel, of the pre-parcelized human body in today's world and, specifically, in today's literature? How can we retain, or restore even, a sense of ethics that both respects otherness and understands its complex residence in "common ground"? How can we then reimagine our own place there? In the conclusion I elaborate the question of contemporary forms of communication and make the case that it is a *reading practice* that can best help us maintain a critical eye toward the discursive production of "sameness" and "otherness," and the consequences thereof.

Let me here briefly allude to the essay that I treat at length in chapter 3, Jean-Luc Nancy's "The Intruder." In this essay, Nancy begins by remarking on how he owes his very life to the fact that when his heart failed, medical science had opened up a "slot" of technological possibilities that included life-saving transplant techniques: "Less than twenty years ago, one didn't graft, especially not with the use of cyclosporin, which protects against the rejection of the graft. Twenty years from now, it will certainly be a matter of another sort of graft, with other methods. A personal contingency thus crosses a contingency in the history of techniques. In an earlier age, 'I' would be dead; in the future, I would be a survivor by some other means. But always, 'I' finds itself tightly packed into a narrow slot of technical possibilities."[32]

In this volume I look at precisely the slot that is opened at a particular moment in South African political history, that liminal period that saw blacks and whites draw together in ways that put unprecedented pressure on racial, political, and family loyalties, of inherited notions of "us" and "them." Coetzee parallels that historical moment by looking at the tectonic shift that is created by conceptually and ethically displacing the animal-human binary, wherein the "nonhuman," marked by its lack of reason, becomes less and less alien, and the possession of "reason" a more and more problematic definition of humankind. Gordimer's text looks at how that same moment in South African history affected notions of gender, sexuality, and the family, as the barriers between black and white, public and private, opened up. In Ishiguro and Nancy, biotechnology and bio*economies* come to open up the heretofore sacrosanct human body to synthetic (re)production and commodification; within this "slot," new possibilities of human trading in otherness, now converted to sameness, takes place unfettered by ethics and barely representable in the literary imagination. Finally, Ozeki's text places us in an era wherein affect is delivered globally via new hybrid media that breach the barriers between private and public, information and entertainment, text and image and sound. Given the "information age," what kind of glossy screen flattens our senses of dimension, depth, character into eminently substitutable data? How does the common digital denominator slot us into software-guided "social networks"?

Fundamentally, I am drawn back to this question: if literary narratives can still help us imagine others across global discourses regarding the commonly held properties of human beings (the mind, the heart, and the body), can they also exceed the ways those specific modes determine the shape and form of understanding, and, if so, does that offer us any greater or more potent way of not only imagining, but also *thinking through* being together in the world? How can we see both "others" and ourselves differently, in ways that live up to the promise and rationale for reading literature, at all? In that sense, we come back to and remain with the idea that literature itself is a kind of otherness, something that is, as George Eliot says, the "closest thing to life," but not life itself. It is precisely that empathetic, imaginative, and critical relation to that thing outside itself that literature rehearses and models for our own selves.

1

When Otherness Overcomes Reason

Realism is an issue not only for literature; it is a major political, philo-sophical and practical issue that must be handled and explained as such—as a matter of general human interest.—BERTOLT BRECHT, "On the Formalistic Character of the Theory of Realism," 1938

There is first of all the problem of the opening, namely, how to get us from where we are, which is, as yet, nowhere, to the far bank. It is a simple bridging problem, a problem of knocking together a bridge. People solve such problems every day. They solve them, and having solved them push on.—J. M. COETZEE, *Elizabeth Costello*

Precisely by drawing together the issues of literary realism and ra-tionality we can get at the issues that Brecht notes: realism is attached to notions of how things work, or don't, how decisions to act in certain ways are motivated by particular forces and have specific effects that are of "general" human interest; it involves, as Coetzee says, not only getting from A to B, but also situating ourselves "some place" in the first place, to occupy a position from which to act. If we are successful, and do move from A to B, we are then enabled and encouraged to "move on" in life, dealing with the world according to those assumptions. Analysis of literary realism allows us to diagnose the reputed commonality of be-havior, how different people might act in concert with others, but also, this literature, *as* literature, contains a critical, self-reflective element. If literature has been charged with delivering the lives of others to us for our enrichment and betterment, how, if at all, does this new other-ness change our assumptions about what is realistic, about what is *common* to all human beings in their behaviors, choices, actions, judg-ments? Finally, does otherness challenge not only our assumptions about how people act in common, in accordance with the protocols of rationality and realism to get from A to B, but also our ability to represent the real world?

Martha Nussbaum is one of the most prominent contemporary advocates of the idea that literature should present us with the lives of others unlike ourselves in order that we may have a fuller understanding of both ourselves and our world. It is no coincidence that the literary examples that she uses are exclusively drawn from realist literature, and this choice of literary genre is indeed shared by most of the proponents of the movement that we can call "ethics in literature." For them, realist literature attempts to describe a world directly, and to describe not only the lives of others in details that we can recognize as part of that larger, shared world, but also how they think, feel, and act in it. The choices they make are reflections of values, capacities, desires, needs. The questions then become whether these needs are shared, whether the choices "they" make are the ones "we" would have. Realist literature, for these critics, is the genre most concerned with the issues of representing otherness accurately, as set within worlds that ground others in our world. The other is delivered to us on that common ground.

In contrast, J. M. Coetzee's novel *Elizabeth Costello* declares itself as part of a postrealist era: things no longer lead inevitably to certain effects; people do not behave in ways that reflect a common rationality that can be transferred from one situation to the other. Just to get by in life seems more difficult precisely because those sequences, those causes and effects, no longer seem to work in tandem. "Bridges" are now fragile things, if they exist at all. Issues of reason, of judgment, of values and their achievement—things intimately attached to the genre of realist literature—now seem impossible to deal with, once the scaffolding of "realism" is found to be unreliable. The political, philosophical, and practical issues of which Brecht speaks are all now stalled, if not destroyed. Why has this happened? What has brought about this inability to successfully plot future action?

Elizabeth Costello is an example of what happens when, ironically, language is *too* common, shared by too many undifferentiated people and things, when reason and rationality are flawed and irregular. Otherness, the very thing that we look to realist literature to deliver to us, causes this paralysis. More precisely, it is otherness of a degree that is fatal to the realist project, and possibly to the project of ethics and literature. However, I do not advocate a move to postmodern literature. That may, or may not, solve the problem. Rather, I want to see if *any* literary narrative can be read in such a way as to both recognize the problem of too much otherness, which instantiates a difference that goes beyond a single, binding realism, and offer insight to an uncommonality that is understood through the uneven effects of what I have named global "delivery systems." In this way, the fraying of the fabric of reality and reason brought about by an overload of otherness lays bare the inadequacy of these delivery systems, which count on commonality and the suppression of difference to function. How have their attempts to make the heterogeneous homogeneous failed, unable to constrain and neutralize that difference, and what are some of the consequences of this implosion?

Before turning to realist literature, I briefly consider rational choice theory, for this theory is premised on a highly influential formula that informs the ways many in the fields of economics, political science, psychology, and sociology think about human behavior, and can be seen as an illuminating project outside literature. Those who subscribe to rational choice theory believe that in it we have a tool for understanding how all human beings, regardless of race, culture, gender, age, make choices: rational choice theory posits a human commonality based on reason and its deployment. According to this theory, people will not only build bridges from here to there in a similar fashion, but will also, in fact, see the need for bridges similarly and use them in similar ways. They will, in short, see the world of choice and action, and behave in it in accord with the same formula. Their stories, therefore, may be understood as logically adhering to, or departing from, this basic formula of rational choice-making. The connection between rational choice theory and notions of storytelling, of accounting for behavior, is not hard to see, and I will touch briefly on the nexus of these two subjects as they appear in the work of Reid Hastie and Jon Elster.

I then discuss how storytelling attempts to "bridge" the distance between self and other via the particular language of literary realism. After a longer discussion of what, exactly, literary realism is with specific regard to otherness, I turn to the novel itself for what I will call the disruption of literary realism by excessive otherness. In *Elizabeth Costello* the nostalgia for realism and the diagnosis of its aftermath is brought on by too high a degree of otherness, which invades and overcomes the

novel and the bounds of literary realism. I locate the crisis of representation brought about by the overflow of otherness at a precise historical
moment created by technological and industrial change that exerts
great pressure on the line of otherness between the human and nonhuman in critical manners. I conclude by examining the political and
historical ramifications of this crisis of representation, tracing that problematic in another novel by Coetzee, *Disgrace*.

Rational Choice and the Imagination

If by "globalization" we mean a newly extensive and intensive connectedness between formerly remote or disconnected peoples, then
certainly notions of such things as a "*global* economy," "*world* culture,"
and "*human* interaction" have to be newly assessed. Our customary
tools for comprehending and representing human behavior, both in the
social sciences and the humanities, no longer have the luxury of focusing only on discrete and separate objects, phenomena, and behaviors,
since these are now mingling and cross-referencing each other in unprecedented and sometimes discrepant manners. Ironically, knowledge
of others appears to have become only more problematic in an age when
the distance between others is continually shrinking.

Yet for some, especially those social scientists predisposed toward
rational choice theory, the matter seems uncomplicated. For instance,
Gary Becker writes,

> The combined assumptions of maximizing behavior, market equilib-
> rium, and stable preferences, used relentlessly and unflinchingly, form
> the heart of the economic approach. . . . I have come to the position that
> the economic approach is a comprehensive one that is applicable to all
> human behavior, be it behavior involving money prices or imputed
> shadow prices, repeated or infrequent decisions, large or minor deci-
> sions, emotional or mechanical ends, rich or poor persons, men or
> women, adults or children, brilliant or stupid persons, patients or thera-
> pists, businessmen or politicians, teachers or students.[1]

In short, the "economic approach" would seem to overcome the unruli-
ness of difference, subordinating it to a universally applicable analytic.

Peter Abell presents a useful sketch of rational choice theory in relation to sociology. As he describes it, rational choice theory strives "to

understand individual actors (which in specified circumstances may be collectivities of one sort or another) as acting, or more likely interacting, in a manner such that they can be deemed to be doing the best they can for themselves, given their objectives, resources, and circumstances, as they see them."[2] Jon Elster argues,

> Ideally, a fully satisfactory rational-choice explanation of an action would have the following structure. It would show that the action is the (unique) best way of satisfying the full set of the agent's desires, given the (uniquely) best beliefs the agent could form, relatively to the (uniquely determined) optimal amount of evidence. We may refer to this as the *optimality part* of the explanation. In addition the explanation would show that the action was caused (in the right way) by the desires and beliefs, and the beliefs caused (in the right way) by consideration of the evidence. We may refer to this as the *causal part* of the explanation. These two parts together yield a first-best rational-choice explanation of the action.[3]

He continues, however, by saying that "the optimality part by itself yields a second-best explanation, which, however, for practical purposes may have to suffice, given the difficulty of access to the psychic causality of the agent."[4] This qualification is important, for my purpose is not to test out rational choice theory as a particular delivery system, but rather to examine the overlap between notions of rational behavior and choice-making, and the imagination and fiction.

While Barthes portrays realist literature as certainly partaking of this formula for moving forward, emphasizing the action- and decision-driven motion of narrative, he notes as well: "The general structure of narrative, at least as this has been analyzed at one time or another up to the present, appears essentially predictive. . . . It can be said that, at each juncture of the narrative syntax, someone says to the hero (or to the reader, it does not matter which): if you act this way, if you choose this alternative, then this is what will happen," it is precisely the "psychic causality of the agent," so opaque within the operations of rational choice theory, that, "exogeneously," literature may be able to explore in its complexity and dimensionality.[5] Otherwise, if "economic behavior" is shared by all humans in all endeavors, then how can literature do anything but record the ceaseless rehearsal of the same formula, perhaps with minor variations? It is in what is necessarily absented from the calculations of rational choice theory that a literary account takes over, in the realm of the psychology of the other, in her or his reasons for different kinds of choices, based on perhaps different sorts of rationality and imagination.

In the process of choice-making, one of the main elements is information. We need a certain amount of information on which to base our choices. But from where do we derive this information? Aside from objective sources of information, we also draw on our memory and imagination. And our imagination is of course not completely unanchored from reality; we cannot simply imagine any kind of information as being valuable. In fact too much information (like too much otherness) clouds the vision. On the other hand, having too narrow a scope of imagination can also be detrimental—we cannot make an "informed" choice. Thus information (data) and the imagination (which data are visible, viable) are joined together in rational choice-making.

If this is inevitable, Hastie notes that therein lie some serious problems: "*Availability to the imagination* influences the estimates of frequency. The problem that arises, just as with the availability of actual instances in our experience or availability of vicarious instances, is that this availability is determined by many factors other than actual frequency. It is quite clear that sometimes the thinking is 'easier' than others and some ideas 'come to mind' more readily than others."[6] In other words, as we attempt to make our choices, we may well draw on information in very particular and perhaps unreasonable ways. What do we imagine can happen (predictably) if we choose this course of action? What are the chances our choice will yield this or that result? This is not an idle speculation—it is a basic risk that informs choice-making. Right or wrong, we tend to be swayed by what seems a plausible narrative, what is "available" to our imagination about the world around us.

Critically, Hastie notes, "Scenarios are even more believable if the components form a good gestalt because they fit into or exemplify some familiar narrative schema."[7] Indeed, in choice-making we access our capacity to sort the world into categories: "Many judgments are concerned with the proper category into which to classify an object or event."[8] We sift through data, slot it into categories, and act with regard to our assumptions about how these categories name things, and indeed how they "behave" in conjunction with each other. Hastie points to "the common tendency to make judgments and decisions about category membership based on similarity between our conception of the category and our impression of the to-be-classified object, situation, or event."[9] In sum, overreliance on what is available to our imagination in certain inherited or predisposed ways causes problems: "The primary behavioral signature of *relying on similarity* is that people miss the critical statistical or logical structure of the situation and ignore relevant information."[10] This echoes Elster's designated weak point in rational choice theory: the psychic disposition of the agent. This disposition, going back to Aristotle, is produced at least in part by an intersubjective encounter mediated by language—we are induced, through language to act on "rational" desires.

To connect this explicitly to narrative, we can say that key constituent elements of choice-making can often draw on biased or skewed data and ignore salient information because of imperfect imaginations. We ignore or discount information that falls outside our categorical schemata, or what we are "induced" to want, to choose. In sorting out the world into similar and dissimilar phenomena, we tend to shape our world to fit our needs. To make the connection to otherness clear: by siphoning off the dissimilar, the different, the other, we risk making essentially bad choices. On the other hand, if we entertain too much information, we will never be able to make a choice—we'll be paralyzed. This is one facet of cognitive dissonance theory, as Elster explains it: "Cognitive dissonance theory predicts that when one motivation is slightly stronger than another, it will try to recruit allies so that the reasons on one side become decisively stronger. The unconscious mind shops around, as it were, for additional arguments in favor of the tentative conclusion reached by the conscious mind."[11] He adds, "The theory states that when a person experiences an internal inconsistency or dissonance among her beliefs and values, we can expect some kind of mental adjustment that will eliminate or reduce the dissonance. Typically, the adjustment will choose the path of least resistance."[12] In short, we can unconsciously see and shape choices in certain ways, according to our imagined needs, categories, beliefs about causes and effects, objects and subjects. We are predisposed, or "induced," to see the world in certain ways. This seems noncontroversial. What interests me here is how literary narrative may perform this induction to rational desire and how that fact colors the way we behave toward and with others who are "placed" into our sense of what is "real" or "realistic" differently. Do we let them in, wary of the narrowness of our imaginations? Or do we hold them at bay, wary of the crippling effect too many choices might have on us?

To get at this problem, Elster explicitly turns to storytelling. In *Nuts and Bolts for the Social Sciences,* his discussions of storytelling and litera-ture provide an important set of observations regarding the goals of rational choice theory, as well as its limitations. He points to both the benefits and dangers of literature (and the kind of thinking it engages) within the rational choice enterprise. In all cases, Elster's remarks bear on the topic of this chapter. Seeming to echo Aristotle, he gives credit to storytelling for its ability to present the individual with a set of choice options and a particular imaginative space for weighing those choices: "Storytelling can suggest new, parsimonious explanations. Suppose that someone asserts that self-sacrificing or helping behavior is conclusive proof that not all action is rational. . . . Could it not be in one's self-interest to help others? Could it not be rational to be swayed by one's emotions? The first step toward finding a positive answer is telling a *plausible story* to show how these possibilities could be realized."[13] But he cautions, "With some ingenuity—and many scholars have a great deal—one can *always* tell a story in which things are turned upside down."[14] In sum, storytelling allows us to increase the body of informa-tion on which we form our beliefs, but fiction also may be deployed to support, or instantiate and indeed proliferate false or irrational beliefs.

On the other hand, if Hastie is correct, these things happen just as well in the real world: people place limits on what is "available" to their imaginations; choice is riddled with fictions we tell ourselves. And just as in literature, where we have to decide how much otherness is required for us to reap the full benefit of being presented with the lives of others, in rational choice-making we have to ascertain how much information we need and how much paralyzes our ability to make a choice. In either case, these choices have clear effects on how we live with each other.

For Elster, storytelling allows the individual to speculate on a range of possible scenarios, to weigh the cost-benefit of not enough, or too much, otherness, to consider exactly how "other-oriented emotions" motivate stories in which the individual might feel the effect of actions on a hypothetical stand-in for him- or herself. With fiction and affect on the table for discussion, Elster completes the circle, speaking of justice and the correlate issue of ethics.

> The . . . feeling of being unfairly treated deserves special mention. Sufficient conditions for the occurrence of this powerful emotion are the following. First, the situation is perceived as morally wrong; second, it has been brought about intentionally, not as the byproduct of natural

causality or the invisible hand of social causality; third, it can be rectified by social intervention. Thus the feeling of injustice rests on the combination of "It ought to be otherwise," "It is someone's fault that it is not otherwise," and "It could have been made otherwise," in addition to the general counterfactual condition "It could have been otherwise."[15]

Note that the conditional elements ("ought," "could") are linked to both the ethics and narrative, better behavior and different stories. The speaker is imagining not a single fact, but a set of interconnected circumstances in which others might live justly. Within this set of discussions of storytelling, affect, and ethics, we are thus caught in a situation wherein stories, and the thoughts they make possible, are all part of choice-making, and yet their "cost-benefit" ratio is uncertain—how many possibilities can or should we entertain, and how much otherness can we invite in from what is not readily available to our imagination? Speaking in "cold," "rational" terms, how can we optimize our choices by accommodating and processing information that we may have habitually ignored or discounted without being placed in a situation wherein we can never choose because there are too many equal, nondifferentiated choices? Speaking in "humanistic" and "literary" ways, how much "otherness" is necessary to gain the benefits of being "exposed" to the lives of others without creating too much distance and alienation from our selves, fragmenting beyond recuperation our sense of reality, attached as it is to reasonable choice, action, bridges between here and there? Indeed, the issue of otherness is, according to one account, there from the birth of realist literature.

Literary Realism among Others

Realism is a paradoxical moment in Western literature when representation can neither accommodate the Otherness of woman nor exist without it.—NAOMI SCHOR, *Reading in Detail*

Literary realism, in short, was a cultural brother of ideology, or more accurately was itself an ideological "operator," performing the primary task of ideology, the function of naturalizing socially and historically produced systems of meaning.—CHRISTOPHER PRENDERGAST, "Realism, 'God's Secret,' and the Body"

On the one hand, one could say that from its inception "realism" had to grapple with a greater diversity of newly recognized actors who tested the cohesiveness of norms and institutions and at times forced their modification. On the other hand, literary critics have asserted that realism was enabled precisely by otherness; the new diversity of the world called for another way of representing reality, hence, realism. In either case, key questions were raised not only in terms of the constitution of the "real," but also regarding the way people were understood to behave, to act in this new world. What did it mean for new, different sets of subjects to interact? What results could be anticipated, good and bad? George J. Becker attaches realism in literature with a new modern social project: "In a general but very persuasive way the development of realism in literature is associated with the effort of leaders of nineteenth-century thought and institution building to update themselves, to create for themselves a social and intellectual ambience in reasonable harmony with the facts of human existence as they appeared then, in short, to become 'modern.'"[16] He continues, "Broadly speaking, these movements, and others like them, attempted to give nonpeople the status of people, in varying degrees enlarging the spectrum of human personality."[17] The "nonpeople" Becker is referring to here include those newly viable populations produced after the Catholic emancipation in England and Ireland, the abolition of serfdom in Russia, and the abolition of African slavery throughout the world, beginning with the closing of the slave trade at the start of the nineteenth century and ending with emancipation in Brazil, in 1888. He asserts that during this period "there was a steadily broadening interest in human beings, a realization that a potential originality—and a potential interest for literature—existed in all strata of humanity."[18]

Nevertheless, two passages from Benito Pérez Galdós, writing in the last years of the nineteenth century, capture both the positive and the negative effects of this new diversity. First, in the realm of literary composition, things become more "real," and the "masks" of conventional representations give way to diverse, and presumably more authentic, finer-tuned modes of writing about the world and its varied peoples.

> In the sphere of Art, generic types, which symbolized major groupings of the human family, are disappearing and losing life and color. Even human faces are not what they were, so it would seem ridiculous to say so. . . . With the breakdown of categories masks fall at one blow and faces

appear in their true purity. Types are lost, the man is better revealed to us, and Art is directed solely to giving to imaginary beings a life that is more human and social.[19]

In short, we find the emergence of the modern individual, in all its particularity and detail, or so it is claimed.

But Galdós also points to the challenges such new constituencies present to social structures and conventions, asserting that "the lack of unity is such that even in political life, naturally organized and disciplined groups, there is clear evidence of the vast dissolution of these large families formed by the enthusiasm of constituencies, by traditional affinities, or by more or less clear-cut principles."[20] It is as if the standing principles of presenting and judging action, choice, behavior cannot operate in the same ways anymore, given these new sets of agents. Radical otherness pushes the limits of any liberal accommodation of "diversity," as Naomi Schor succinctly points out. How much otherness is incorporable into this newly realized world, and in what manner? How can literature serve as not only a "reflection" of the real, but also an instrument whereby the real, or what passed for it, could be judged, debated, reimagined? Amid multiplicity, was there any commonality? How could "others" be "delivered" and managed across this vast uneven terrain of the real?

Indeed, Erich Auerbach takes up precisely this problematic as it extends into twentieth-century modernist writing, which incorporates the new multiplicity of subjectivities into its formal presentation of reality. Auerbach's well-known example is found in Virginia Woolf.

> The essential characteristic of the technique represented by Virginia Woolf is that we are given not merely one person whose consciousness is rendered, but many persons, with frequent shifts from one to the other—in our text, Mrs. Ramsey, "people," Mr. Bankes, in brief interludes James, the Swiss maid in a flashback, and the nameless ones who speculate over a tear. The multiplicity of persons suggests that we are here after all confronted with an endeavor to investigate an objective reality, that is, specifically, the "real" Mrs. Ramsey.[21]

Crucially, Auerbach places his analysis within the broader sociohistorical context that put new pressures on the capacity of realist literature.

> It is easy to understand that such a technique [the reflection of multiple consciousnesses] had to develop gradually and that it did so precisely

during the decades of the First World War period and after. The widening of man's horizon, and the increase of his experiences, knowledge, ideas, and possible forms of existence, which began in the 16th century, continued through the 19th at an ever faster tempo—with such a tremendous acceleration since the beginning of the 20th that synthetic and objective attempts at interpretation are produced and demolished every instant. A tremendous tempo of the changes proved the more confusing because they could not be surveyed as a whole. . . . Furthermore, the changes did not produce the same effects in all places, so that the differences of attainment between the various social strata of one and the same people and between different peoples came to be—if not greater—at least more noticeable. The spread of publicity in the crowding of mankind on a shrinking globe sharpened awareness of the differences and ways of life and attitudes, and mobilized the interests and forms of existence which the new changes either furthered or threatened. In all parts of the world crises adjustment arose; they increased in number and coalesced.[22]

Here we see slow but irreversible change spreading globally, albeit unevenly. This unevenness creates variegated peoples, each affected differently by mass historical shifts, and, critically, these differences, this new production of otherness, is disseminated by "publicity" in all manner of print media that struggle to cognitively map this new world.

Most important for my study of the mapping of rationality, action, and the representation of how different people might act the same way (or not) is how Auerbach develops this line of inquiry. In a manner not dissimilar to that of Galdós, who noted the dissolution of conventional categories and the birth of more variegated, "precise" modes of representing reality, Auerbach notes that in modernist fiction, the essential aim of realism abides, though now delivered via a new mode of writing which could disclose the new surface variations of life. But Auerbach adds a crucial dimension. He argues that beneath *any* surface, at *any* time, one would discover a *common* human "reality."

Something new and elemental appeared: nothing less than the wealth of reality and depth of life in every moment to which we surrender ourselves without prejudice. . . . It is precisely the random moment which is comparatively independent of the controversial and unstable orders over which men fight and despair; it passes unaffected by them, as daily life. *The more it is exploited, the more the elementary things which our lives have in common come to light.* The more numerous, varied, and simple the people are who appear as subjects of such random moments, the more effectively must what they have in common shine forth. In this unprejudiced and exploratory type of representation we cannot but see to what extent—below the surface conflicts—the differences between men's ways of life and forms of thought have already lessened.[23]

Modern life has produced a dizzying and seemingly untotalizable proliferation of new effects—technological, scientific, economic—that has linked people together in new ways, even while impacting different populations unevenly. Nonetheless, broad heterogeneity is paradoxically accompanied by profound homogeneity; the newly connected modern world reveals a diversity of modernities that nonetheless harbor something essentially common. Modernist literature focused on a seemingly contradictory project: to entertain, accommodate, even solicit a multiplicity of points of view and angles of vision, and at the same time to attempt to ascertain, from all those randomly chosen perspectives, what they held in common. Auerbach seems to be challenging the world: set aside the large, obvious categories of belonging and identity —ideology, religion, nation, language itself—that place people into discrete groups all too easily. Instead, pick a moment, any moment, and you will find, from that unprejudiced sampling, that the cards are all the same.

So thoroughgoing is this commonality that Auerbach audaciously asserts there are no longer any exotic peoples—not only are swarthy "Corsicans" and "Spaniards" now decidedly un-exotic, but even Chinese seem equally part of the common human family.

> The strata of societies and their different ways of life have become inextricably mingled. There are no longer even exotic peoples. A century ago (in Mérimée for example), Corsicans or Spaniards were still exotic; today the term would be quite unsuitable for Pearl Buck's Chinese peasants. Beneath the conflicts, and also through them, an economic and cultural leveling process is taking place. It is still a long way to a common life of mankind on earth, but the goal begins to be visible. And it is most clearly visible now in the unprejudiced, precise, interior and exterior representation of the random moment in the lives of different people.[24]

More than a century before Thomas Friedman's flat-earth theory, Erich Auerbach seems to have recognized a harbinger. But we need to be more precise about what he says, for Auerbach isn't speaking of these people, but rather about the *representation* of them, and by specific literary figures, from Mérimée to Pearl Buck. The tension between heterogeneity and homogeneity is lessened, if not obviated, by the work of art, which dialectically presents the surface variations of the underlying reality of a common life. People may act differently on the surface, unevenly impacted as they are by sweeping historical changes, but their motivations and desires and the thinking that goes into different choices are not so uncommon—discrete economic and cultural worlds no longer exist. Nevertheless, in Auerbach the presentation of reality is complicated by both its anchoring in history, which of course is not static, and in literature, whose forms and goals are precisely not simple or uniform, and this dialectic is one of the basic insights of *Mimesis*.

Today the functionality of literary language, as it attempts to present the reality of others, is made intensely problematic precisely because the "leveling" effect of globalization, the famous "flatness" trumpeted by Friedman and others, is only perceptible from a *certain* angle of vision. However, otherness of a certain degree, presented in literary texts, disrupts that angle of vision. In short, the uneven impact of history that Auerbach notes has not been dissipated and leveled out, and neither have their forms of representation. This unevenness has of course deeply affected how people have come to act according to different imaginings of their situatedness in "globalization." Their differing positions in turn naturally alter the way they interact with others, the choices they make based on sometimes radically different conceptions and performances of "rationality." Literary realism, seeking to make sense of choices, actions, behaviors of and toward others, is now involved with a new sort of social contract. Brook Thomas, describing the sociocultural world of the American realist novel, says, "Readers who enter such a world participate in a moral economy in which people potentially stand on an equal foot with each other."[25] I want to underscore the word *potentially* and up the ante in this "multicultural," "global" world. I map this immanence on to our temporary age of globalized delivery systems, to see their hegemonic logic at work in ordering facts, choices, consequences, across the board. The idea of American literary realism's connection to the idea of a "contract," which Thomas uses as a key word in his study, can, I think, be more broadly applied. Thomas connects the unfolding of syntagmatic sequences along the horizontal plane, the chain of reason and action and fulfillment—Coetzee's "bridge-building," in other words—to the drawing up and execution of a contract. In the realist text, we have nothing less than the building of epistemological relations to form a world: "Contract's promise to generate an immanent, rather than transcendental, ordering of society suggests that how 'facts' are ordered is more important than simple attention to them."[26]

Indeed, most critics and theorists of realist narrative regard the syntagmatic unfolding of literary narrative as its chief structural characteristic. The movement from one moment to the next, from cause to effect, has been seen to be particularly present in realist narratives; the "real" is manifested as a certain logic unfolds, as choices appear, as actions are taken which lead to certain results, and as contracts are fulfilled or breached. According to a common critique of "realism," these results also serve as judgments; there is a sort of "poetic justice" that is repeatedly rehearsed, a certain ideology underscored and reaffirmed. However, while I will certainly attend to the syntagmatic unfolding of the narrative contract, I also attend to the vertical axis, and in particular to which sorts of agents can occupy the linguistic slot of "subject" or "agent." Updating the relation between actor and act in this new historical frame is essential.

According to liberal ideology, and Gary Becker's "economic behavior" model, it should not matter who stands in the role of "agent," at least not enough to disrupt the formula. I disagree. Different peoples crowding into the position of "subject" affects not only the narrative constitution of the literary world being narrated, but also the very mode of presenting reality. Different models of reason and rationality are set forth as different subjects occupy the same linguistic slot; but more important than realizing the "rich variety" of other perspectives, these literary narratives show the fragility of such norms when a radical degree of otherness is perceived, if not entirely contained. Ultimately, this should prompt us to read these texts in different ways—in fact, this is required by these new kinds of narratives, which critique both the claims of commonality that allow "others" to be delivered to us and how those claims, founded on the "proper" or "acceptable" ratio of self to other, are themselves predicated on certain assumptions about not only what it means to be human, across the board, but also how human beings connect. Coetzee's novel offers a complex critique of the ratio of self to other, and the capacity and nature of interaction at a dizzying degree of otherness, all captured in the novel's emplotting of choice, behavior, and judgment.

But before turning to Coetzee's novel, I want briefly to evoke the work of the linguist Roman Jakobson and the literary critics Lawrence Scherer and Pamela Morris, to illustrate more concretely what I am concerned with regard to the vertical axis. From their very different angles, each considers the case of excessive otherness in terms of an "overload" within the paradigmatic axis. What happens when too many subjects crowd into that space, too many possible agents exist? How does the linguistic, and the literary narrative system, accommodate that overflow? That is, as we follow Becker, Galdós, and Auerbach in linking literary history to the proliferation of otherness and other perspectives, what sort of adjustments are necessary, both systemically and in terms of our understanding of the reality of human interaction?

To begin with, Jakobson importantly takes note of how language is used according to common understandings and assumptions. Again, a social contract is at work. Crucially, the fulfillment of the contract participates in the construction of a world, built up from the combination of speech acts that cross-reference each other. There is no "freedom" to say just anything; rather, the conversation builds an understanding about reality based on a common stock of terms, locutions, lexical items between mutually recognized speakers.

> Speech implies a selection of certain linguistic entities and their combination into linguistic units of a higher degree of complexity. At the lexical level this is readily apparent: the speaker selects words and combines them into sentences according to the syntactic system of the language he is using; sentences in their turn are combined into utterances. But the speaker is by no means a completely free agent in his choice of words: selection (except for the rare case of actual neologism) must be made from the lexical storehouse which he and his addressee possess and comment.[27]

Again, "everyone, when speaking to another person, tries, deliberately or involuntarily, to hit upon a common vocabulary: either to please or simply be understood or, finally, to bring him out, he uses the terms of his addressee. There is no such thing as private property in language:

everything is socialized. Verbal exchange, like any form of intercourse, requires at least two communicators, an idiolect proves to be a somewhat perverse fiction."[28] What happens when people are not able to fulfill that contract, even if they wish to?

Jakobson's study of aphasia is well known; in it he extrapolates from case histories of what he calls "similarity" and "contiguity" disorders a poetics of poetry and prose. Critics such as David Lodge have famously evoked Jakobson's analysis of "contiguity" to describe the basic structure of realist narrative.[29] Lodge and others interested in the description and analysis of narrative look at how worlds unfold in the "projection of similarity upon contiguity," that is, the process of selection from a paradigm of like items and the insertion of that selected term onto the horizontal axis, to join its now contiguous neighbors in making a sentence. But what happens when one cannot easily choose from that menu of like items? What happens when too many things seem too similar, or when what is "available to the imagination" is excessive, rather than narrowed down, when there is no clear choice, no finally convincing determining reason to choose one term rather than another, when seemingly wildly different words can easily stand in the place of each other? Again, while one can dwell in that dysfunctional world by dubbing it "poetry" or "the poetic imagination," in the linguistic contract of realist literature, this has potentially devastating consequences.

Jakobson's study focuses on what happens when a language user's capacity to make choices fails, that is, when he or she cannot decide either which term to select from the vertical axis or how to put words together on the horizontal plane. The inability to distinguish between paradigmatic elements—for example, "Tom," "man," "real-estate agent" all appear to be equivalent, no one term seeming more appropriate than the other—evinces "similarity disorder," a malfunction of the process by which one selects terms from a paradigm; the major deficiency "lies in selection and substitution, with relative stability of combination and contexture." Conversely, a "contiguity disorder" describes the inability to fit words together, wherein the deficiency lies in "combination and contexture, with relative retention of normal selection and substitution."[30] Such disorders make the basic performance of language extremely difficult; language users suffering from such dysfunctionality struggle to fulfill the basic "contract" between speakers. Their deficiencies on one axis force them to compensate by taking recourse to the one axis still available to them in an attempt to fulfill, to use Thomas's term, their linguistic contract.

The instability (or even impossibility) of being able to choose which words to slot into the horizontal frame (Tom, businessman, male, wolf, seducer, Boy Scout, balding, tall) places greater pressure on the contiguous terms to shore up the sentence. That is, if one cannot see the sense of this or that word in a particular slot, one leans on its neighbors for direction, a hint at possible meanings to be made.

> Aphasia with impaired substitution and impact and texture, operations involving similarity, yield to those based on contiguity. . . . Goldstein's tests justify such an expectation: a female patient of this type, when asked to list a few names of animals, disposed them in the same order in which she had seen them in the zoo; similarly, despite instructions to arrange certain objects according to color, size, shape, she classified them on the basis of the spatial contiguity as home things, house materials, etc., and justifed this grouping by reference to a display window where "it does not matter what the things are," that is they do not have to be similar.[31]

What does this have to do with otherness? My adaptation of Jakobson argues that when too many unlikely subjects "take place" in the vertical paradigm, when, according to the genesis of literary realism laid out by George Becker, an incrementally larger number of new and different subjects can vie for position in the slot of "subject," when new, different, and incommensurate perspectives all can be seen to count as "a perspective," this puts greater pressure on the sequence of choice-action, cause-effect, and so on to help us make sense, and more reliance is put on the fictional account of how the world is held together. The old familiar "home things" are relied on in more necessary ways than before. There is thus a testing out of the capacity of new subjects to fit into conventional norms of behavior; radically "other" people need to be understood in "normal" contexts. If they are scrambled together and inaccessible in the subject position (the vertical paradigm), the words that join them to form a predicate have to be anchored in normal discourses syntactically. In the case of radical otherness, when anybody or anything can seem to occupy the vertical paradigm, it is thus all the more important that they appear "reasonable" as manifested in the unfolding of the horizontal axis, that is, the logic of the predicate.

Otherwise, the sentence will collapse under the weight of the person's difference—and it is exactly this that we find in *Elizabeth Costello*.

Interestingly, in addition to the greater reliance on the syntagmatic axis, Jakobson describes a second key effect of similarity disorder as involving the reduction of the multiplicity of terms that fill the paradigmatic axis—there has to be more certainty, stability, absoluteness on that axis. Put briefly, this results in monolingualism: "Loss of bilingualism and confinement to a single dialectal variety of a single language is a systematic manifestation of this disorder."[32] The connection I draw here, perhaps too metaphorically, is that in this linguistic/poetic analysis of "ordinary" language and its poetic dysfunction we can find as well a commentary on two key themes of this chapter: the "contract" that realist literature enacts and perhaps enforces between actors (characters, authors, readers) according to a commonly agreed on language and its norms and protocols; and the manner in which that progressive unfolding of "realism" may be troubled by too much otherness as more and more visible subjects test out the norms of realist representations of "the world."

What happens when one cannot easily select or choose, because too many formerly dissimilar subjects now vie for equal status, for, in other words, similarity, commonality? In that stalled, confusing moment, when it is no longer as clear as it was before which terms are viable or even preferable, not only is more and more reliance placed on the neighboring words—that is, the verbs, predicates, propositions, modifiers—to give a hint as to what, or who, can fit into that "subject" position, there also is a reduction of the static or dissonance occurring along the vertical axis; multiple languages, each offering their own possibilities, are muted or excluded, and a single determinant language remains. Turning now to literary history and criticism "proper," we find another, not dissimilar, way of describing the dissonance created by excessive otherness, this time in terms of literary history and ideology.

Lawrence Schehr argues that realism is involved in a contradictory project: even as it includes "the other" in its universe, it tries to maintain the particularity of the other while making itself universal.[33] That is, to fulfill its liberal ambitions, it invites "the other" in (for variety, diversity, enrichment), while all the time holding itself above and beyond the other as a perpetually dominant force. In the unfolding of its narrative logic, realism normalizes textual relations that reflect this relationship.

But, Schehr continues, the other can bring her own law, undercutting the process of domination.[34] What we find, then, is the setting forth of a contract (a convention for accommodating and situating the other) and a reply (a contestation of that assignment).

In either case, to make this "real," there has to be some common, legible ground that includes both the dominant and the minor, and it is history, uneven as it may be. Different people's different behavior has to be seen as occurring at the same time, under similar, if not identical, constraints and possibilities. We find people understood via the historical praxes of the real that surround them. Schehr asserts, "In realist narrative, being human means having a locus in which to speak, a language to speak, and possibility of interacting with others."[35] Naturally, for this to occur, the other has to be granted the rights of language: "The Other has to be posited first as having the possibility of language and of being a subject."[36] But at this moment, membership into the club means exclusion from otherness, and this has dire consequences: with the loss of "the truly other" the very possibility of unrepresentability is erased. Thus, the unfolding of realist narrative—its "epistemological progress," to use Pam Morris's description—is stalled, at least temporarily, as it has to do the work of accounting for behavior that is supposedly like, and unlike, our own.

The conventional account of what follows, in the transition from nineteenth-century realist fiction to late-twentieth- and twenty-first-century works, is that the postmodernist narratives of the latter evince an intense skepticism toward the notion of realist "progress" and the "knowledge" that comes from it. I suggest that the proliferation of points of view emanating from increasing numbers of "other" people finally exerted so much pressure (and not only literary, of course) that new modes of literary representation had to be found. "Master narratives," for all sorts of aesthetic and ideological reasons, were suspect and frail. Nevertheless, besides the fact that I believe the reports of the death of realism are (for better or worse) in many ways premature, my concerns here are not to rehearse or reevaluate the move to postmodernism.[37] Rather, I want to examine how the weakening of the realist claim does not take place in isolation from the critique of the systems of delivery that it draws on. That is to say, if in a literary text people no longer act in common, according to one or another formula for human behavior (rational choice theory, social choice theory, game theory, etc.), then how does that disclose the unevenness, the problematic nature, of the very notion that commonality can be formulated? Furthermore, and essentially, what consequences does this have for the ways we might reassess the general notion that people can be "delivered" to us with our understandings of "us," "them," and the system intact? How should we act differently, informed now with a different understanding of how we have come to be together in the first place? The fact of the matter is that we *do* act as if we share some common properties, even knowing that that commonality is "constructed." Donald Davidson writes,

> One might, in a metaphorical mood, describe my method for understanding someone else as putting him in my shoes; but this would certainly be a misleading metaphor if taken seriously. While plenty of imagination is called for in a good interpretation, I am not asking anyone to imagine he is playing another's part. I simply call attention to the fact that the propositions I use to interpret the attitudes of another are defined by the roles they play in my thoughts and feelings and behavior; therefore in interpretation they must play appropriately similar roles. It is a consequence of this fact the correct interpretation makes interpreter and interpreted share many strategically important beliefs and values. . . . [I]f it is true that the basis of interpersonal comparison already exists when we attribute desires to others, then we can, after all, make a fairly clear distinction between interpersonal comparisons and the normative judgments based on them.[38]

Pamela Morris glosses Davidson thus: "if experiences, beliefs of one community are transferable into the language of another community, then it cannot sensibly be claimed that the two communities constitute wholly self-contained, incommunicable epistemological and linguistic worlds. On the other hand, if they are wholly incommensurate, it would not be possible even to make a claim for being incommensurate. If another world were to be totally unknowable we would not logically be able to know if it was different."[39] This seems clear. However, I want to shift the focus slightly. Along with examining how claims to commonality are staked, and then tested in the literary narratives I look at in this study, we need to think of what adjustments come into play as one struggles to find, or maintain, common ground. What steps are taken to establish, or prop up, the notion that people are the same, or at least on

some basic level "commensurate," in their humanity? This is the argument of Dudley Shapere, who writes,

> If two scientific theories (or more general contexts of scientific thought,
> such as "traditions" or "communities") differ in so many respects, as
> they certainly seem to do, in virtue of what do we compare them?
> Rather than deny that such comparisons can be made, what we need to
> ask is how it is possible to do so, and what the implications of our way of
> doing it as we do are: how we manage to compare and even evaluate
> such scientific usages and the contexts in which they occur.[40]

That is to say, the focus will shift from the possibility of making com-
parisons to the conditions of possibility.

Jürgen Habermas's appreciation of Davidson is founded on his shift
from the "fixation on the fact mirroring function of language."[41] In terms
of the current study, we move from a concern with how realist texts
name real things to a more performance-based, possibility-making angle, or what I am calling "delivery systems." How is language used to test
out commonality, self-identity, otherness? And I am talking about not
only "ordinary" language, but also the language of two specific discourses: that which is found in Becker's "economic behavior" model
and embedded in rational choice theory, and that which is found in
literary realism. This all will hinge on how people act together. In spirit
then, I follow Habermas: "As soon as we conceive of knowledge as
communicatively mediated, rationality is assessed in terms of the capacity of responsible participants to orient themselves in relation to validity
claims geared to enter subjective recognition," with the important quali-
fier that "subjective recognition" is "delivered" in complex and sometimes contradictory ways that actually test even Habermas's communicative action model.[42] This "orientation" follows the trajectory of
"deliverance," of media that rely on a set of common properties to assure
transposability, communication, contract, bridge-building.

And this brings us exactly to our discussion of *Elizabeth Costello*. As
indicated in the epigraph from the novel that begins this chapter, in the
course of the narrative Coetzee tracks the move from realism, the correspondence of words and things and rational action predicated on a faith
in such correspondence, to a postrealist world in which language and
things no longer connect, when actions lead to unexpected results, and
in fact people become paralyzed. This all occurs not because of some

weird delinkage in the universe, but because rational choices are made impossible when placed in an intersubjective realm populated by too much otherness. The world we find in *Elizabeth Costello* is thus the mirror image of the world of common ground posited by Auerbach. Ultimately, the very thing that binds humans together is shattered, as all living beings, including nonhuman animals, now qualify for a position in the same paradigm.

At the very beginning of the novel, we are presented with the passage I used as an epigraph for this chapter. It is a statement on literary realism that brings together the topics of narrative art, rationality, choice-making, and otherness. Coetzee borrows precisely the discourse of problem-solving and choice-making: "There is first of all the problem of the opening, namely, how to get us from where we are, which is, as yet, nowhere, to the far bank. It is a simple bridging problem, a problem of knocking together a bridge. People solve such problems every day. They solve them, and having solved them push on."[43] We find here two key elements that tie together the issue of rationality and otherness. First of course is the idea of choice—in the poetics of realism one identifies one's preferences, one's utility, and then works out the ways to remove obstacles and maximize efficiencies toward that end. But, second, the poetics of realism is also a poet(h)ics, for that bridge is built not only between discrete choices and actions but also between people and other creatures of the earth. In fact, the latter connection is implicated in the former. The connection between *those* two relies and puts tremendous pressure on the imagination, so much so that it may strain against the constraints of reason. It is no accident that Coetzee's fictional protagonist, the speaker of these lines, presents him with this key problem of otherness and imagination: how to bridge the distance between his biological and biographical self and the sixty-six-year-old Australian female author who is his chief character and organizing point of view. How will he solve the engineering problem he sets forth for all realist literature?[44]

Costello confidently asserts that for realism the task is to "supply the particulars [and] allow the significations to emerge of themselves" (4). However, the problem set forth in the novel is a historical one: it relies on a reader who is able to see the bridge and to connect the particulars into a meaningful unit. Moreover, the novel will proceed to outline a problematic in which it is precisely the difficulty of envisioning a broader, global set of readers, each bringing her or his set of interests and values to the text, that makes signifying a fraught and unsure venture. Time and again in this text we find that the significations do not easily or unambiguously "emerge of themselves." Coetzee suggests that the audience for realist literature may be deaf to those connections and significations, and this is in no small way attached to a different and problematic condition of understanding why and how different people who now exist within our sphere of life (as opposed to existing as distant and distinct) act.

From the very start, the novel sets up the conditions of its success and failure. On the one hand, Costello opines, "Realism is driven to invent situations . . . in which characters give voice to contending ideas and thereby in a certain sense embody them. The notion of *embodying* turns out to be pivotal. In such debates ideas do not and indeed cannot float free: they are tied to the speakers by whom they are enounced, and generated from the matrix of individual interests out of which their speakers act in the world" (9). On the other hand, the characters so invented by Coetzee embody chaotic and inconsistent ideas, and the entire notion of an identifiable individual is shown to be questionable, just as the line between Self and Other is seen to be radically blurred. As such, characters are intensely problematic anchors for any realist position, and as a consequence of this, the "matrix of interests" thus turns out to be anything but coherent; rather, we are confronted by a matrix composed of conflictual gestures and aspirations. It is critical here to insist that the problematic of the novel itself is not (simply) an arbitrarily invented series of paradoxes—the problematic is indeed produced by the twin failures of artistic realism and rationality.

Both the failure of "bridging" and the incoherence of interests stem from the same source: the essential inability to imagine an other. This ability has been a cornerstone in Western philosophical aesthetics since Kant, and has an intimate connection with ethics. It shows up especially in Kant's notion of the *sensus communis*, a term which is difficult to translate fully, but which might be called a common sense: "For the principle [of sensus communis,] while it is only subjective, being yet assumed as a subjective universal (a necessary idea for every one), could, in what concerns the consensus of differing judging Subjects, demand universal assent like an objective principle, provided we were assured of our subsumption under it being correct. This indeterminate norm of a common sense is as a matter of fact, presupposed by us" (Kant, 85). As Antoon Van Den Braembussche argues,

> Kant tries to construct sensus communis as an operation of reflection which enables us to free ourselves from our own prejudices by comparing "our own judgment with human reason in general." . . . Here, Kant, clearly, is making a stance for a kind of *maieutics*, a sort of thought experiment, in which we compare our judgments not with the actual but rather with the merely possible ones of others in order to put ourselves in the position of someone else.[45]

It is, in short, a particular form of empathy that tries to intuit the universally shared affect of a work of art. One's disinterested free play of the imagination is thus an image of the morally good; the sensus communis is connected to acting in such a way that one's actions can be the basis for a universal order. In short, the private is connected to the intersubjective and the public.[46] And within the first dozen pages of the novel we find that the imagining of others is articulated precisely as a core element of Costello's dicta: "It is otherness that is the challenge. Making up someone other than yourself. Making up a world for him to move in" (12).

What becomes clear as the novel progresses is that the true difficulty of this challenge is to create a *plausible* world for the fictional character, a "realistic" one which, according to what we have learned thus far, must be able to present a matrix of interests and behaviors associated with that person as a unified subject that can speak to others. The reader's imaginative construction of that "bridge" between discrete acts and events forms the crux of the realist project, but it must be supported at base by a faith in the consistent behavior of an individual character. However, *Elizabeth Costello* blurs the line between human beings not only as greater numbers of "other" kinds of people invade the privileged space of "the subject," but also as the line between humans and animals disintegrates. Costello ups the ante in her next articulation of realism, presenting a lecture titled "What Is Realism?" and alluding to a parable by Kafka in which an ape (or so it appears) stands before an audience and delivers a speech. Costello uses this as a challenge to her own audience: can they reside in that space in which the human and the ape can cohabit a form of the imagination? What is our capacity to imagine otherness in a transspecies fashion? What do our senses of the real and the rational rely on as foundational, and how does that foundation act as a barrier to other modes of reasoning or imagining? Turning precisely to the act of writing fiction, she questions the bounds of rhetoric, the tropes and figures that stand outside its signifying protocols: "For all we know, the speaker may not 'really' be an ape, may simply be a human being like ourselves deluded into thinking himself an ape, or a human being presenting himself, with heavy irony, for rhetorical purposes, as an ape" (18).[47]

This is not a transhistorical question regarding the elasticity of the imagination and poetic language. Coetzee locates the problem of poetics, realism, and imagination at a specific moment in time, when we witness a particular strain placed on the logic and reason of realism, a crisis predicated by the expanding field of otherness.

> There used to be a time when we knew. We used to believe that when the text said, "on the table stood a glass of water," there was indeed a table, and a glass of water on it, and we had only to look at the word-mirror of the text to see them. But all that has ended. The word-mirror is broken, irreparably, it seems. About what is really going on in the lecture hall your guess is as good as mine: men and men, men and apes, apes and men, apes and apes. . . . There used to be a time, we believe, when we could say who we were. Now we are just performers speaking our parts. The bottom has dropped out. (19)

There is no way to avoid the radical quality of the last statement especially, for if "we" as human subjects are simply performers playing parts set forth by history, then with the blurring of boundaries, the evaporation of the containers of the real, with the flooding-in of otherness, comes too the dissolution of human subjectivity. And yet this dissolution is regarded in *Elizabeth Costello* as not necessarily a bad thing. There is a wonderful and at the same time terrible price to pay for meeting the challenge of inventing something truly other than oneself.

To fully embrace the potential of this terrible success of the "fusion" of self and other, one must first abandon reason as absolute: "Both reason and seven decades of life experience tell me that reason is neither the being of the universe nor the being of God. On the contrary, reason looks to me suspiciously like the being of human thought; worse than that, like the being of one tendency in human thought. Reason is the being of a certain spectrum of human thinking" (67). To maintain the belief that reason is universal rather than particular is to maintain the boundaries of the imagination and the limits of the Self.

> Might it not be that the phenomenon we are examining here is, rather than the flowering of a faculty that allows access to the secrets of the universe, the specialism of a rather narrow self-regenerating intellectual tradition whose forte is reasoning, in the same way that the forte of chess players is playing chess, which for its own motives it tries to install at the centre of the universe? Yet, although I see that the best way to win acceptance from this learned gathering would be for me to join myself, like a tributary stream running into a great river, to the great Western discourse of man versus beast, of reason versus unreason, something in me resists, foreseeing in that step the concession of the entire battle. (69)

Costello resists this concession because it would not only acknowledge the assumptions that undergird that dichotomy, but also because it would also leave intact the illusion that the question of reason and its separation from unreason is a neutral, unmotivated one. Instead, she sees behind the very posing of such questions a continuing program of subordination, of dominance that allows precisely for the maintenance of the boundary between Self and Other in the entire animal realm. She uses the psychologist Wolfgang Köhler's treatise of 1917, "The Mentality of Apes," as a prime example. Köhler tries an experiment on an ape he names Sultan, withholding food until the ape is forced to use his intelligence in a way that confirms Köhler's assumptions of what an animal *should* think: "As long as Sultan continues to think the wrong thoughts, he is starved. He is starved until the pangs of hunger are so intense, so overriding, that he is forced to think the right thought, namely, how to go about getting the bananas. . . . From the purity of speculation (Why do men behave like this?) he is relentlessly propelled towards lower, practical, instrumental reason (How does one use this to get that?)" (73).

Thus, as Costello says, "A carefully plotted psychological regimen conducts him *away* from ethics and metaphysics towards the humbler reaches of practical reason" (74). Indeed, to put it more bluntly, as long as the ape thinks in any other fashion than pragmatically, his behavior confirms his status as animal (and not human), and the creature is punished. This critique has, of course, a broader application: as long as

any animal or sentient creature defies its placement in the schematization of reason, it will be forcefully disciplined. What does this tell us
about our stance toward other human beings? Conversely, and this is
Costello's next topic, much as we seek to maintain a careful watch over
the borders between human and animal life, policing the line with
reason as our yardstick, we can also relegate other human beings to the
other side when our motives require. This is only possible, Costello
claims, when we deny ourselves the faculty of sympathy. And this brings
her discussion fully back into the realm of her declared topic: realism
and literature. At this point in Costello's disquisition the demand for
rationality placed on others is replaced by a demand placed on ourselves
to be able to feel sympathy.

We recall that the key challenge presented to the author is to create
fictional others and worlds in which they would act. And yet this challenge seems insurmountable precisely because it puts us face to face
with a number of imperatives: for example, how to displace (or at least
"bracket") oneself enough to allow for the imagining of an other that
endows that other with her or his (or its) own sphere of action and
choice, without mandating that the other has to act as we do? And yet
how can we make a bridge between their discrete acts and our realm of
understanding reasonable, that is, "realistic," if we do not retain (as if we
could truly give it up) our own particular sense of the real, the rational,
the reasonable? This line of questioning thus links the ethical aspect of
writing to that of being human in general. Costello is moved to make a
bold assertion: "If I can think my way into the existence of a being who
has never existed, then I can think my way into the existence of a bat or a
chimpanzee or an oyster, any being with whom I share the substrate of
life" (80). And yet we are forced to wonder if mere "sharing" is all we
(can) do in life, for both practical and moral reasons. The move into the
realm of the real and historical exerts tremendous critical pressure on
Costello's idealism (though from what we have learned about her, that
word does not exactly fit), not to mention on her politics.

Using the Holocaust as her historical example, Costello argues, "The
question to ask should not be: Do we have something in common—
reason, self-consciousness, a soul—with other animals? . . . The horror is
that the killers refused to think themselves into the place of their victims, as did everyone else. . . . In other words, they closed their hearts.
The heart is the seat of a faculty, *sympathy*, that allows us to share at

times the being of another" (79). Taken alone, this argument seems noncontroversial. It is when Costello makes more explicit what she means by "other animals" that her audience rises up in protest: how can she compare the slaughter of humans with the "culling" of livestock? Is she not desecrating the human in order to elevate the animal and to create a world in which we "share" the planet? The issue thus recedes from being a purely ethical one and emerges full force as a historical and eminently political one. Along with this forced entry into the realm of the political, we note, as well, a logical problem. An audience member thus questions Costello: "The very fact that you can be arguing against this reasoning, exposing its falsity, means that you put a certain faith in the power of reason, of true reason as opposed to false reason" (100). Behind every critique of reason is another sort of rationality that founds that critique. It is at this point in the novel that, as if this line of reasoning were exhausted, the scene abruptly shifts to a new locale: Africa.

Costello there meets her sister Blanche, now Sister Bridget, and finds herself defending precisely reason, beauty, and choice. We find that Costello's beliefs respond to this new environment and to her tenuous relationship with her sister. Costello finds herself unwittingly recruited to be the defender of not only humanism, but also the faculty of reason. And reason is no better borne out than in choice. Emblematic in this section is the episode of Joseph the woodcarver, a person revered by the religious community for his absolute dedication to God, which he manifests every minute by his laborious carving, over and over again, of crucifixes. In response to her sister's comment that Joseph can take gratification in Jesus' joy over this "choice," Costello replies sardonically, "I would think Jesus would be gladder still . . . if he knew that Joseph had some choice. That Joseph had not been dragooned into piety" (138). In the same way that Sultan the ape is "dragooned" away from ethical questions and into the sheer practicality of remaining alive, Costello claims that Joseph has been lured away from choosing a broad range of aesthetic life (which she relates to the ideal aesthetic of the ancient Greeks) and into the mere repetition of a single figure, repeatedly depicted in exactly the same pose and posture. To her, this makes no sense. Yet to Blanche it not only makes perfect sense to adhere to this constraint, which is a source of joy, not suffering, but is also senseless to abandon it in order to gain something so pointless in her sister's aesthetic: "I do not need to consult novels . . . to know what pettiness, what baseness, what cruelty human beings are capable of" (128). That is to say, even in sheer economic terms, the cost is hardly worth it; in fact, it is to trade down one life choice for another. Frustrated by the failure to win the argument with her sister, Costello undergoes another transformation.

Performing first the role of aesthete against the hegemony of cold reason, then the role of liberal secular humanist armed with reason against the hegemony of cold, choiceless religious passion, Elizabeth next takes on the role of a moralist who will constrain the very realm of artistic choice that she has just championed against religious constraint. She is invited to give a talk in Amsterdam on "Witness, Silence, Censorship," and during that period becomes deeply disturbed by Paul West's novel *The Very Rich Hours of Count von Stauffenberg*, in which the author offers a horrifyingly graphic account of the final, tortured existence of the conspirators against Hitler. If previously she championed literary art for its aesthetic humanistic value, and for its ethically critical ability to put us in touch with others of all species, now Costello draws back and blocks off certain "realities" from our scope of empathy, for our own sake: "She is no longer sure that people are always improved by what they read. Furthermore, she is not sure that writers who venture into the darker territories of the soul always return unscathed. She has begun to wonder whether writing what one desires, any more than reading what one desires, is in itself a good thing" (160). We have come some distance then from the imperative to be able to choose one's poetic investments, as seen in the episode of the crucifix maker, to the delimiting of aesthetic choice found in this passage. Indeed, choice is taken out of the realm of aesthetics and placed squarely into the realm of ethics: "She no longer believes that storytelling is good in itself. . . . If she . . . had to choose between telling a story and doing good, she would rather, she thinks, do good" (167). Nevertheless, this transition is not founded in anything logical or rational. With neither aesthetic nor rational criteria to guide her, Costello is cast into the realm of sheer faith, or belief. And this is indeed the subject of the penultimate sequence of the novel.

Costello finds herself in a Kafkaesque situation, in a remote Italian village, petitioning before an anonymous tribunal to cross over to "the other side," and we seem to have come full circle back to the novel's initial statement: "There is first of all the problem of the opening, namely, how to get us from where we are, which is, as yet, nowhere, to the far bank." We have come, in other words, to the final "bridge" to be crossed, the final solution to be arrived at, and it is a problem precisely of crossing over, between events, locales, and subjectivities, between life and death. In this state of limbo, Coetzee plumbs the depths of language and articulation, of intersubjectivity, of Costello's adamant individual will and the social nature of writing and of speaking to and with an other.

The judges have one and only one question: what does Costello believe in? The novel is about nothing if not the inventory of possible modes of belief: in reason, in art, in religion, in other human beings, in our capacity to imagine lives other than our own, and in the reasonableness of choices we ourselves would perhaps not have made (poetic and otherwise). Here, near the very end of the novel, we find Costello unable, or unwilling, to admit to believing in anything, even if it means release—a highly irrational choice, if her intent is to reach the other side. Naming her belief will mean release precisely because, according to the belief of the tribunal, it will attest to nothing less than her humanity: "Without beliefs we are not human" (200). But Costello rejects this statement, interpreting it as requiring that beliefs be rational: "Beliefs are not the only ethical supports we have. We can rely on our hearts as well. That is all. I have nothing more to say" (203). Yet, crucially, the retreat is not from rationality to sentimentality, and the reliance on "our hearts" leads rather to an evacuation of self and a merging with the other. Costello's refusal to state her beliefs is paradoxically founded on a belief in an indistinct and fluctuating self. She defiantly asks the tribunal, "But who am I, who is this *I*, this *you*? We change from day to day, and we also stay the same. No *I*, no *you* is more fundamental that any other. You might as well ask which is the true Elizabeth Costello: the one who made the first statement or the one who made the second. My answer is, both are true. Both. And neither. *I am an other*" (221).

At this point in the novel the "bridge" to be made between individuals and the significance of their choices and actions collapses, and this also marks the implosion of the enclosure of the Self. However, this is a riposte that has been with us since the beginning of Costello's lecture on realism. We can thus read *Elizabeth Costello* as following the vacillating, inconsistent trajectory of reason, emotion, belief, art and religion, all ultimately tied to the problematic of otherness: how do we "know" or understand other living beings? What constitutes our emotional response to their lives? How can reason, art, religion form the foundations on which we meet the other? And, crucially, are we capable of conceptualizing ourselves either as apart from, or as indistinct from, the other? And what are the costs of both conceptualizations? While the novel spends the bulk of its time challenging us to imagine otherwise, the end of the novel presents the vertiginous descent into a maelstrom not only of oneness, but also of paralysis.

This conclusion is dramatically articulated in the text that introduces the postscript to the novel, Hugo von Hofmannstahl's "Letter to Lord Chandos from Lord Bacon": "It is as if everything, everything that exists, everything I can recall, everything my confused thinking touches on, means something" (226). This statement achieves its full significance only in light of, again, Costello's opening comments on realism: for realism the task is to "supply the particulars, [then] allow the significations to emerge of themselves" (4). The problem now before us is precisely that there is an overabundance of particulars, so much so that everything "means something," and that the discriminations and hierarchies secured by reason are under attack: with the proliferation of diversity reason turns to con-fusion.

The coextensivity of language and being, of rational discrimination and ontological indistinction, is paralleled in the companion piece to Lord Chandos's agony over the influx of irrationality. I am referring to Lady Chandos's agony over the influx of otherness, as found in the "Letter of Elizabeth, Lady Chandos, to Francis Bacon": "All is allegory, says my Philip. Each creature is key to all other creatures. A dog sitting in a patch of sun licking itself, says he, is at one moment a dog and at the next a vessel of revelation. But I ask you can I live with rats and dogs and beetles crawling through me day and night, drowning and gasping, scratching me, tugging me, urging me deeper and deeper into revelation—how? *We are not made for revelation*" (229). This seems to be a final rebuttal of Costello's project of writing, a rebuttal of the challenge of projecting oneself outside oneself and of "sharing" the planet with all other life forms. Whether through art or religion, this project or challenge and the attendant revelation are to be rejected, for they will ultimately strip one of reason and selfhood at once. And yet even as language itself is dragged along unremittingly by a flood of otherness, as each creature allegorizes another, and each word then bleeds into another ("It is like a contagion, saying one thing always for another"), the final appeal is made precisely through language, and more precisely through writing, to a man who is known to the writer of the letter as one who "selects" his words and "sets them in place" and "builds his judgments" with discretion and discernment. And here, in this linguistic freefall, we can see the trace of Emmanuel Levinas's call to radically reconceive our ontological presumptions and see the emergence of self as always preceded by an irreducible other. Levinas himself uses language as a key corollary for this: "Everything depends on the possibility of vibrating with a meaning that is not synchronized with the speech that captures it and cannot be fitted into its order; everything depends on the possibility of a signification that would signify in an irreducible disturbance."[48] In this passage from *Elizabeth Costello*, I would assert, we find such a disturbance perpetrated by the constant slippage of signifiers, unmoored from "order" and madly referencing themselves and not things (anymore).

And thus we note that the structure being built at the end of this novel is not the realist bridge between particulars ("It is a simple bridging problem, a problem of knocking together a bridge"), but rather a wall: "Yet he writes to you, as I write to you, who are known above all men to select your words and set them in place and build your judgments as a mason builds a wall with bricks. Drowning, we write out of our separate fates. Save us. Your obedient servant, Elizabeth C. this 11 September 1603" (229). This wall is the barrier between radical irrationality, as found in the vertiginous semantic slippage into and among otherness ("But I ask you can I live with rats and dogs and beetles crawling through me day and night, drowning and gasping, scratching me, tugging me, urging me deeper and deeper into revelation—how?"), and a specific kind of realism signaled by linguistic stability ("You select your words and set them in place and build your judgments as a mason builds a wall with bricks").

Coetzee's text rearticulates the ardent hope that literature can deliver others to us, and us to others, in an unreasonable, irrational, and eminently total manner, and yet it shows behind the dissolution of distance and of singular being, behind a successful poet(h)ics, a maddening slide beyond the ken of the mind, a journey across a bridge that leads into a horrible mystery that can only be intimated with trepidation. Dissatisfied with the rational because of its hegemonic dominance of mental activity, its monopoly on the definition of what it is that separates humans from humans and humans from animals, and the cruelty that follows in the wake of such a separation, *Elizabeth Costello* nonetheless draws no conclusion, ultimately, only a wall, and in so doing forces on us, the readers, a choice of rationality enabled by linguistic fixity and "realism," or madness brought about by too much otherness.

Or perhaps this is a matter of too much ethics. For Coetzee is pressing us to rethink in radical terms the notion of rationality as it is used to segregate us from nonhuman animals. If Costello has punctured the illusion of the rational as somehow transcendent and pure, then she has also laid bare the logical and ethical consequences of embracing otherness absolutely. For Coetzee, the appearance of this issue comes about at the appearance of a particular "slot" of possibilities opened up in our recent avatar of globalization: "Whatever is wrong (in the relations between human beings and other animals) has become wrong on a huge scale in the last 100 or 150 years, as traditional animal husbandry has been turned into an industry using industrial methods of production."[49] The perpetuation of inhuman acts on those who are only available to us as objectified others on a mass scale because they have been denied the attribute of a problematic and nonnatural rationality is what draws Coetzee's attention, as it exposes our mass complicity.

> The vast majority [are those people] who in one way or another support the industrial use of animals by making use of the products of that industry but are nevertheless a little sickened, a little queasy, when they think of what happens on factory farms and abattoirs and therefore arrange their lives in such a way that they need to be reminded of farms and abattoirs as little as possible, and do their best to ensure that their children are kept in the dark too, because as we all know children have tender hearts and are easily moved.[50]

How does this particular choice of action—not just to kill, but to breed to kill—rely on a slot of technical possibilities (industrial technologies) coupled with a particular "delivery system" that diverges from and *contorts* our relations to nonhuman animals? How are affect and sympathy, those hallmarks of eighteenth-century literature which we contemporaries still feel are part of what literature "delivers" to us via otherness, blocked in this particular case? The crisis in literary form coincides with the crisis in ethics and animal rights. Everything depends on how we secure our position as writing subjects, as human beings, on the notion of possessing something the nonhuman animals lack: rationality. The overflow of otherness is therefore attributable to the breakdown of this barrier, as reason is dethroned. The debunking of reason as the absolute determinant of exceptional *human* being and also of human *rights* forces us to address the issue of the "sameness" of nonhuman animals at this point in history when technology has allowed for mass extermination of both the human and nonhuman animal. How are we to act ethically in this new world?

Elizabeth Costello's cynicism can be traced, ultimately, to an observation she makes early on, one that we now need to revisit.

> There used to be a time when we knew. We used to believe that when the text said, "on the table stood a glass of water," there was indeed a table, and a glass of water on it, and we had only to look at the word-mirror of the text to see them. But all that has ended. The word-mirror is broken, irreparably, it seems. About what is really going on in the lecture hall your guess is as good as mine: men and men, men and apes, apes and men, apes and apes. . . . There used to be a time, we believe, when we could say who we were. Now we are just performers speaking our parts. The bottom has dropped out. (19)

This remarkable passage contains, indeed, nearly the entire trajectory of the novel, moving from an age when knowledge was sure, when rationality did its work, and, coextensively, when literary language did its work as well: when the text said something, it conjured up that thing in our minds and in our system of belief. Words mirrored things, and projected them into our consciousness as well. In short, literature could do its work because the reader was able to make the connections between words and images, particular events and actions and some intended significance. One could, in short, have a particularly realistic set of beliefs and assumptions underwrite one's choice-making.[51] But the breaking of the word-mirror has to be seen not only in the context of a rupturing of literary functionality, but also in the context of a spill-over effect from the text to the world in general, and it is a world which itself contains too much alterity, a world in which the global intrudes and insists on being fully recognized as other. This is where the ethical comes into play. And it does so through an ontological crisis concerning not just the social, but also the species. In this crisis, realism itself seems to fall victim to unbridled otherness. Who are "we" (to go back to the testimony delivered to the tribunal)?

It is this aspect of the novel, beyond the simultaneous dissolution of both rationality and art, that is most troubling. For Coetzee seems to be saying that the dissolution of the rational and the aesthetic occurs within a systemic meltdown that takes along with it the ethical and political. And all this is attributable in no small degree to the invasion of otherness and the failure of the liberal imagination to make good on its aspiration to accommodate it. For as much as romantic liberal humanists welcome the opportunity to share the planet, the novel suggests that without a foundation of reasonable belief to secure the project, we are at a loss to survive the tidal wave of difference, because it will have taken effective political action with it. The "globe" will outdo us, not because of its mass or multiplicity, but because we have no workable political instrument with which to mediate and negotiate a settlement. That underpinning is taken away precisely by the exhaustion of realism and the dethroning of rationality in the face of the nonhuman animal. If rationality no longer absolutely skewers our difference from them, everything has to be renegotiated. And that is precisely the work Coetzee sets out for us.

Let me urge us to read this problematic in a different, though I think related, history, which is exactly what Coetzee does in his most celebrated novel, *Disgrace* (1999), which locates itself very specifically in the transitional era in South African history when blacks begin to take on more and more rights. It is only by reading *Elizabeth Costello* in concert with *Disgrace* that I believe the full weight of either can be felt. The abstractions of one illuminate the political and historical precision of the other, and vice versa; the dilemma of "animal" otherness is linked surely to the issue of racial otherness. The plot of *Disgrace* is well-enough known. David Lurie, a professor forced to resign his teaching post in Cape Town for sexually harassing a young undergraduate woman, takes up residence at his daughter's smallholding in the country. Lucy maintains a sustenance-style farmhouse and dog kennel; she is the last of a group of young people trying to make a go of living off the land. David is brutally beaten and Lucy violently raped by a group of young black men. During the rape, she is impregnated. In the course of the novel, the identity of at least one of the perpetrators becomes known. However, although David urges her time and again to lodge a formal complaint against the boy, Lucy refuses. Just as Elizabeth Costello attempts to finesse the rationality of the tribunal, whom she stands before on the passage from life to death, so, too, do both David and Lucy, in separate instances, refuse to give testimony before two different tribunals. Lurie refuses to mouth the confession and apology tacitly set up as requisites for him to be able to retain his teaching position; Lucy refuses to press charges. Why is that? Why make that choice to relinquish rights and justice? Although I am not prepared to argue that the ethics or logic of father's and daughter's refusal to speak are the same, I do believe they share an appreciation of the fact that they are caught out of step with their historical moment. For Lurie, the age of romanticism, of literature, of aesthetics, is gone, as are the days when rape could pass easily for seduction. For Lucy, to keep to her original bargain to live off the land requires that she compromise and become not a landowner, but a tenant, effectively switching places with the black African Petrus, who will take over her property, as she, traumatized by her victimage and by the new laws, must acquiesce to the fact that "her" land is inevitably, one day or another, going to revert to the ownership of black Africans.

Like her father, who leaves Cape Town and withdraws into a seemingly endless and futile attempt to finish a libretto, Lucy performs her own retreat from the protocols of filing a charge of rape with the authorities. For her, the rape becomes purely a "private matter" precisely because the historical moment has changed—what would have been a reasonable, rational course of action now has to be reassessed, given history and, in particular, her new relation to the other. This in turn transforms her sense of herself and her role as an actor in the world. She tells her father,

> This has nothing to do with you, David. You want to know why I have not laid a particular charge with the police. I will tell you, as long as you agree not to raise the subject again. The reason is that, as far as I'm concerned, what happened to me is a purely private matter. In another time, in another place, it might be held to be a public matter. But in this place, at this time, it is not. It is my business, mine alone.[52]

Conversely, her father relentlessly pursues the cause and culpability of the act, interrogating Lucy's tenant, Petrus, suspecting that Petrus's involvement could have ranged from simply turning a blind eye to the invasion, to actually planning the crime as a way to drive Lucy off the land and acquire it himself. Was it simply a random act of racism against whites or a carefully planned and executed act of violent dispossession? "Do you know, Petrus," he says, "I find it hard to believe the men who came here were strangers. I find it hard to believe they arrived out of nowhere, and did what they did, and disappeared afterwards like ghosts. And I find it hard to believe that the reason they picked on us was simply that we were the first white folk they met that day. What do you think? Am I wrong?" (118). For both David and Lucy, there is a gradual yet final realization that history has brought a profound and irreversible change to South Africa, and no "normal" remedy or action is possible, given the radical change in the delivery system. While Lucy declares, "As for Petrus, he is not some hired laborer whom I can sack because in my opinion he is mixed up with the wrong people. That's all gone, gone with the wind" (133), David asserts that his daughter's dream of staying on and farming the land alone is doomed to fail: "Yet [Lucy] too will have to leave, in the long run. As a woman alone on a farm she has no future, that is clear. Even the days of Ettinger, with his guns and barbed wire and alarm systems, are numbered" (134).

David presents this "rational choice": "Lucy, it is really time for you to face up your choices. Either you stay on in a house full of ugly memories and go on brooding on what has happened to you, or you put the whole episode behind you and start a new chapter elsewhere. Those, as I see it, are the alternatives. I know you would like to stay, but shouldn't you at least consider the other route? Can't the two of us talk about it rationally?" (155). The problem, of course, is that they cannot talk about it rationally, for each sees the future of South Africa from a radically different angle—if only for the fact that David cannot not act as a father, a role he has heretofore only performed occasionally and without full consciousness of who his daughter is. For him, this situation calls not only for him to protect his daughter and gain justice for her, but also for him to negate the horrible truth that his grandchild will be the bastard child of a black rapist. If David's promiscuous reenactments of "romance" in a cynical age yield only barren and alienated pleasure, Lucy's motherhood will be a wretched symbol of the new position of whites in South Africa.

The outcome of David's presenting the rational choice to Lucy actually predicts the resolution to the tale: Lucy cannot stay on "alone," and the solution to that is for her to marry the black African Petrus and have him claim the child she is to bear as his. If this is the new realism in

South Africa, the new way actions will unfold with this radical revision of the subject paradigm, it is a heavy irony that Lucy asks her father to present her contract to Petrus—as if echoing Coetzee's own assumption of the voice of Elizabeth Costello, David ventriloquizes Lucy. She gives him the script for the presentation of, as Brook Thomas puts it, the new contractual agreement of a post-apartheid South Africa, one where the other is allowed to determine the narrative.

> Go back to Petrus. Propose the following. Say I accept his protection. Say he can put out whatever story he likes about our relationship and I won't contradict him. If he wants me to be known as his third wife, so be it. As his concubine, ditto. But then the child becomes his too. The child becomes part of his family. As for the land, say I will sign the land over to him as long as the house remains mine. I will become attendant on his land. (204)

It is crucial to note that with this new power to tell "whatever story he likes," Petrus is not totally unencumbered, for with that power comes the obligation for him to acknowledge as well his responsibility—this "fiction" will now contain a symbolic real, and he must accept the child of the rape as his product. In Lucy's case, it is clear that "otherness," in this case blackness, has merged into the paradigm of privilege and ownership heretofore denied it. Within the specific "delivery system" that now incorporates blacks and whites, what used to be an area of exclusion and separateness has become, at least in potential, common ground.

A tectonic shift in rights, ownership, results in a different kind of voicedness.[53] Crucially, what we are presented with is not the age of apartheid or of some revolutionary post-apartheid world, but, as Nadine Gordimer says, life "in the interregnum." If in *Elizabeth Costello* the outcome of too much otherness flooding the paradigm of "human" is a general paralysis of that category, in *Disgrace* the result is an overwhelming sense of resignation to history as well. The great accomplishment of that novel lies in the characters' attempts to salvage from it all some moment of grace, in terms of both racial and animal being. The line between resignation and grace, however, is very thin.

Disgrace ends with the most radical vision of commonality, the same found at the end of *Elizabeth Costello*: human and nonhuman animal have merged. Here is the final exchange between David and Lucy.

> "Yes, I agree, it is humiliating. But perhaps that is a good point to start from again. Perhaps that is what I must learn to accept. To start at ground level. With nothing. Not with nothing but. With nothing. No cards, no weapons, no property, no rights, no dignity."
>
> "Like a dog."
>
> "Yes, like a dog." (205)

However, we should note a key difference between this notion of a human and nonhuman fusion and the one found in *Elizabeth Costello*. Unlike *Elizabeth Costello*'s absolute, transcendent merging of human and animal, in *Disgrace* the relationship between humans and animals is historically precise—it is not *all* humans who are now *like* dogs, but specifically the older white male intellectual in post-apartheid South Africa.

I now turn to another South African novelist's treatment of the same era, Nadine Gordimer's *My Son's Story* (1990). In it, we find another meditation on the role and nature of narrative at a time of radically increased contact with the other. Here, however, "the political" is placed in the foreground, and its possibilities read specifically as involved in an interracial problematic. Crucially, Gordimer powerfully installs gender as a key element that allows a different kind of political action to take place. Its altogether startling conclusion suggests a feminization of politics and a complex, ambivalent stance toward literary art. In short, we find a compelling and qualitatively different address to these twin "delivery systems."

2

Whose Story Is It?

At a key moment in her novel *My Son's Story* (1990), Nadine Gordimer describes a particular convergence of whites and blacks at a political rally.

> An avenue of black faces looked into the windows, pressing close, so that the combis had to slow to these people's walking pace in order not to crush them under the wheels. No picnic party; the whites found themselves at once surrounded by, gazed at, gazing into the faces of these blacks who had stoned white drivers on the main road, who had taken control of this place out of the hands of white authority, who refused to pay for the right to exist in the decaying ruins of the war of attrition against their presence too close across the veld; these people who killed police collaborators, in their impotence to stop the police killing their children. One thing to read about them in the papers, to empathize with them, across the veld; Hannah felt the fear in her companions like a rise in temperature inside the vehicle. She slid open the window beside her. Instead of stones, black hands reached in, met and touched first hers and then those of all inside who reached out to them. The windows were opened. Passengers jostled one another for the blessing of the hands, the healing touch. Some never saw the faces of those whose fingers they held for a moment before the combi's progress broke the grasp. In the crush outside faces gleaming in welcome bobbed up.[1]

The passage lends itself to be read allegorically. As the whites attempt to express their solidarity with blacks, their gesture is stalled for a moment: blacks themselves block that expression and draw attention to themselves not simply as abstract political objects of identification, but as real, embodied, human beings. That interruption, that stalling, carves out a time and a place for mutual observation: each group gazes into the other's faces, not past them. At the same time that blacks are recognized as agents of both violence and resistance, whites are identified as existing within a specific relationship to that violence and resistance. That is how the two groups "know" each other. Critically, this encounter is emphatically historicized—the "war of attrition" marks a key element in Gordimer's later novels. Gordimer describes herself at a certain moment as, borrowing from Gramsci, living "in the interregnum," that is, in the slow transitional period into a post-apartheid age.

This new contact zone differs as the political relation shifts, from that of damage done by rocks hurled from a distance, to the laying on of hands through the windows of the combis, and finally to physical togetherness and political solidarity. The new proximity requires a new way of sensing human social space, from one in which certain humans are brought together exclusively under a specific logic of political economy, to another, which produces and contains a different community.

> The blacks were accustomed to closeness. In queues for transport, for work permits, for housing allocation, for all the stamped paper that authorized their lives; loaded into over-crowded trains and buses to take them back and forth across the veld, fitting a family into one room, they cannot keep the outline of space another, invisible skin-whites project around themselves, distanced from each other in everything but sexual and parental intimacy. But now in the graveyard the people from the combis were dispersed from one another and the spatial aura they instinctively kept, and pressed into a single, vast, stirring being with the people of the township. The nun was close against the breast of a man. A black child with his little naked penis waggling under a shirt clung to the leg of a professor. A woman's French perfume and the sweat of a drunk merged as if one breath came from them. And yet it was not alarming for the whites; in fact, an old fear of closeness, of the odours and heat of other flesh, was gone. One ultimate body of bodies was inhaling and exhaling in the single diastole and systole, and above was the freedom of the great open afternoon sky. (110)

This emphatically is a moral and political moment, eminently collective, as individual faces are blurred and indistinct, almost irrelevant, signaling a broad historical sweep. But alongside this image of solidarity, of fusion, there is nonetheless a residual difference. The whites have been blessed by the laying on of black hands, in a moment of redemption and reconciliation, and hence are granted absolution from the "old fear of closeness." Yet even in the construction of this celebratory and indeed utopian "body of bodies," the same is not said of blacks. Indeed, "freedom" as it exists resides above, not among them. It is as if the image leading up to this "body of bodies" has not faded into the historical past; it is an image of language that is not quite yet able to be shared as easily as it is pronounced. And the reason for this is that its historical function is still too deeply rooted in one linguistic, social, and racial community whose segregation from the rest has been too deeply rooted and persistently enforced to be forgotten. This stubborn historical fact forces a rereading of "unity" and a reinterpretation of political language, spoken and gestural.

> There were the cries, Amandla! Viva! and joy when these were taken up by the whites, and there were the deep dreamy intonations of the old-time greetings, "nkos" from people too ancient to grasp that this, granted to whites, now represents shameful servility. In the smiling haze of weekend-drunks the procession of white people was part of the illusions that softened the realities of the week's labour, and made the improbable appear possible. The crowd began to sing, of course, and toyi-toyi, the half-dance, half-procession alongside the convoy bringing, among the raised fists of most in the combis, a kind of embarrassed papal or royal weighing-of-air-in-the-hand as a gracious response from others. (109)

In this novel are two images that refuse to resolve into one: the image in which otherness is dissolved, subordinated by a larger inclusivity in which differences are at least conditionally erased; and another in which history refuses to be so easily swept into the past and replaced by a new order. The question then becomes whether the literary imagination, and literary art, can envision a set of new historical conditions under which that emergence of solidarity between self and other might take place. Can it work against the grain of a history of segregation and separateness, of a material history that is not ready yet to accommodate such a vision? Can it provide a picture of anything else but the silence found at the end of both of Coetzee's novels, at the same historical moment?

My Son's Story announces its attention to these themes in its very narrative conceit: Gordimer places the narration (largely) in the hands of a young adolescent black man, named "Will" by his father in homage to Shakespeare. The boundaries of gender and age are thus imaginatively crossed as Gordimer takes on the voice of the other, inventing it not out of the ether, but from a literary imagination informed by historical memory and present-day contact. As in *Elizabeth Costello*, in *My Son's Story* the protagonist happens to be a writer of fiction, but this bond between the actual author and the protagonist-as-author is not the only link that appears to reach across their differences in gender and age: it is also critical to note that there is the essential link of national identity. It is precisely in playing out its negotiations of otherness within this eminently national framework that the story is grounded; its characters and their relations are situated in a highly particularized time, place, and set of interests. The questions that form the core of this book's discussion of writing, imagination, and the ways people are brought together—which include their historical relation as well as their imagined relation to the world, what Althusser famously calls "ideology"—demand to be understood within this frame, even as they point outward to larger, universal thematics.

My Son's Story provides a comprehensive portrayal of all these issues, addressing the transgression of sexual, racial, moral, political, national, and gender boundaries that keep different peoples separated out into various groups of "others." At base, the novel's problematic seems to argue a zero-sum game: as boundaries are destabilized, as players change position, new points of balance and equilibrium are established. It is as if the world cannot tolerate too much change, of any sort, and that shifts in the political, sexual, racial landscape end up settling into other, but similar, patterns of empowerment and disempowerment. Before moving into my reading of *My Son's Story* along these lines of inquiry, it would be good to first listen to what Gordimer has to say about writing, otherness, and South African history.

Writing, Identification and Disidentification, Otherness

Let's begin with a very basic question: how does Gordimer "identify" with her topic and the people, real and fictional, that go into the making of her novel? If literature is to bring us into contact with distant others across geographic, cultural, class, gender, racial differences, how does the writer begin to form some idea of what that other might be, and what constraints—aesthestic, intellectual, ethical—might pertain? In the introduction to a 1976 collection of her short stories, Gordimer describes the genesis of her writing process: "I have written *from the starting point* of other people's 'real' lives; what I have written represents alternatives to the development of a life as it was formed before I encountered it and as it will continue, out of my sight. . . . Fiction is a way of exploring possibilities present but undreamt of in the living of a single life."[2]

Gordimer then focuses on the intimate connection between writing and ethics.

> Powers of observation heightened beyond the normal imply extraordinary disinvolvement; or rather the double process. Excessive preoccupation and identification with the lives of others, and at the same time a monstrous detachment. For identification brings the superficial loyalties (that is, to the self) of concealment and privacy, while detachment brings the harsher fidelities (to the truth about the self) of revealment and exposure. The tension between standing apart and being fully involved; that is what makes a writer. There is where we begin. The validity of this dialectic is the synthesis of revelation; our achievement of, or even attempt at this is the moral, the human justification of what we do.[3]

This resembles nothing as much as Adam Smith's detached observer. But Gordimer develops this ethical notion further, in relation to the act of writing fiction.

According to Gordimer, writing's "double process" involves not only a fascination with the lives of others, but also both identification and its opposite. And yet, she continues, the focus becomes not the other, but the self. Identification, it seems, has become complete—the other has become identical, however contingently and momentarily, to the self, which now itself requires the loyalty and discretion owed to the other. At the same time, to even be able to write demands forgoing that right to privacy and the "exposure" of the secret understanding forged between other and self. This is what writers do, ultimately: they not only invent but also expose the imagined union between the other and the self. And yet it cannot be lost to readers that the "other" in this formulation has a rather ephemeral existence. Almost instantaneously, it disappears and the "tension" of disclosure exists purely within the right to hide the self and the impulse to disclose it. The issue could be one of simple, unreflective egotism, but I think that is too easy an interpretation. It might be more useful to consider seriously what allows that precipitous, seemingly unconscious slip. It would be better to delve more deeply into the act of writing. On the one hand, this act seems simply to involve dipping into the "real" life of others in order to grasp a small moment of it, then setting it back on its way into the flow of "real" history, having mined it for a particle of life to be recast in the forge of the literary imagination. On the other hand, writing seems to be caught between the desire to discreetly protect from view this newly minted imaginary construction of a new self and the compulsion to "expose" and in fact share that figment with the world. This latter option is a politically motivated one.

In Gordimer, the compulsion to express the internalized encounter with the other—that is, this newly arrived at imaginative world—is highly specific to the political situation in which she finds herself and the other.

> A writer is a being in whose sensibility is fused what Lukacs calls "the duality of inwardness and outside world," and he must never be asked to sunder this union. The coexistence of these absolutes often seems irreconcilable within one life, for me. In another country, another time, they would present no conflict because they would operate in unrelated parts of existence; in South Africa now they have to be co-ordinates for which the coupling must be found. The morality of life and the morality of art have broken out of their categories in social flux. If you cannot reconcile them, they cannot be kept from one another's throats, within you.[4]

In this quotation, Gordimer connects the act of writing fiction to the specific challenge of South Africa. More particularly, she brings forward a term missing from the previous passages we have considered; the issue is now more than simply "art" and "life," the inward and the outward, concealment and disclosure. Along with the insistence that these dynamics be located in time and space is the assertion that *morality* colors all, and that morality is tied to social phenomena. We now are asked to consider the ethicopolitical demands that intrude on what might otherwise be regarded as only a debate within oneself as to whether to express or repress the contents of one's imagined encounter with another, one's projection of that image into the world.

The imagination is now to be seen as irrevocably linked to a consideration of time and place and a larger social context. This context is not fixed, but in motion and variable, creating a shifting terrain across which to read the lives of others and one's relation to them.

> Part of these stories' "truth" does depend upon faithfulness to another series of lost events—the shifts in social attitudes as evidenced in the characters and situations. . . . The change in social attitudes unconsciously reflected in the stories represents both that of the people in my society—that is to say, history—and my apprehension of it; in the writing, I am acting upon my society, and in the manner of my apprehension, all the time history is acting upon me.[5]

In any imagining of the lives of others, and in any attempt to imaginatively forge from that a trajectory of life, a writer thus reads as well the traces of the past and the present—history weighs in on one's understanding of one's material, and constrains and colors one's working with it. We therefore see, from the minimal outline of self and other, an expansion of the act of writing into a wider consideration of historical, political, ethical, and social (rather than simply intersubjective) life.

With that widening sphere, with such considerations now also extending outward to encompass a larger sphere of responsibility and accountability, in Gordimer's South African case is the inevitable question of race and material history. In a speech delivered in 1979, "Relevance and Commitment," Gordimer draws all these elements together in a forceful and precise account of the arts in South Africa, insisting that "it is at the widest level of the formation of our society itself, and not at any specific professional level, that the external power of society enters the breast and brain of the artist and determines the nature and state of art."[6] This is probably her single most comprehensive and indeed passionate statement on writing, race, and South Africa, and thus bears substantial citation and discussion. First, there is her declaration that any consideration of "culture" in South Africa cannot be discussed seriously or comprehensively without attending to race relations, and those relations in turn are irrevocably linked to material history and economics.

There is a question that bursts with the tendency of a mole from below the surface of our assumptions at this conference: Do men and can men make a common culture if their material interests conflict?

... The nature of art in South Africa today is primarily determined by the conflict of material interests in South African society. We gather, rent by that conflict, in this auditorium. On the very ground of one of South Africa's institutions, this 150-year-old university, we gather within a philosophy of spiritual liberation that requires, among other fundamentals, a frank appraisal of the institutions and policies of the white communities that affect the arts in South Africa.

... For I take it we acknowledge that as racial problems, both material and spiritual, can hope to be solved only in circumstances of economic equality, so the creative potential of our country cannot be discussed without realisation and full acceptance that fulfillment of that potential can be aimed for only on the premise of the same circumstances.

Equal economic opportunity, along with civil and parliamentary rights for all 26 million South Africans, is rightly and inevitably the basis for any consideration of the future of the arts.[7]

This is a straightforward weaving together of much of what my book is about: the intimate connection between culture and material history, the profound effects of the latter on the former, and the critical role that institutions play in the "deliverance" of others across those terrains— how it is that people are drawn together and kept apart at the same time by the uneven applications of laws, economic practices, political power, and disenfranchisement. In another essay, "Living in the Interregnum," Gordimer writes, "It is not a matter of blacks taking over white institutions, it is one of conceiving of institutions—from nursery schools to government departments—that reflect a societal structure vastly different from that built to the specifications of white power and privilege."[8] Importantly, she reflects on how the shifting national landscape of race relations affects the ways one envisions one's art as it regards the other and one's relation to that other. Indeed, it is exactly the liberal vision of art as reconciling the discordance between the real and the ideal that has to bear the particular contradictions of national racial politics.

For a long time—a generation at least—the white artist has not seen his referent as confined within white values. For a long time he assumed the objective reality by which his relevance was to be measured was somewhere out there between and encompassing black and white. Now he finds that no such relevance exists; the black has withdrawn from a position where art, as he saw it, assumed the liberal role Nosipho Majeke defined as that of the "conciliator between oppressor and oppressed."[9]

Under such conditions, when asked the question "Where do whites fit in in the New Africa?," Gordimer is forced to reply, "*Nowhere*, I'm inclined to say."[10]

Nonetheless, later in the same essay Gordimer cannot refuse a conjecture on the preconditions that might allow some "place" for whites in the new Africa. And these preconditions involve exactly that whites take on the imagined existence of an other. She does not venture as far as to say that whites must imagine themselves as subjugated, colonized people—that would be inappropriate on a number of levels, certainly. Rather, she assigns another imagined identity for them to occupy: "The white man who wants to fit in in the new Africa must learn a number of hard things. He'd do well to regard himself as an immigrant to a new country; somewhere he has never lived before, but to whose life he has committed himself. He'll have to forget the old impulses to leadership, and the temptation to give advice backed by the experience and culture of Western civilization."[11] In this situation of reidentification, whites must disabuse themselves of both their sense of ownership and control, but also of the cultural capital that they have heretofore been reliant on and confident in deploying. What Gordimer has done, in inventing the necessary reimaging of the self and its relation to the other, has demanded that whites identify themselves within another imaginative narrative. Critically, their entrance into Africa is not that of colonizers but of subaltern immigrants. Only by reidentifying themselves in an other's narrative can they achieve the mental and political humility now required for them to exist in South Africa.

In the subsequent decades Gordimer shifts ground and argues that despite the clear differences in economic and political life that separate her experience of South Africa from that of blacks, they have both a shared national history and a shared experience of political, if not material life. This has given her the privilege to write about blacks. After all, she says, echoing the problematic found in the scene of the mixed crowd, "we have been not merely rubbing shoulders but truly in contact with one another; there is a whole area of life where we know each other, despite the laws, despite everything that has kept us apart. . . . I have gone through the bit of falling over backwards and apologizing because I am white. . . . If I write about blacks I feel I have the right to do so. I know enough to do so. I accept the limitations of what I know."[12] This switch in position might be attributed to several things, not the least of which are the changing political climate in South Africa and the invention of different tactics and strategies of resistance. Change is upon South Africa, but it is a slow and uneven change, which, as it tears at the roots of apartheid, pulls up other things as well. The national landscape is marred with suspicion and hope at the same time; we see both the intimations of a new South Africa and the stubborn residual effects of the old.

Ultimately, a quote from Gramsci that Gordimer uses as the epigraph for her novel *July's People* defines the imaginative project—it is one of diagnosis: "The old is dying, and the new cannot be born; in this interregnum there arises a great diversity of morbid symptoms."[13] This diagnosis presses into precisely the literary imagination, and the imagining of a multiplicity of relations between the self and other. Perhaps this investment in symptomology drives Gordimer to at the very least bracket the notion of an unbreachable wall between self and other and to put in its place a hollowed out space for the literary imagination. Crucially, this is not simply a blank check to write at will; it is "paid for," if you will, by the writer's ability to sense deeply and live within exactly that space and time outlined at the start of this chapter, wherein a fusion of black and white might be at least contingently produced. But the writer's role there is not simply one of inhabitant, but also one of diagnostician, critic, and reimaginer. The synaesthetic image found in the following passage is heady and vertiginous, exhilarating and liberating, and at the same time the novelistic structure that embeds it contains as well its negation. The flow and flux of self and other is channeled and compelled in critical ways by the human and the historical. And it is the fictional text that captures all of this, for an instant: "A woman's French perfume and the sweat of a drunk merged as if one breath came from them. And yet it was not alarming for the whites; in fact, an old fear of closeness, of the odours and heat of other flesh, was gone. One ultimate body of bodies was inhaling and exhaling in the single diastole and systole, and above was the freedom of the great open afternoon sky." The central question for Gordimer would take on not just the nature of such a seemingly transcendent moment, but also its roots, its uneven effects, and its longevity, and all this springs forth from a specific national historical moment.

My Son's Story (?)

In *My Son's Story* Gordimer examines this collective coming together microcosmically, her sociological sampling being the family unit. It is in the interface between the members of this family, and between the family and the outside world, that she tests out the viability of political struggle in South Africa. It is important to note how the connection between private and public space is so well developed in the novel, serving as an index of the shifting social relations, freedoms, and unfreedoms that are manifested in the daily lives of South Africans. The key question is how these various social, political, communal forms are to be occupied, invested with new and different possibilities for living together. For living together compromises the clear demarcations between private and public, social and political, history and the imagination, the self and the other. Indeed, at a key moment of the novel it becomes clear that not only are the walls of the family house porous, but porous, too, are psychic, ontological, and epistemological categories. In response to an interviewer's question regarding her novel *None to Accompany Me*, Gordimer remarks on the relationship she constructs between a white woman and a black man; this relationship bears a strong resemblance to one found in *My Son's Story*.

> There's something special about their relationship; it's really not possible to define it. I think the whole thing is, she doesn't try to define it; she accepts it: it is there. It's an irrational thing, because—if you look at his background and the way that they met—here is a man coming out of the squatter camp. But, of course, if you're looking at it in a political way, it's connected with what is quoted on the jacket of the book: that with the passing of an old regime, perhaps there is a possibility of living a new way, of discovering a new self. So that is the connection with the fact that he is a prominent black man. He's living in a way quite different from the way anybody in his world has lived before—as a businessman, an entrepreneur. And yet he comes from the heart of the struggle, living there in the squatter camp. So he is becoming someone who can answer what he sees as the demands of his time. Some people can never change.

They may be wonderful in a certain situation and totally impotent in another. It is always difficult to analyze your own books, but if I try to analyze it, what Vera and Zeph have in common is that they are both moving into a different life and perhaps, with it, there can be a different kind of relationship.[14]

Let's begin by looking at *My Son's Story* in a "political way." After all, we can gather from its author's remarks that the political texturing of ordinary existence is unavoidable, if not overdetermining. At this precise moment in history, along the calibrations of the "interregnum," the new "self" is not only made possible, but certain old selves are also rendered untenable, or only tenable in new ways. The relationship between Vera and Zeph is one between two individuals whose lives are caught in this new historical configuration, a still-in-between state. The old Africa has shaped them, and they are carrying that identity into a new territory, one that will encase and redefine their relationship. The question will become whether the loss of old demarcations of self and other, brought about in the name of solidarity, has truly been liberating. Is it possible to break out of old categories in ways that control against the too-great influx of people and new forms of political and social behavior?

The first scene of *My Son's Story* brings all these issues together within what appears to be a rather mundane scene. Gordimer draws us into an understanding of apartheid, its shifting historical permutations, its effects on the everyday, and the way the everyday taps into the deep racial divides and psychic effects of apartheid. The novel opens onto a scene outside a movie theater. The narrator, Will, a young black African, is playing hooky from his exam preparation, enjoying a brief respite of freedom at a theater that has recently opened its doors to blacks. Gordimer is keenly attuned to the ways in which everyday "institutions" manifest the imagined relation (hence ideological relation) between blacks and whites. Indeed, in one essay she uses precisely the cinema as an example of the interlacing of institutions, laws, and perceptions of everyday life for blacks and whites.

A more equitable distribution of wealth may be enforced by laws. The hierarchy of perception that white institutions and living habits implant throughout daily experience in every white, from childhood, can be changed only by whites themselves, from within. The weird ordering of the collective life, in South Africa, has slipped its special contact lens into the eyes of whites; we actually see blacks differently, which includes not seeing, not noticing their unnatural absence, since there are so many perfectly ordinary venues of daily life—the cinema, for instance—where blacks have never been allowed in, and so one has forgotten that they could be, might be, encountered there.[15]

At this precise moment, on leaving the movie theater, Will runs into his father, Sonny, who is with a white woman. Will's first reaction is that he has "discovered" his father. This discovery is not simply about his father's assumed infidelity with regard to Will's mother and family; it is a discovery which Will imagines and narrates via a conventional and racist narrative, that of a black man lusting after a younger white woman, foregrounding the racial nature of that lust and the power politics that would drive his father to break his marriage vows for the sake of making love to a woman Will describes in these terms.

> Pinkish and white-downy-blurred; her pink, unpainted lips, the embroidered blouse over some sort of shapeless soft cushion (it dented when she moved) that must be her breasts, the long denim skirt with its guerrilla military pockets—couldn't she make up her mind whether she wanted to look as if she'd just come from a garden party or a Freedom Fighters' hide in the bush? Everything undefined; except the eyes. Blue, of course. Not very large and like the dabs filled in with brilliant colour on an otherwise unfinished sketch. (15)

In fact, Will freely admits his reliance on racial and sexual stereotypes: "And even if I hadn't known her, I could have put her together like those composite drawings of wanted criminals you see in the papers, an iden-tikit. The schoolboy's wet dream. My father's woman" (15).

It is as if the floodgates were opened suddenly, with the liberalization of the laws that prohibited blacks from entering the cinema. Now that they can, the "rubbing of elbows" can lead to anything. If they can now be drawn into a common cultural experience—watching the "foreign" film—what else might happen? What has *already* happened? If the loosening of barriers can be read positively, then Gordimer also asks us to read the negative potential as well. Take for instance, the basic notion of ethics and personal deportment. How are people to act among themselves? What is the nature of the new social contract in South Africa? At the start of the novel, after this opening scene announcing the change in the rights of blacks to attend this theater, we return to an account of what preceded that change, of what life was like before, and how that shaped one's sense of community and interpersonal relations.

Speaking of Will's family in the early days, Gordimer writes, "They found that for them both the meaning of life seemed to be contained, if mysteriously, in living useful lives. They knew what that was not: not living only for oneself, or one's children, or the clan of relatives. They were not sure what it was; not yet. Only that it had to do with responsibility to a community" (9). The passage begins as a laudable but conventional statement regarding practical useful lives, and that usefulness was to be targeted to a "community." But the sentence continues in an extraordinary manner, transforming the platitudinous tone into a sinister one: "And that could only mean the community to which they were confined, to which they belonged because the law told them so, in the first place, and that to which the attachments and dependencies of daily life and the shared concerns that came from living within it, made them belong, of themselves" (9). Community is therefore not freely chosen, it is mandated—where one lives is determined by where one cannot live. Confinement is a soft term for imprisonment, after all.

The traffic between discrete and segregated spaces is thus carefully controlled and contained, and within the individual consciousness is interpolated a psychic barricade.

> During the week, the throng vanished, obediently pushed back to the areas set aside for them outside the town. The workers were in the factories, the schoolteacher went to his designated school; men, women, children—everyone kept to the daily pathways worn within that circumscribed area. . . . [I]t was as if the municipality left some warning odour, scent of immutable authority, where the Saturday people were not to transgress. And they read the scent; they recognized it always, it had always been there. There was no need for notices spelling it out. (11–12)

And yet the fact that this community is a coerced one does not impede the growth of real human attachments; "shared concerns" are thus the instigators of a sense of sameness and indeed belonging, albeit a belonging confined to that space and that lived experience. The real task is to determine the prioritization of shared concerns within the community, as well as the proper relation to the "outside." For most, behavior is largely geared toward survival and maintaining the status quo.

But because of the universality of liberal sentiment and institutions, of course the blacks need schools—there must be inculcated in them a sense of (and even obligation for) improvement. Where that improved self will go and what it will do is, under apartheid, a cruel circle—back to the segregated community or out into the broader world to take up a subaltern position. In the face of such expectations, Will's father, Sonny, attempts to debunk the notion, held by the parents in the community, that their children's education is indeed impractical, a "luxury," a dalliance for a short period in the lives of whites, which will be rechanneled back into the black community to little effect. On the contrary, Sonny wishes to connect the state apparatus back to the community it serves, however partially and ineffectively: "Sonny felt his way was obviously through a special responsibility to the children in the school: it opened out from conscientiousness in teaching his own classes to an accountability for the welfare of all the children at the school. He saw the need to bring together the school and the community in which it performed an isolated function—education as a luxury, a privilege apart from the survival preoccupations of the parents" (9). It is no understatement to say that this is the foundation of Sonny's politicization. The community that is his by law nonetheless produces moral and ethical responsibilities that ironically demand that blacks turn against the state sponsors and, armed with the knowledge conveyed within those very structures, militate to change structural injustices.

Like the cinema, schools are spaces in which culture is disseminated and in which, just as important, people mix to receive and produce culture, with different goals and effects. Sonny teaches the children Shakespeare, an author he has always loved, as a literary artist he admired enough to name his only son after him, but also as a token of the cultural capital he assumed would facilitate his upward mobility. But at a critical moment in the text he also teaches them how to design and paint protest signs. Swept up in the anti-apartheid movement, the children have begun following another tutor—the movement. They start becoming (re)producers of another language, and marching on another path.

EDUCATION APARTHEID SLAVVERY POLICE GET OUT OUR SCHOOLS. They were copying the real blacks, the headmaster told his staff meeting, and he would have none of it. They would not grow up to carry passes, their schools were better than the blacks, they were advantaged—no, he did not say it: they were lighter than the blacks. But the hardest-working, best member of his staff was thinking how children learn from modeling themselves on others, mimicking at first the forms of maturity they see in their parents and then coming to perform them cognitively as their capacities grow; why should they not be learning something about themselves, for themselves, by mimicking the responsibilities recognized precociously by certain other children—their siblings. To recognize the real blacks as siblings: that was already something no irritated, angry head-master could explain away as a schoolyard craze, wearing bottle-top jewellery, passing a zoll round in the lavatories. (26)

In this transformative historical moment, the relation between student and teacher is inverted, and they are "delivered" to each other in a radically different way across the same channel. Soon a synthesis is achieved, as their personal and political wills are inculcated in Sonny and he bends his training to their purpose.

> The schoolteacher walked back to his empty classroom; stood there at his table alone; then picked up a red marker with a broad tip and went out among his boys and girls. They stirred with bravado and fear; they had had many calls for silence from teachers who came to harangue them with orders and even to plead reason to them. But he went from cardboard to cardboard correcting spelling and adding prepositions left out. Giggles and laughter moved the children now, like one of the gusts that kicked dust spiralling away in the trampled yard.—Let's take your placards into class and rewrite them. When you want to tell people something you have to know how to express it properly. So that they will take you seriously.—And they followed him. (26)

Sonny thus embarks on a different kind of education for himself, and this produces a greater and a different kind of contact not only with blacks, but with whites as well. Compare these parallel reports on his activities.

> He was approached to form a local committee, he was elected to a regional executive, he studied government white papers in the tin-trunk archives of township proclamations, and title deeds old people had kept; he stood on the creaking boards of a church hall and made his first speech. (32)

> He bought books that kept him from Shakespeare. He read them over and over in order to grasp and adapt the theory that recognized social education of the community, the parents and relatives and neighbours of the pupils, as part of a school's function. He started a parent-teacher association and an advisory service for parents, collected money for

special equipment for handicapped children, took groups of senior boys and girls to do repairs in the yard rooms of pensioners. What else might he do? For the uplift of the community he enterprisingly approached the Rotary Club and Lions' Club in the white town with respectful requests that they might graciously send their doctors, lawyers, and members of amateur theatre and music groups to lecture or perform in the school hall. (9)

It is crucial to note that as Sonny is transformed from teacher to political activist, his remaking takes place by putting him into contact with whites in different manners, via specific institutional connections, with a set of motivations that in turn prompt him to act and speak differently in order to enter the political discourse of power. Indeed, it is words and language, now embodied differently, that lead to this graphic change in identity: "Unexpectedly, he proved to be one of the best speakers in the movement and at weekends was needed to address gatherings around the province. His name appeared on posters in dorms where they were scrawled over obscenely or torn down by local whites. 'Sonny,' in quotes, was printed between his first and surnames, in the lists of speakers, the childish appellation became a natural political advantage, stressing approachability and closeness to the people he would address" (32).

In this study, of course, the "deliverance of others" is being examined for its "delivery system." This means not only how others are represented in fiction, but how the very designation of other (and same) is produced via specific instruments and discourses—schools, laws, political struggle, and, yes, sex—that shape how identities and human connections are formed and reformed. In this interaction, in Gordimer there is a mixed sense of purpose and coincidence, fatality and historicity. Why did Will and Sonny happen to be at the same theater, at that moment? How did the liberalization of the laws allow this tiny window to open? Recall how Gordimer describes the protagonist of *None to Accompany Me*: "He's living in a way quite different from the way anybody in his world has lived before—as a businessman, an entrepreneur. And yet he comes from the heart of the struggle, living there in the squatter camp. So he is becoming someone who can answer what he sees as the demands of his time. Some people can never change. They may be wonderful in a certain situation and totally impotent in another."[16] This unsteady ebb and flow of historical change and effect demands a political strategy built to accommodate it. Sonny remarks, "'Taking into account changing circumstances' is a tenet like that of a farmer taking into account the weather" (138). The confines of community are slowly set aside, as he declares to his family, "We're going to move among whites. It's a tactic decided upon, and I'm the one who's volunteered. . . . Working-class Afrikaners want to move up in the world and they'll sell for a high price" (41). "Circumstances" thus dictate the family's decisions; moving house becomes a "tactic." The penetration of the public into the private, social, and personal history seems complete, and the flow of otherness is channeled precisely along these new pathways, these new "slots of possibility."

Let us gather up some of these threads—as before, the very composition of "community" is determined not by any organic growth, but by the changing demands of institutions of power and resistance. Here, the "shared concerns" that influence who lives where include the aspirations of poor whites to move up (measured against the resulting need to "sell high," the cost-benefit analysis of race and class identifications). The historical opportunity thus is shared, if inexactly, across racial lines. For as poor whites move out, driven by class considerations, blacks move in for both class and racial considerations. Sonny "volunteers" to move his family into this precarious and still untransformed territory, this liminal zone, for the sake of the movement. And as he does so he establishes a contact zone not only with the remaining poor whites and newly admitted blacks, but also on the political front, a zone of engagement with sympathetic whites. This is precisely how he will encounter the white woman who will become both his political ally and his lover.

As Sonny becomes more and more involved in the public life of politics, his involvement with the private space of family life shrinks, as if in some zero-sum game. Indeed, despite the fact that at first the entrance of the political into Sonny's house seems a straightforward matter, a noble confluence of interests, in Will's eyes it seems more like an invasion. In Will's story, this is the moment when his father is lost to the cause; it is the beginning of the end of the family. Indeed, the appearance of Sonny's soon-to-be-lover, Hannah, is linked to Sonny's disappearance.

> Of course "we know each other." She entered our house when he was in detention. I let her in. I opened the door to her myself; I always went to the door, then, the schoolboy was the man of the house for my mother

and sister, now that he was not there. Each time, I prepared my expression, the way I would stand to confront the police come to search the house once again. But it was a blonde woman with the naked face and apologetic, presumptuous familiarity, in her smile, of people who come to help. It was her job; she was the representative of an international human rights organization sent to monitor political detentions and trials, and to assist people like my father and their families. We didn't need groceries, my school fees were paid; my mother and Baby (after school) were both working and there was no rent owed because when we moved to the city my father had bought that house in what later was called a "grey area" where people of our kind defied the law and settled in among whites.

So we didn't need her. She sat on the edge of our sofa and drank tea and offered what is known as moral support. (14)

The simple social nicety of his opening the door for Hannah becomes in Will's eyes an act retroactively regarded as the betrayal of the family. The simple "visit" from Hannah is likewise connected to a whole set of actions proper to her relation to the family. She is there to "assist" according to a carefully scripted and rationalized set of expectations of how whites of a certain political persuasion and profession behave toward blacks of the same. The interlinkage between the personal and political is concisely summed up in the last phrase—"She sat on the edge of our sofa and drank tea and offered what is known as moral support"—and yet Will has already determined the superfluous nature of that support, based on his assessment of black-white relations and the cost and benefits of accepting support.

One thing has been apparent since the very beginning of the narrative: perhaps more than any other commodity, except bodies themselves, the thing most valued, and at the same time most misapprehended, is knowledge. In the course of the narrative, the domestic sphere, supposedly the sanctuary of the private and shared intimacies of families, is shattered by the intrusion of the public world of politics. Knowledge of Sonny's infidelity, knowledge of his wife Aila's knowledge (or lack of it) of the affair, knowledge to be passed down to the children at the school or up to Sonny from those same children, knowledge of the political and legal systems can become cross-referenced when the private and public commingle. Hannah is critical to the family (as much as her affair with Sonny proves fatal to it in a profoundly unexpected manner) because she has "inside knowledge" that Will says "she must have gathered from interviews with the lawyers and furtive exchanges in court with the accused in trials she had already attended, exchanges made across the barrier between the public gallery and the dock during the judge's tea recess" (15). The silent, secretive, hidden knowledge passed between the accused and their supporters sitting behind the barriers in the public section of the courtroom is something Hannah in turn absorbs as knowledge. This is a private, but seemingly routine use of a language invented to deal with that specific "circumstance," to use Sonny's word. It is a language that not only connects the accused with a select public, but also connects Hannah to that relation, and one which she and Sonny will deploy at his trial, as they take on those positions and that relationship. It will also bind Aila to her family across exactly that same space.

However, as insistent as Gordimer is that we understand the connections that the political and the legal set up between blacks and whites, in the case of Sonny and Hannah, the sexual and racial are imbricated through and through, and this presents another compelling site for the interpenetration of self and other across formerly sacrosanct racial barriers. Gordimer has Will repeat the phrase "of course," this time as he describes Hannah as a racialized, sexual object, understood through long-standing conventions and stereotypes of race and gender. Why repeat that phrase, that assessment? Because it signals a natural or habitual way of perceiving and representing others via a stereotype. But in a literary text it also calls attention to itself as precisely as a stereotype, and demands to be questioned. What does this tell us about Will, and about the ways race and sex are insinuated together in his apprehension of his father's adultery? The repetition of "of course" signals both ironic distance and a habit of seeing that Will cannot completely distance by this ironic tone:

> Of course she is blonde. The wet dreams I have, a schoolboy who's never slept with a woman, are blonde. It's an infection brought to us by the laws that have decided what we are, and what they are, the blonde ones. It turns out that all of us are carriers, as people may have in their bloodstreams a disease that may or may not manifest itself in them but will be passed on; it has come to him in spite of all he has emancipated himself from so admirably—oh yes, I did, I do admire my father. People talk of someone "coming down" with a fever; he's come down this; to this. (14)

Why and how is Sonny's sexual relationship with a white woman inevitable? How is desire produced not simply between blacks and whites, but between blacks and whites constructed as such by "the laws" which are here anthropomorphized, given a will and intention of their own? These laws have decided not only identities, but also behaviors that both constitute and manifest "who" other people "are." And Will's diagnosis of Sonny is precisely of a spirit with the diagnosis of "morbid symptoms" of which Gordimer speaks in her essay "Living in the Interregnum."

Counterposed to Will's diagnosis of the affair as both externally driven and narcissistic, we have Sonny's version, which comes off as self-ennobling. Instead of being mediated and indeed determined by "the laws" which have produced internalized laws of attraction ("of course"), Sonny's version insists on the political and ethical motivations that he and Hannah share. He sees their relationship as mediated and determined by both their political will and the institutional apparatuses that frame that will. Any emotional content is sublimated into a higher purpose. He regards himself and Hannah as operating in parallel fashion: as his new relation to his new community is one of political activism and self-sacrifice, her relation to his family is also put in terms of sacrifice for the greater good of an expanding community.

> As the picture of the first time he saw her—the young woman monitoring the trial—was reconstructed only later, so the meaning of the moment when she came to comfort his daughter was interpreted by him only later, growing in its power over him, a sign. It was then that it began, that it was inescapable. Needing Hannah. He could not think of what had happened to him as "love," "falling in love" any more than, except as lip-service convenience, political jargon expressed for him his decision to sacrifice schoolmastering, self-improvement, and go to prison for his kind. A spontaneous gesture quite in the line of her professional concern for prisoners and their families: she walked across the gallery of Court A into a need that clanged closed, about the two of them. It was the creation myth of their beginning. That it was not recognized as such at once, by them, added to its beauty. (53–54)

This jibes with Hannah's own representation of the affair to herself. In the following passage she meditates on how her moral and ethical beliefs, coupled with her profession, put her into specific kinds of contact with blacks, and consequently with Sonny. And as with his recitation, Hannah's describes their love as indistinguishable from their shared political desires.

> The hands of the accused across the barrier while they joke about their jailers; visiting the wives, husbands, parents, children, the partners in many kinds of alliances broken by imprisonment—all this extended Hannah's feelings in a way she would not have known possible for anyone. In love. She was in love. . . . In love, a temperature and atmospheric pressure of shared tension, response, the glancing contact of trust in place of caresses, and the important, proud responsibility of doing anything asked, even the humblest tasks, in place of passionate private avowals. A loving state of being. (90)

Most concisely, "In her . . . sexual happiness and political commitment were one" (125). As the affair takes hold, Sonny's transformation is made complete. Will notes the end of whatever happiness the family might have enjoyed, as the zero-sum game between private and public, family and national politics, is played out: "When he had to stop being a teacher and his profession and his community work were no longer each an extension of the other, something that made him whole. Our family, whole. . . . He no longer had a profession; his profession had become the meetings, the speeches, the campaigns, the delegations to authorities" (35–36). What allows Hannah and Sonny to legitimize their affair is their belief that it is necessary to the political struggle. Indeed, their coupling seems to symbolize for them the overcoming of racial barriers and thus serves as an allegory as well of the triumph of anti-apartheid struggles: "Hannah was, after all, a comrade. Always had been, from the first; and as well. The cause was the lover, the lover the cause" (223).

Yet when Hannah, in political solidarity, lets a compatriot stay in the cottage that is both her home and their trysting place, Sonny feels betrayed, not only by the intrusion of a third party, but the fact that Hannah has disclosed their secret password to another:

> —He slept here. I used to come in and see him snoring there on your bed. . . . [W]hy did you give him that password, Hannah? Why couldn't you have thought of something else?
> —What else could I have sent that would make you absolutely sure? What else is there that belongs only to us?
> —Well now there's a third person. (173)

The "intrusion" of the third person puts the lie to Sonny's depiction of his love affair with Hannah as synonymous with their political struggle. The love nest he has constructed and now privatized shows the hypocrisy of his narrative. We see that the connections, real and imagined, between the characters are in fact different ways of knowing, and acting, with regard to their imagined relationships with the other. These circuits of knowledge and action rely not only on desire, politics, family alliances, and loyalties—but also the connections and overlaps between each of these.

But now the "private" relationship between Sonny and Hannah is breached by someone else besides the anonymous young man who is the initial "third person." Since Sonny and Hannah's relationship is, according to their construction of it, intimately connected to, and even synonymous with, political struggle, then there is no keeping out other participants in that struggle. Besides the young man, this will include Will himself, designated by Sonny as their messenger, and later the secret police. The political allies, too, have earned the right to enter into the relationship with Sonny and Hannah—how could they not? The boundary between the love affair and the political intrigue is porous, if not impossible to maintain. If what links Sonny and Hannah is a common political cause—if that is their mode of deliverance to each other across the borders of race and gender difference—then anyone of the same political sympathy and purpose should be able to join that relationship. And that is exactly how Aila comes to figure into it. Crucially, and poetically, she enters the struggle to protect the daughter she and Sonny conceive together—"Baby." Poetic, because their first child, the first moment in which they become a nuclear family, grows up to be the instrument and agent of political struggle that links the personal to the political once again. And, to achieve an even higher degree of irony, Gordimer sets down a narrative thread suggesting that Baby joins the struggle because she has discovered her father's affair.

Once Aila joins the cause, she becomes privy to and conversant in exactly the strategic and tactical language of the courtroom. Her coming to acquire this skill, which parallels her political action, takes place as a zero-sum game: the more expertise and power she acquires, the less power Sonny retains.

> She had been briefed on how to deal with interrogators. My father clasped fist in hand as if stunning himself, his knees spread and his head

sunk over his sagging body. The lawyer was embarrassed and alarmed. He tamely filled a glass of water; could not offer it to a man who had been through detention and imprisonment himself, a veteran of challenge to jailers of all kinds. My father looked up all round, wanting to know from somewhere, from me, because I was there, I was always there at home, her boy, mother's boy, how it happened? When? Where did my mother learn these things? How, without his having noticed it, had she come to kinds of knowledge that were not for her? And what was it she knew? Whom did she know whose names she couldn't reveal? What was Aila doing, all those months, without him? (222)

Aila's independence is thus directly linked to the keyword *knowledge*, and the zero-sum game is patently clear: Aila knows, and Sonny has no clue as to how she has come to know "these things."

But it is not just Aila who ascends to knowledge. At the same moment, Hannah's knowledge is coupled to Aila's. In a stunning movement, the power of women is consolidated in Hannah, Baby, Aila, as the men (Sonny, Will, even the astounded lawyer) stand apart and ignorant. Indeed, the communication between Sonny and Aila is made possible only by Hannah. However, unlike the first instance, wherein Hannah was helping Aila to communicate with the imprisoned Sonny, here the positions are reversed: Aila is the accused.

It was Hannah who found out where Aila was being held. Hannah's connections. It was Hannah who got a note from Aila's husband smuggled to her. Hannah had helped this family in trouble before. Many families. She had visited the father and husband in prison. The note was a minute tightly-rolled piece of paper—Sonny knew how such things had to be slipped in stuck to the bottom of a tin plate at meal time or under the inner sole of a shoe. Hannah did not read the note before she passed it on for delivery. A note came back in Aila's hand-writing. The scrap of paper was the label soaked off an aspirin bottle. There were four words. *Don't contact Baby. Wait.* (223)

But more than this functional, professional relationship between the two women, which has now displaced and superseded Hannah's relation to Sonny (precisely because of a change in "circumstances"), there develops out of this mode of "delivery" or connection an affective, emotional one, qualitatively different from the sexually grounded relationship that had sprung up between Hannah and Sonny. And Sonny, rather than being pleased by this new relationship between Hannah and Aila, is both astounded by its unlikeliness and jealous: "Hannah's concern about Aila was a comfort; and could not be. It seemed to him she lay beside him now as if in her professional capacity, as she had come to see him when he was in detention, one among others her persistence in devotion to the cause enabled her to get to visit, and to whom, as to him, she wrote morale-building letters" (223). The unique relation between Hannah and Sonny now seems to be set within a general category of those aided and abetted by Hannah. The very notion that Sonny uses to assuage his guilt and rationalize his infidelity comes back to haunt him—Hannah has (and should have) *many* "comrades." Again: "Sonny was amazed, intruded upon. Hannah wept. The tears moved slowly down her broad cheeks and she did not turn from him or cover her face in decency with her hands. She had no right to weep for Aila!" (235).

Sonny's jealousy extends not only to the relation between Hannah and Aila, but to that between Aila and the public at large—Aila's fame has trumped his: "Aila! In that role . . . to imagine the freedom songs and salutes for poor Aila!" (226). This is an exact reversal of Will's early assessment of how Sonny arrives at his priorities: "My mother's not in the struggle so my mother has no priority" (136). Now, however, she is, and now Sonny's hypocrisy and great egotism become obvious and undeniable. This leads to a general categorical breakdown for Sonny.

> If he had been the one with the right to judge her. As her husband? As a comrade? The construction he had skilfully made of his life was un-inhabitable, his categories were useless, nothing fitted his need. Needing Hannah. His attraction to Hannah belonged to the distorted place and time in which they—all of them—he, Aila, Hannah, lived. With Hannah there was the sexuality of commitment; for commitment implies danger, and the blind primal instinct is to ensure the species survives in circumstances of danger, even when the individual animal dies or the plant has had its season. In this freak displacement, the biological drive of his life, which belonged with his wife and the children he'd begotten, was diverted to his lover. He and Hannah begot no child; the revolutionary movement was to be their survivor. The excitement of their mating was for that. But Aila was the revolutionary, now. (241–42)

With that displacement of the familial by the political, the very displacement initially wrought by Sonny, we find the erosion of the "center of life," and in his greatest act of selfishness and egotism, and moral evasion, Sonny blames his lover for the loss of his wife: "The centre of life wasn't there, with her, the centre of life was where the banalities are enacted—the fuss over births, marriages, family affairs with their survival rituals of food and clothing, that were with Aila. Because of Hannah, Aila was gone. Finished off, that self that was Aila" (243).

And it is not just the "center of life" that has been evacuated by this gendered reversal—it is also Sonny's political and sexual power: "Since when did Aila decide what was politically expedient? Since when did she think she understood such things?" (169). With Aila's new understanding and decision-making power comes the collapse of Sonny's sexual power. On the same page, Gordimer writes, "His bundle of sex hung there like something disowned by his body" (169), and this loss extends from the physical to the emotional. Sonny rethinks his relation to Hannah: "What was he going to get her to say: I love you Sonny, I love you so much—but she's like Aila, now, she can't say it" (211).

Conclusion: Whose Story?

The ability to say, or not, to write, or not, to resurrect or keep alive certain modes of knowing others and oneself—all these questions, and others, have been raised in the novel. It is thus no accident that Gordimer ends where she began—with Will, whose name not only references, as his father intended, William Shakespeare, but also, I would argue, the will to write. As such, Will's meditation at the end of the novel, a reflection on writing, continues the logic and thematic of the novel, and in it we can imagine literature as a delivery system that is inexact, open, and excessive in generating meaning, as it uncovers and helps articulate the changing nature of the relationships between self and other. This problematic is deeply embedded in the social and historical networks that connect people variously, and often at cross-purposes. Here we find individual will, individual imaginings of these connections, placed into flux, as "circumstance" changes, sometimes, but not always, due to the actions of the characters. In this regard, we can recall the issue of "situation." How is it that we can imagine (or not) ourselves in the situations in which others find themselves? How is it that Aila "becomes" Sonny, Sonny Aila, Hannah Aila, Will Baby, et cetera? Critically, how do people feel they "know" the world of others through these identifications and disidentifications, which may or may not be anchored in anything like reality? And, to link up emphatically to the issue of ethics that is at the heart of this study, what kind of responsibility comes with this so-called knowledge? Will asks, "Why should I be the one who had to know. Is it supposed to be some kind of privilege?" (44). Further on in the narrative, he finds this "privilege" too much to bear: "I wish I didn't have so much imagination, I wish other people's lives were closed to me" (79).

Now what, exactly, has his imagination presented to him, and what status does the imagining of others' lives have to knowledge of others' lives?

> I've imagined, out of their deception, the frustration of my absence, the pain of knowing them too well, what others would be doing, saying and feeling in the gaps between my witness. All the details about Sonny and his women?—oh, those I've taken from the women I've known. "Sonny is not the man he was"; someone has said that to me: his comrades think it's because Aila's gone. But I'm young and it's my time that's come, with women. My time that's coming with politics. I was excluded from that, it didn't suit them for me to have any function within it, but I'm going to be the one to record, someday, what he and my mother / Aila and Baby and the others did, what it really was like to live a life determined by the struggle to be free, as desert dwellers' days are determined by the struggle against thirst and those of dwellers amid snow and ice by the struggle against the numbing of cold. That's what struggle really is, not a platform slogan repeated like a TV jingle. (276)

Here Will clearly declares what has been evident all along—his outsider status with regard to the struggle. Is it by default or destiny that he is thus the one whose story it is? But lest we get too taken with the notion of individual destiny, Gordimer reminds us that there is another "witness" to the action, one embodied not by an individual but by a state agency: "There was someone who always knew where Sonny was, the Security Police. He knew that, Hannah knew that. . . . The third presence in the lovers' privacy is the Security Police; anonymous, unseen: a condition of the intimacy of political activists" (81–82). Gordimer later makes clear the connection between the state and artistic imagination: "There was Will. What would he have done if there hadn't been Will.

Only to Will could he find some way of indicating where he could be found if something happened. Like the Security Police, Will would be in on it" (84). If Sonny has designated Will the messenger for the family—"You're the family Mercury now" (85)—he has also at once made him the Hermes, thus linked to hermeneutics. As he conveys, he interprets, imagines, resignifies, creates their lives as well as reports them. Gordimer thus doubles up and condenses the lives of the family—as a social unit, and as a political one, open to the eyes of family members (albeit those eyes might well be selectively blind), and to the state.

Gordimer's epigraph for the novel comes from Shakespeare's thirteenth sonnet, and by the end of the novel we understand her logic.

> O, that you were yourself! but, love, you are
> No longer yours than you yourself here live:
> Against this coming end you should prepare,
> And your sweet semblance to some other give.
> So should that beauty which you hold in lease
> Find no determination: then you were
> Yourself again after yourself's decease,
> When your sweet issue your sweet form should bear.
> Who lets so fair a house fall to decay,
> Which husbandry in honour might uphold
> Against the stormy gusts of winter's day
> And barren rage of death's eternal cold?
> O, none but unthrifts! Dear my love, you know
> You had a father: let your son say so.

It is the last line that Gordimer uses for her epigraph, but the sonnet as a whole gives a fuller and more urgent context. The legacy of the father, his entire lineage before him, is at stake, and we can read into that equation a sense of "house" that extends beyond the family, to the community and to the nation. The discontinuity that would befall all this would be brought about precisely by the son not fulfilling his duty—to pronounce an identity on his father as a son. Language must pass through the other here—one's identity is determined by the figure of a future generation. But in the unfolding of the narrative that commences after the epigraph we are not given a great deal of confidence in Will's ability, or inclination, to bestow this identity on his father and to continue his name and his line, at least not directly and not singularly.

To understand why this is so, we have to consider two things. First, the last words Will addresses to his father take place in a poem which speaks of nothing as much as betrayal. Adapting what we can take to be Sonny's voice, Will writes,

> Come, lover, comrade, friend, child, bird
> Come
> I entice you with my crumbs, see—
> Dove
> Sprig of olive in its beak
> Dashes in swift through the bars, breaks its neck
> Against stone walls. (277)

Sonny's disloyalty to his family, and his comrades, certainly would not merit reward; in fact, Will's poem seems a pointed response to the epigraph's benediction and charge to him. It is as if Sonny has indeed allowed his house to fall into disrepair, and the rupture of his name and his line is the consequence. Along with this is the fact that Will is now a writer, but a writer with a particular blend of purposes. He admits that he may not know certain details of the lives of others, but he has no problem with "filling in the gaps between my witness." As a "family Mercury," he does as Gordimer says she does—takes the lives of others as a starting point. To what? To, Will says, come into a life of politics. He will report "what it really was like to live a life determined by the struggle to be free, as desert dwellers' days are determined by the struggle against thirst and those of dwellers amid snow and ice by the struggle against the numbing of cold. That's what struggle really is, not a platform slogan repeated like a TV jingle." Thus, while Will might well include Sonny in his report, it will not be Sonny's story exclusively, but Sonny's story as imbricated with those of many others in the struggle.

But we should put some pressure on the notion that he will simply be a reporter, and this is again noted in his imaginative construction of how things happened, things that were part of the experience of others. In this sense, Gordimer blends art and politics in a way that indeed builds a bridge between self and other, or, more precisely, discloses the delivery systems that situate both, in sameness and difference. This relation is thoroughly historicized, as will also be the case in the texts we examine in the following chapter, this time centering on art, but with an eye toward the moment when bodies can be shared.

3

Art: A Foreign Exchange

[The Organization for Economic Co-operation and Development] aim[s] to "construct scenarios 'to image' the bioeconomy in the future landscape" in order to draft a policy agenda for governments in respect to this sector. They define "the bioeconomy" as that part of economic activities "which captures the latent value in biological processes and renewable bioresources to produce improved health and sustainable growth and development."—ORGANIZATION FOR ECONOMIC CO-OPERATION AND DEVELOPMENT, "Proposal for a Major Project on the Bioeconomy in 2030"

The bioeconomy is doing very well, thank you. In 2003, the U.S. biotech sector was a $33.6 billion industry. In that subfield of the bioeconomy that has to do with organ transplants, the body itself has become like Mother Earth, as the Doors put it—raped and pillaged, or as Dorothy Nelkin has it, "Body parts are *extracted* like a mineral, *harvested* like a crop, or *mined* like a resource."[1] More than reason, more than emotion, bodies are taken as the most concrete and irrefutable common human coin, relatively constant across its multiple iterations. We all have bodies, of sorts. We may not agree that a thought is a thought, or a feeling a feeling, as vaguely defined as those things are. Their powers to affiliate radically disparate others are hampered by language, by representation. On the other hand, bodies simply exist in time and space, the here and now. We can argue that those that stand before us don't think like humans should, or react emotionally as humans normally would, but there are reasonable ways to push back against each of these arguments and adjust the ratio of "sameness" and "otherness." People are bound together across institutional media and discourses (political struggle, economic rationality, literary realism, advertising, and visual media) which count on persuading minds and hearts of a common human "nature," over and against the particular interests that abide. To best allow that human nature to flourish (whether it be to act rationally, to acquire the greatest quantity of its preferences, to seek freedom and happiness, to "feel" bonded to the human world, etc.), we have had to see our individual manifestations of humanness as somehow in conversation with those of others, alive or dead.

And yet this dynamic of negotiation employs otherness to both strengthen claims to legitimacy and to sometimes destroy it. At some point in literary history we were instructed to read the lives of those different from us in order to obtain a broader, richer, and more real and indeed more global sense of life, and to increase our human capacities. Yet that has been coupled with a political and ethical question: how much otherness is required for this lesson to be learned, for value to be added, and how much "excessive" otherness has to be jettisoned? Bodies would seem to present a different case. And in this chapter my address to "bodies" is solely in the most intense form of body-sharing: organ transplants. This issue disrupts and troubles two key works of philosophy and literature. In organ transplantation we are faced with the most unflinching instance of the delivery of a part of another's body into our own, within a bioeconomic field that has at its core an engine of alienation and dispropriation that ultimately forces a question as to the nature of life, living, self, and otherness: "Vitality has been decomposed into a series of distinct and discrete objects, that can be stabilized, frozen, banked, stored, accumulated, exchanged, traded across time, across space, across organs and species, across diverse contexts and enterprises, in the service of bioeconomics. Inevitably, it raises questions about the borders of life, and those troubling entities—notably embryos and stem cells—whose position on the binaries of life/nonlife and human/nonhuman is subject to dispute."[2]

So as to be perfectly clear from the very start—I am no purist. If I were Jean-Luc Nancy, or just my plain self, I would leap at the chance to extend my life by accepting the organ of another human being. I am not against this type of medical procedure in general. However, my intention is not to make an ethical pronouncement on the industry, but rather to see how this phenomenon has provided two major writers of the twenty-first century, Jean-Luc Nancy and Kazuo Ishiguro, the vehicle through which to explore radical otherness, the binary of self-other.

Their efforts bear not unproblematic fruit, and I will demonstrate how a similar contradiction abides in both, one that involves precisely ideology and history.

Both of the texts I have chosen for examination here seem to be doubly split. Nancy's work *L'intrus* (The Intruder) builds on his long-standing meditation on being alone with others. What does it mean to be "singular" when, according to Nancy, this singularity always already appears as plural, conjoined, and indistinct? For Nancy, death is the one common point of recuperating that vision of being together; each person's death is a death of others as well, and all the efforts of human beings to defer or avoid death bespeak to Nancy an effort to postpone that grand recuperation. I couple this idea of singularity/plurality with his aversion to notions of "operative" communities, those that are geared toward making manifest some always different and better thing at the expense of reflecting on what already exists in common but is glossed over in the name of fulfilling some greater purpose. Yet Nancy's own heart transplant is predicated on exactly those two activities—that of "operatizing" a biotechnical apparatus or community for the purpose of forestalling Nancy's own demise. Therefore, we are left to make a choice, or at least pragmatically to bracket one in favor of the other: we can wax philosophical, critiquing the operative, death-postponing "community" of technicians and surgeons; or we can enjoy the time granted us by those less-than-optimal activities.

This issue can be rephrased thus: we can detemporalize (universalize, generalize) the problem, or see it as an eminently historical problem of the constitution of communities, in particular communities that "deliver" otherness to the self in the form of migrated organs. Can philosophy, in other words, provide us with a "big picture" that renders the specifics of "deliverance" irrelevant and in so doing disarm the contradiction between the ideal vision Nancy offers of "*in*operative communities" and the operative community that allows his life to continue? Similarly, Kazuo Ishiguro's novel *Never Let Me Go* is split between a deep and indeed even insurmountable commitment to art as providing an at least temporary escape from the shadow of mortality, an interlude of transcendence, so to speak, and an equally profound sense of bad timing—here history matters, a lot. On the one hand, Ishiguro directs our eyes to an entirely abstract "lesson in growing up" (as he calls it); on the other hand, that lesson is predicated on erasing two key distinctions, that between the human and nonhuman, and that of the precise relation of exchange between those two groups. Only if we perform this act of double erasure can we luxuriate in the wisdom Ishiguro proffers. In both these cases, the relation between self and other, and the media that connect the two, cannot remain unaffected by this inner split. We constantly see, on both these authors' parts, an attempt to adjust that relation. This adjustment, rather than being critiqued for its adequacy or not, is better seen as an index to the abiding contradictions that make philosophy and literary art so very frustrating and rich.

The history of tissue and organ transplants in Western medicine has always been involved with questions of singularity, otherness, sharing, and politics. As early as the sixteenth century, Gaspari Tagliocozzi, a surgeon who was also a professor of anatomy and of medicine at the University of Bologna, wrote of grafting skin to form a nose on those who were noseless (in those days nasal amputation was a common form of punishment—we are speaking thus of the reconstitution of a citizen, of reconstruction as a political and ethical act). While proud of his accomplishment in fabricating a nose from an individual's own tissue, Tagliocozzi warns against grafting noses from one body to another. His warning is based precisely on the idea of individuality: "The singular character of the individual entirely dissuades us from attempting this work on another person. For such is the force and power of individuality, that if anyone should believe that he could accelerate and increase the beauty of the union, nay more, achieve even the least part of the operation, we consider him plainly superstitious and badly grounded in the physical sciences."[3] Inherent in the sense of individual bodies is the notion that there are specific individual properties that cannot be transposed. Indeed, as Sherwin Nuland notes, the story of transplantation became "the story of our evolving comprehension that the cells of each of us harbored within them something that is theirs alone." The question then becomes, "How can a potential recipient be made less xenophobic, less destructive of protoplasm from a donor? In other words, how can one person be made more tolerant of the transplanted tissues of another?"[4]

It is precisely with the discovery of cyclosporin that an entirely new horizon opens up; cyclosporin becomes the chemical of tolerance, one which enables doctors to manage the immune system and selectively accommodate the foreign, or quell "xenophobia." Thus, in 1986, William

Winslade and Judith Wison Ross re-pose the question of individuality, but this time with a radical alternative in mind.

> Are we spirits who happen to possess bodies and in fact need those bodies in order to manifest ourselves in this particular material world? If so, then it is not much concern whether we are inhabiting a pure or mixed-parts body. Are we, instead, minds-and-bodies, a kind of computer-like system in which the bodies are our hardware and the minds our software, our operating systems, as it were? If so, then the software, like any software, can run on any compatible body, although often not as well on the body-hardware for which the mind-software was originally intended.... [I]ndividual integrity lies presumably in the brain or in the more complex parts of the nervous system culminating in the brain (although even here a serious problem lurks as researchers investigate the transportability of brain tissue). The rest, outside and inside, is mere packaging of operating parts, to be used, and, when exhausted, to be replaced.[5]

Thanks to modern technologies of medicine, we have come the distance from unimpeachable individual specificity to wide-open interchangeability. And it should be clear by now that throughout these meditations on the distinct, unique, and nontransferable properties of individual bodies is a corollary ontological value pertaining to the notion of individual identity as something inherent, unchanging, and nontransferable.

The historical possibilities of entertaining such a profound re-evaluation of individuals and their bodies creates complex questions of technology and ethics, ontology and otherness. It is in this context of opportunity and crisis that we can read Jean-Luc Nancy's *L'intrus*, which precisely situates itself historically.

> Less than twenty years ago, one didn't graft, especially not with the use of cyclosporin, which protects against the rejection of the graft. Twenty years from now, it will certainly be a matter of another sort of graft, with other methods. A personal contingency thus crosses a contingency in the history of techniques. In an earlier age, "I" would be dead; in the future, I would be a survivor by some other means. But always, "I" finds itself tightly packed into a narrow slot of technical possibilities.[6]

The notion of historical contingency, this "slot of possibilities," deeply informs not only *L'intrus* and *Never Let Me Go*, but also the entire project of the study of the deliverance of others: the self and the other are seen here as brought together under very specific, historical delivery systems.

Central to the philosophical writings of Jean-Luc Nancy is the precise nature of human being and the ontological status of material subjects. Nancy has focused on the manners in which being has been framed in two different but not mutually exclusive ways, each of which has negative consequences for thinking through the issue of being. First is the dominant tendency to read human being as immanent—some individual essence is always at the verge of appearing. The manifestation of essence (whenever and however it appears) is assumed to then be able to ratify an entire philosophical program of reading the human as such. Until then, we must be satisfied with evaluating human history and contemporaneity as indexed by that immanence. Second, and most germane to the topic of this chapter, is the will to operationalize human being—human being and its various actions in the world are meant to accomplish something, to bring something into existence, to change the world and human being in it. There is the sense that such operationalization will, directly or indirectly, be related to the immanent unfolding of human being: we are human in the way that we act in the world, transform the world to our purposes, make it be "us," and the manifestation of such actions takes place through institutions and discourses that codify and rationalize these transformations and their intentionality. The nature of human organization in communities is intimately related to both these frames. Ideal communities are traditionally thought to manifest the perfect negotiation and reconciliation of individual and collective identities, of self and other. This is their immanence— supposed convergences and consolidations are operationalized, their collective "being" quickly used either to reflect back on their perfect enactments or made to be a sign of something else to come. In contradistinction to this kind of purposeful framing and tracking of human being (philosophically and pragmatically so), Nancy proposes that we look at human being in the present as simultaneously singular and plural. The key issue is neither the emergence of being as "individual," nor the emergence of "community" as the harmonizing of individual beings, but rather the notion that all being is best described as a coextensive and contemporary "being with," the focus being at once the singular entities and their common properties of being with each other.

Certainly, one can regard Nancy's meditation on his heart transplant as the near-perfect occasion in which to dramatize this philosophical premise.

In my treatment of Nancy's text, I argue that advances in medical technology have created another kind of human community, one framed precisely by operationalization. Its operationalization is keyed into the project of making possible the immanent realization of immortality. This operationalized community of biotechnical workers has devastating consequences for Nancy's ontology, even as it extends his life. (In a similar vein, in Ishiguro's novel, the invention of life to sustain life raises huge ethical issues when those invented lives have feelings and emotions and bodies just like ours. It is the institutional genesis and logic that gives them birth that creates precisely a deadly schism between donor and receiver, benefactor and beneficiary. Thus, the very possibility of delivering otherness delivers to the donor a death sentence, and to the receiver a morally contaminated, albeit extended, existence.) From this, I believe, we can derive a lesson about human "connectedness" via the logic and economics of exchange and otherness.

Being cannot be anything but being-with-one-another, circulating in the with and as the with of this singularity plural existence.
—JEAN-LUC NANCY, *Being Singular Plural*

Throughout his writings, Nancy insists that any attempt to define singular being as ontologically isolatable from others is bound to fail. Being is always "being-with-one-another." This "co-appearance" is the "fundamental ontological structure" (*Being Singular Plural*, 61).[7] The closest Nancy will come to naming Being as distinct is to place it in coextensive relation to his concepts of the "singular" and the "plural."

> Being singular plural: these three apposite words, which do not have any determined syntax . . . mark an absolute equivalence, both in an indistinct *and* distinct way . . . *Being singular plural* means the essence of Being is only as co-essence. . . . Because none of these three terms precedes or grounds the other, each designates the coessence of the others. This coessence puts essence itself in the hyphenation—"being" "singular-plural"—which is a mark of union and also a mark of division, a mark of sharing that effaces itself, leaving each term to its isolation *and* its being-with-the-others. (*Being Singular Plural*, 28, 30, 37)

Just as he is loathe to isolate Being as separable from (and valorized over) being-with-others, Nancy is set against aggrandizing "otherness": "All forms of the capitalized 'Other' represent precisely the exalted and overexalted mode of propriety of what is proper, which persists and consists in the 'somewhere' of a 'nowhere' and in the 'sometime' of a 'no time,' that is, in the *punctum aeternum* outside the world" (*Being Singular Plural*, 13). We end up with a schematization of Being as no less and no more than the Other; both are in turn removed from any singular "exalted status."[8]

Crucially, Nancy's proposal is different from the Hegelian dialectic in which there is a mutual dependency of being and other, ultimately to be resolved in the florescence of the subject of absolute Being. Instead, Nancy argues for a shared ontology that refuses both an origin in singularity and an immanent resolution into singular Being: "A like-being resembles me in that I myself 'resemble' him: we 'resemble' together, if you will. That is to say, there is no original or origin of identity. What holds the place of an 'origin' is the sharing of singularities. This means that this 'origin'—the origin of community or the originary community —is nothing other than the limit: the origin is the tracing of the borders upon which or along which singular beings are exposed" (*The Inoperative Community*, 33).

Nancy extends this notion far beyond the "human" to delineate a global notion of the shared property of a nondialectical being-with-otherness.

> Both the theory and the praxis of critique demonstrate that, from now on, critique absolutely needs to rest on some principle other than that of the ontology of the Other and the Same: it needs an ontology of being-with-one-another, and this ontology must support both the sphere of "nature" and sphere of "history," as well as both the "human" and the "non-human"; it must be an ontology for the world, for everyone—and if I can be so bold, it has to be an ontology for each and every one and for the world "as a totality," and nothing short of the whole world, since this is all there is (but, in this way, there is *all*). (*Being Singular Plural*, 53–54)

In particular, and with specific import for my discussion of *L'intrus*, Nancy insists on maintaining our focus on the interstitial spaces of shared "being with": "There is no Other. 'Creation' signifies precisely that there is no Other and that 'there is' is not an Other. Being is not the Other, but the origin is the punctual and discrete spacing *between us*, as *between us and the rest of the world*, as *between all beings*" (*Being Singular Plural*, 19).[9] I will return to this notion of the spacing of the in-between, and the possible infringement thereof created by the heart transplant, but first it is necessary to consider what this notion has to do with the idea of community, and, by extension, ethics and politics.

In Nancy, the notion of being-with is intimately occasioned in a spatial and temporal metaphor, which, once again, "scales back" both the isolatability of "individual being" and the telos of immanence: " 'With' is the sharing of time-space; it is the at-the-same-time-in-the-same-place as itself, it itself, shattered. It is the instant scaling-back of the principle of identity: Being is at the same time in the same place only on the condition of the spacing of an indefinite plurality of singularities. . . . We are each time an other, each time with others" (*Being Singular Plural*, 35). Given both this simultaneity and this coappearance, the idea of a slowly evolving social subject with an attendant, developing social community is erased, as are traditional notions of community as the collection of preexisting individuals. Stated flatly, "Community means that there is no singular being without another singular being" (*The Inoperative Community*, 28). The point of ontological articulation is thus "coappearance" as it occurs in the in-between, shared spaces of being-with.[10] And it is precisely the dis-position of this shared space that characterizes the political and ontological activity of community. This connection is encapsulated in this sentence: "Being is put into play among us; it does not have any other meaning except the dis-position of this 'between' " (*Being Singular Plural*, 27). And it is made universal here: "Being is not the Other, but the origin is the punctual and discrete spacing *between us*, as *between us and the rest of the world*, as *between all things*" (*Being Singular Plural*, 19).[11]

Consistent with his insistence that Being not be reduced to the mere immanence of something other to come is Nancy's argument that "community" be freed from immanence. Such thinking leads one always to think of community as less-than itself. Importantly, one effect of this devaluing of being-together is the operationalizing of community. Under the imperative to become something better, to reach some other, more satisfying state, communities are asked to manifest progress toward those goals, to be effective instances of human social development.

The political, if this word may serve to designate not the organization of society but the disposition of community as such, the destination of its sharing, must not be the assumption or the work of love or of death. It need neither find, nor regain, nor effect a communion taken to be lost or still to come. If the political is not dissolved in the sociotechnical element of forces and needs (in which, in effect, it seems to be dissolving under our eyes), it must inscribe the sharing of community. . . . "Political" would mean a community ordering itself to the unworking of its communication, or destined to this unworking: a community consciously undergoing the experience of its sharing. (*The Inoperative Community*, 40)

Community, in Nancy's sense of the word, is thus tied absolutely to the idea of inoperation, a refusal to be drawn into a "higher" purpose (of love, of death, or finding, or regaining, or efficacy). It is only then that we can apprehend its location and experience it in this dis-positional space, a lateral and coextensive motion that refers to nothing. Crucially, in Nancy's work we also find a very similar discourse on the body, and this forms a crucial perspective on what will occur in *L'intrus*.

Just as he rejects the operationalizing of community, its being pressed into service always to symbolize (and act toward) something other and beyond, so too does Nancy critique the constant, seemingly inevitable symbolization of the body. Against this current in Western philosophical thought, he asks instead for "a *corpus*, a *catalog*, the recitation of an empirical logos that, without transcendental reason, would be a gleaned list, random in order or in its degree of completion, a corpus of the body's *entries*: dictionary entries, entries into language, body registers, registers of bodies. . . . All this would be possible only if we had access to bodies, only if they were not impenetrable, as physics defines them. Bodies impenetrable to language" (*The Birth to Presence*, 189). Just as he wishes us to regard community as simply and always a distinct disposition of space in-between, and Being as the coappearance (always) of the singular and the plural in and as this space, so too does he seek to prevent the body from constantly being drawn into speaking of something else, or signifying beyond itself. Instead he would place it into a simple catalog, an inventorying of itself and its others, such that it is given over to writing itself. Then what we will find are "no longer bodies that make sense, but sense that engenders and shares bodies. No longer the semiological, symptomatological, mythological, or phenomenological pillage of bodies, but thought and writing given, given over to bodies. The writing of a *corpus* as a separation and sharing of bodies, sharing their being-body, shaped out by it, and thus divided from itself and from its sense, exscribed all along its own inscription" (*The Birth to Presence*, 197).

Nevertheless, and crucially for my reading of *L'intrus*, both Nancy's desire for us to see community as "inoperative" and his hope that we can regard the body as something other than a symbolic space are jeopardized precisely by the historical occasion of the transplant. For, in this instance, Nancy is confronted by, and his body drawn within for its very survival, a technological community with a precise intent—the deferral of death. And in this community, immanence reappears as immortality. If the negative image of the body for Nancy may be seen in this fragment wherein "the body remains the organon, the instrument or the incarnation, the mechanism or the work of a *sense* that never stops rushing into it, presenting itself to itself, making itself known as such and wanting to tell itself there" (*The Birth to Presence*, 192), then in the medical scientific and technological community in which he finds himself inscribed we find the invasion of a specific sense, a saturation of particular meaning, operationalized and put into service to make the body survive. But survival is possible only within its unique regimes, values, and assumptions.

In the instance of the heart transplant, we find that the "rushing in" is not just that of the other's organ, which is substituted for one's own, but the entire sense-making operation of which this substitution is the end and the beginning. This instance may be read as diametrically opposed to Nancy's description of the shared space between singularities, a sharing that constitutes precisely the singular as singular/plural. Nancy argues that this "between" "does not lead from one to another; it constitutes no connective tissue, no cement, no bridge. . . . [I]t is that which is at the heart of a connection, the *interlacing* of strands whose extremities remain separate even at the very center of the knot" (*Being Singular Plural*, 5). Instead, in *L'intrus* we find the intense and inescapable pressure to discern whether this particular interlacing, interpenetration, does not fuse Nancy into the other, and vice versa. Does this instance of fusion not provide a counterexample to that of sexual intercourse, which Nancy often cites as the positive example of such unfused interlacing?

Frustratingly and provocatively, one could indeed argue in either direction. On the one hand, one could say that the instance of the transplant negates the positive assertions we find throughout Nancy's writing on being and otherness, that it points us to a new historical moment wherein bodies are inscribed and fused (for the sake of their very survival) within a community of science, technology, and the particular values that operationalize the heart in their service. On the other hand, it is possible to argue that this opening up to receive the other, and the subsequent re-relation of singularities, the radical upsetting of a sense of separateness, exemplify instead the perfect realization of Nancy's ontology, that the technologically affected "fusion" actually only reverses the self-other relation and accentuates their mutual identity within the interstitial space of indeterminate ownership of the heart. Herein, the stranger and Nancy share a liminal space or dis-position of organs and identity.

This microcommunity is well described in Rabinow's notion of "biosociality." Nikolas Rose explains.

> Paul Rabinow was the first to recognize this phenomenon—he coined the term "biosociality" to characterize the new forms of collective identification that are taking shape in the age of genomics. His research had led him to identify new types of group and individual identities and practices arising out of the new techniques of genetic diagnosis and monitoring of risks and susceptibilities. Such groups meet to share their experiences, lobby for funding research into "their" disease, and change their relations to their children, their environment, and their forms of life in the plight of genetic knowledge. He also foresaw the ways in which they would develop novel kinds of relations with medical specialists, clinics, laboratories, and with medical knowledge, surrounded by "a heavy panoply of pastoral keepers to help them experience, share, intervene, and 'understand' their fate."[12]

Nancy Scheper-Hughes's articulation of the concept nicely taps into the long-distant, non-face-to-face nature of the liaison between self and unseen other: "New forms of social kinship (and a promise of biosociality) must be invented to link strangers, even at times political 'enemies,' from distant locations who are described by the operating surgeons as 'a perfect match—like brothers,' while they are prevented from seeing, let alone speaking to, each other."[13] This, then, is the particularly operationalized community into which Nancy enters as the heart of the other "intrudes" into the cavity in his chest. In this instance, of course, no conversation between the two people is possible, as the very condition on which the donor "gave" his heart was the condition of his death.

Not only is Nancy's survival "inscribed in a complex process woven together with strangers and strangeness," but this strangeness is of a particular, instrumental nature (*L'intrus*, 21). Nancy describes the intimate and concrete practices which invade his body, "the intrusion . . . of this space: tubes, pliers, sutures, and catheters" (*L'intrus*, 26).

> There is an opening there through which passes an incessant flux of strangeness; immune depressant drugs, other drugs charged with combatting certain so-called secondary effects, effects which they do not know how to fight (such as the degradation of the kidneys), repeated check-ups, all of existence set in a new register, swept completely through. It is life scanned and reported in multiple registers, each one of which inscribes other possibilities of death. . . . It is thus I myself who becomes my intruder, in all of these accumulated and opposing ways. I feel it well: it is far stronger than a sensation. The strangeness of my own identity, which was always so much alive and vivid, never before touched me so acutely. "I" has clearly become the formal index of an unverifiable and impalpable chain. (*L'intrus*, 35–36)

All this bespeaks the fact that the "strangeness" here consists not only of the other's heart, but of the entire apparatus that makes the operation possible, that is, in the final analysis, the intrusion itself.

If one recalls Nancy's critique of Western philosophy's constant transformation of the body into a sign of something else, we cannot but be shocked at the present transformation of Nancy's body into this "new register." In the regime of the transplant, the body has become both the object of a thoroughgoing redefinition and, in that process, is persistently and necessarily read as a symbol of the efficacy of those operations and its legitimizing token. The analytical struggle in *L'intrus* is to tease out the properly philosophical, ontological dimension from the pragmatic, technical, and medical scientific dimension—where does one stop, and the other begin? Again, does this operation enable Nancy's ontological claims to be manifested, or does it negate them?

The weight of the pragmatic is indisputable; Nancy unrelentingly notes the pervasive presence and profound reach of the discursive community which mandates and governs the practices which keep him alive, which enable and facilitate these processes for Nancy's "own" sake.

> To taking drugs more than once a day and going back to the hospital for check-ups there added the dental consequences of radiotherapy, the loss of saliva, the food restrictions, the restrictions on contact for fear of contagion, the weakening of muscles and kidneys, the reduction of memory and of the strength to work, the reading of analyses, the insidious recurrence of mucositis, candida, polyneuritis and this general feeling of no longer being dissociable from a network of measures, of observations, of chemical, institutional and symbolic connections which never allow themselves to be ignored like the connections intertwined in ordinary life are. On the contrary, these connections expressly hold life unremittingly aware of their presence and supervision. (*L'intrus*, 40)

Such awareness extends to incorporating Nancy himself, transforming him into the very material intrusions that now are necessary elements of his body: "The intruder exposes me excessively. It extrudes me, exports me, expropriates me. I am the malady and the medicine; I am the cancerous cell and the transplanted organ; I am the immune depressant agents and their palliatives" (*L'intrus*, 42).

In such dramatic and graphic passages, we find a dramatic and intense instance where one has operationalized the heart, the body, and thereby rendered them outside themselves altogether. Is it not the case that "when one puts the body on the program, on whatever program, one has already set it aside" (*The Birth to Presence*, 190)? Again, the critical question is whether or not this pragmatic program is consistent with Nancy's ontological program, or quite different from it. Do science and technology radically alter (or even pervert) the ontological situation, or dramatically enhance it?

Nancy addresses the relation of technology to being: "We regard ['technological' nature] as an autonomous instrument. We do so without ever asking ourselves if it might not be 'our' comprehension of 'ourselves' that comes up with these techniques and invents itself in them, and without wondering if technology is in fact essentially in complete agreement with the 'with'" (*Being Singular Plural*, 70). He continues the idea that *techné* is consistent with ontology: "Even 'in nature' species proliferate and live alongside one another. *Techné* would always have to do with what neither proceeds from nor to itself, with disparity, continguity, and, thus, with an unachieved and unachievable essence of the 'with'" (*Being Singular Plural*, 202n.61). But is this not an altogether different version of technology than the one we find in *L'intrus*? While the positive version of techné finds it, along with everything else, alongside everybody and everything else, in *L'intrus* is not techné intrusive and violent, transformative? Doesn't Nancy's heart transplant present a radically different, historically specific, instance? The specific, historical case of technology is one which he mentions emphatically in *The Inoperative Community*:

> But for us, by now beyond even the "totalitarianism" that was to be the monstrous realization of this promise, there remains only the play of imperialisms against the background of still another empire, another techno-economical imperative, and the social forms that such an imperative creates. It is no longer even a question of community. But this is also because the techno-economical organization or "making operational" of our world has taken over, even inherited, the plans for a communitarian organization. It is still essentially a matter of work, of operation, of operativity. (23)[14]

The question we have been asking all along—is this operation a dramatization of Nancy's ontology or its worst nightmare—can be situated and read across multiple sites. Each, however, touches on the question of whether the operation allows us to see, graphically and profoundly, Nancy's ontology, or whether its very conditions of possibility do not irredeemably place it in the circuits of a technological operationalization that hijack the human body into a project of immanence. And this immanence would be nothing else than the immanence of immortality.

It is now that we must finally turn to the role of death: "Thus, the multiple stranger who intrudes on my life . . . is nothing other than death, or rather life/death: a suspension of the continuum of being, a scansion where there is not a lot for 'me' to do" (*L'intrus*, 25). Nancy names the intruder, completely and absolutely, its multiplicity now gathered under a single signifier. Crucially, this naming gives a new name as well to the paradoxical question that we have laid out in this chapter: is this operation to be seen as a positive or negative event? If we see it as the latter, it is solely because of the operationalizing of the heart, which comes on its insertion into a technoscientific (not to say economic) community of immanence. Parallel to this network is a network where "life/death is shared, where life connects with death, where the incommunicable communicates" (*L'intrus*, 30). Yet in the course of his essay (and drawing on other of his writings on death), Nancy gives us more grounds on which to answer for the positive, that is, to construe this instance as providing the most intense experiencing of being. His use of language makes this perfectly clear: "To isolate death from life— to not let the one entwine itself intimately with the other, each one intruding into the heart of the other—that is what one must never do" (*L'intrus*, 23).

We can thus look afresh at passages such as those from *Being Singular Plural*, and see in *L'intrus* a particular concretization of Nancy's notion of death and others. The sharing of the heart, the creation of a particular instance of being-singular-plural, is intimately acted out on the communal topos of death and life.

> Community is revealed in the death of others; hence it is always re-vealed to others. Community is what takes place always through others and for others. It is not the space of the *egos*—subjects and substances that are at bottom immortal—but of the *I's*, that are not *egos*. It is not a communion that fuses the *egos* into an *Ego* of a higher *We*. It is the community of *others*. . . . A community is the presentation to its mem-bers of their mortal truth (which amounts to saying that there is no community of immortal beings: one can imagine either a society or a communion of immortal beings, but not a community). (*The Inopera-tive Community*, 15)

The death of others is always a death revealed to others; death "hap-pens" to one, and at once constitutes yet another sign of the shared space of being.

The language of this passage from *The Inoperative Community* graphi-cally names the process of laceration and singular being and death.

> What tears apart is the presentation of finitude in and by community— the presentation of the triple mourning I must go through: that of the death of the other, that of my birth, and that of my death. Community is the carrying out of this triple mourning. . . . What is lacerated in this way is not the singular being: on the contrary, this is where the singular being coappears. Rather, it is the communal fabric, it is immanence that is lacerated. And yet this laceration does not happen *to* anything, for this fabric does not exist. There is no tissue, no flesh, no subject or substance

of common being, and consequently there is no laceration of this being. But there *is* sharing out. Properly speaking, there is no laceration of the singular being: there is no open cut in which the inside would get lost in the outside. . . . "Laceration" consists only in exposure: the entire "inside" of the singular being is exposed to the "outside." (30)

Seen in these terms, the transplant operation changes exactly nothing (and this is a good thing). The immanence of some marvelous communion is taken away from the scene—there is no triumph, or, indeed, defeat (since this laceration happens to nothing, either in the present or in the future). Voided of substance as we are used to regard it, the singular being simply stands exposed to and with the other. The positions of self and other are interchangable, any "essence" (whose heart is whose?) becomes replaced by a global notion of commonplacedness.

And yet this reading is to take only one dimension as the totality of *L'intrus*. The simple fact is that sharing in this instance is enabled and mediated by a structured community intent on immanence, the immanence of its own perfection, the immanence of death-lessness (or at least, the ability to create the possibility for the deferral of death). Read in this regard, this operationalization of bodies (on all sides, from all directions) reinstantiates immanence and recodes bodies in its own logic. In this sense, the historical question which has been with us all along emerges with a vengeance: are we now living at a time when the one thing that brings about recognition of community—death—is forestalled in the name of a specialized community operating under the basis of the eternal imperative to find immortality? And is this immortality to be found only by perverting the ontological precepts Nancy sets forth, that is, ironically, by making possible this laceration that is not a laceration? And, most sharply, is this "operation" not the sole privilege of a select few who can afford to engage in this system, and what of those who are unable to, and those whose organs are donated, in other words, of those who underwrite the system? As Scheper-Hughes notes,

> The entry of free markets (black and grey) and market incentives into organs procurement has thrown into question the transplant rhetoric of "organs scarcity." There is obviously no shortage of desperate individuals willing to sell a kidney, a portion of their liver, a lung, an eye,

or even a testicle for a pittance. But while erasing one vexing scarcity, the organs traffic has produced a new one—a scarcity of transplant patients of sufficient means and independence and who are willing to break, bend, or bypass laws and longstanding codes of medical ethical conduct.[15]

A powerful and early admonition is offered by Richard Titmuss.

> The commercialism of blood and donor relationships represses the expression of altruism, erodes the sense of community, lowers scientific standards, limits both personal and professional freedoms, sanctions the making of profits in hospitals and clinical laboratories, legalizes hostility between doctor and patient, subjects critical areas of medicine to the laws of the marketplace, places immense social costs on those least able to bear them—the poor, the sick, and the inept—increases the danger of unethical behavior in various sectors of medical science and practice, and results in situations in which proportionately more and more blood is supplied by the poor, the unskilled and the unemployed, Blacks and other low income groups.[16]

In my discussion of *L'intrus*, I have tried to maintain a focus on the "narrow slot of technical possibilities," as it draws together self and other, that is historically arrived at and institutionally delivered. This historic occasion brings about the tension within Nancy's writings that I have outlined between a transcendent philosophical statement and a historical materialist reading of life. *The Intruder*, in other words, intrudes into and disrupts the continuity of Nancy's writings and forces a reevaluation. In Kazuo Ishiguro's novel, we find another tension and contradiction, also situated between an abstract paean to art and the question of why and how otherness is delivered to us. The tension of *Never Let Me Go* is located at the nexus of an ideology that portrays art as offering a "bubble" in which to live in productive blindness to death, and a notion that the highest human tragedy is to live in the wrong historical moment, when the ethics that guide the proper relations between self and other are hopelessly inoperative. Ishiguro's case, like Nancy's, forces a rethinking of otherness and one's relation to others. We have, in other words, an inescapable ethical question that accompanies any life-extending operation that involves not only the "intrusion" of the other but also, in this case, the sacrifice of his or her life as mandated by this particular delivery system.

Never Let Me Go

The basic plot of this novel is simply enough told. A young woman reminisces about her childhood at boarding school and her days beyond it. After not too long a time we realize that this is a rather special institution. The children are actually clones, bred to grow to a certain age and then to start donating their organs to actual human beings, again and again, until they, in the language of the institution, "complete."[17] In this discussion, I will use two "takes" on Ishiguro's fiction, from the author himself, to outline the basic contradiction in the novel. First, Ishiguro has repeatedly insisted that this is a sad, but ultimately affirmative novel. In one interview he provides the response he wishes to hear: " 'This is a very sad novel. But there was something also quite affirming in it, because the characters are so decent. But, it's terribly sad.' That response is probably closest to what I was trying to get at. You know, the fact is, yes, we will all fade away and die, but people can find the energy to create little pockets of happiness and decency while we're here."[18] In this perspective, with the evocation of "while we're here," this is simply a novel about growing up: "It was a way of exploring certain aspects—psychologically for instance—of what happens when you leave childhood, face up to adulthood, and then face up to your own mortality."[19] So far, so good: we are all mortal, after all, and under the gun of the same death sentence. Why not delve into the way the novel offers some solace for that universal condition, specifically as that solace takes the form of education and art? This is just what a liberal sentimentalist, such as myself, would want to hear.

But then things get both more interesting, and more dicey: "I thought I could discuss certain aspects of facing death. I didn't want them to worry about how to escape. I wanted their concerns to be more or less the same ones that all people had. What are the things important to us while we are here? How do we fit things like love, work, friendship into what is surprisingly a short period of time?"[20] It is precisely here that we have the first glimmer of recognition that there is a problem with imagining that these characters are "just like us." These "beings," who are so like us, are not really exactly so. From the sentence, "I thought I could discuss certain aspects of facing death," to the next one, "I didn't want them to worry about how to escape," we have the insertion of "them," not "us," and the differential just becomes more entrenched after that point, if vacillating. This opens up a question: how are they like and unlike us? Yes, they are alive, and they die, just like us. But are we all told that our death is predicated on giving our life-sustaining organs to other people? This seems a hard fact to ignore so easily. What lessons, then, can be shared across that divide?

In this scenario, art education and practice (and education in general) forms a useful illusion; it perpetuates the "bubble" of protection we need to enjoy life before we inevitably die. Referring to death, Ishiguro asks, "What really matters if you know that this is going to happen to you? What are the things you hold on to, what are the things you want to set right before you go? What do you regret? What are the consolations? What are the things you feel you have to do before you go? And also the question is, what is all the education and culture for if you are going to check out?"[21] He asks the question more pointedly: "If they had known they would die in the way they do, would they have embraced this arts education? They might say, 'What's the point? Why are we making all this effort?' I don't mean just in arts, but in their relationships. Would we make any effort to be decent human beings?"[22] In sum, the prescription is veiled ignorance, inculcation of aesthetic and ethical sensibilities, and then knowledge of impending doom, softened by those acquired sensibilities. In other words, it's "life and life only." The notion that this is just about growing up is expressed in its most banal and intimate manner as Ishiguro speaks of this as not only something one's parents do for one, but also as a collective human act, performed almost instinctively: "It struck me how quickly even total strangers would enter into this conspiracy with myself and my wife to keep her [their daughter] in this bubble. Everybody wanted to censor out the sadness of the world. They desperately wanted this little child to be deceived about how nice a place the world was."[23]

But there is a difference that goes to the core of this book: the actual "otherness" of the clone children and the delivery system that links them to "real" humans in a deadly unfair ratio of charity and purpose. Ishiguro knows this difference intimately, yet he continuously seeks to elide it. How can he actually imagine such an elastic metaphor as this? "The overall story is of the clones and the fact that they give up their organs, one by one, and they die. They think about why they've been educated and what's important in their lives. That's all a metaphor for what we all do in the real world. Indeed, the same fate awaits us."[24] Yes, and no. We all die, but we do not all die at an early age because our bodies have been slowly depleted of their vital organs for somebody else's sake. Or, more graphically: "There is a countdown. By creating a situation where to us—the reader and me the writer—their lives seem cruelly truncated, inside their world, that's what's normal. I thought by creating that kind of situation for them, we could get a perspective on our own situation, where we hope to live to eighty if something doesn't strike us down. These people operate the same way. They've been given this fate and they accept it. There is a cruelty about it, but they don't see it to the same extent."[25]

After seeing the number of times Ishiguro mentions this equivalence, which acts as a kind of alibi, it becomes clear why he is so attached to side-stepping the central conceit of the novel, the exchange system. He does so to deliver its central ideology: that if the clones don't know they are going to die, not in that way at least, there is no real cruelty, or when that recognition comes, it will be softened by art and education. At that point, "they try to do the best to make it good. They don't really try to get outside of that. They say with varying degrees, 'This is my life. I'm going to do the best with what I've been given. I will try to gain dignity and worth, to try and conduct my relationships with the people who are important to me in the right way.' "[26] Again, I am not trying to deprive the novel of this intended reading; what I am trying to do is show how radically partial it is, if we recognize the counterdiscourse of material history and the actual exchange system that is, in effect, inoperative. The clone children were spawned at this point, in this, to use Nancy's words, "narrow slot of technical possibilities" and sociohistorical needs and desires, to deliver themselves up to gradual, ritualized, and rationalized slaughter. That this could take place requires that "good people" think they are doing good things. And this goodness (this "decency") is in fact what is to be bestowed on the children as an act of grace before their organs are ripped out (all the extractions are scrupulously performed off-screen). This involves us in a deliberation of questions such as "Good in what sense? To whom? For whom?" To answer these and other questions requires us to go into that territory of history, and specifically material history, that Ishiguro wishes to bracket off.

Initially, Ishiguro's novel was titled "The Student's Novel" and had nothing to do with clones. And then the world discovered actual (not imagined) cloning: "It was the final dimension that helped the story to come alive. Around that time, in 2001, there was a lot of stuff about cloning, about stem-cell research, about Dolly, the sheep. It was very much in the air. . . . I was looking for a situation to talk about the whole aging process, but in such an odd way that we'd have to look at it all in a new way."[27] The "odd way" is thus an invented metaphor. The problem is, it is not just a metaphor. With this very real possibility, people's lives were ineluctably altered, as was human history. The discovery of cloning allowed Ishiguro to transfigure the already well-established practice of organ transplants. Now we could imagine nonhuman "others" created for the purpose of giving up their vital organs. The gap between clones and human donors thus allows, indeed it forces a discussion of otherness precisely within the boundaries of a radically operative community that is at once "nonhuman" and more pernicious—it creates life to destroy life, and the sole compensation for sacrifice is "decency." The point of this discussion again is not to deny the metaphor; if anything, it is to extend its reach and significance, but in the opposite direction. I would like to use this opening to reflect back, not only on our mortal status (we are all the same in death and in life, and art helps us all get along ethically and spiritually), but also on how this narrative cannot so easily slough off the issue of difference and history.

> I am drawn to periods in history where more values in society have undergone a sudden change because a lot of the things I am interested in tend to find a cutting edge in those situations. I am interested in how people who tried to do something good and useful in their lives suddenly find that they had misplaced their efforts. Not only have they perhaps wasted their talent and their energies, but perhaps they have contributed unknowingly to something that was evil all the time, thinking they were doing something good.[28]

More than the specific remarks Ishiguro makes about *Never Let Me Go*, the sentiment found above forms a litany that runs throughout even his earliest interviews. In this view, people are inherently good and decent, but as often as not their sense of right and wrong behavior is out of sync with their historical moment, their "slot of possibilities." In my discussion of this topic, I focus on how biotechnology creates a historical demand for an ethics that always lags behind. Ishiguro instead substitutes an anachronistic liberal sentimentality. The problem is, of course, that to do this he has to erase history, and the difference history makes, in contradiction to his avowed sensitivity to the way it can skew ethical behavior.

This problematic is found forcefully in the final confrontation between the characters Kathy and Tommy and the directress of their boarding school, and the terms in play are art, and life, and their narrow slot of possibility. In Hailsham boarding school, art is a sign of creativity and compliance at once; students are instructed to operationalize their creative talents. Those who do not are considered both untalented and uncooperative—rebellious in fact. But as the children grow, and grow closer to the time when they will "graduate" to start their donations, and hence start to die, a rumor circulates that the artwork appropriated by the directress, Madame, for her "gallery" serves as an index to the children's proximity to the human. If their art reveals a capacity for love, so the legend goes, they may be granted a "deferral," an extension in life. The mystery of the purpose behind art seems to become less opaque now. Kathy and her lover Tommy thus make a journey to ask for just such a deferral from Madame. She in turn asks,

> "Now why, young man, explain it to me. Why would my gallery help in telling which of you were really in love?"
>
> "Because it would help show you what we were like," Tommy said. "Because. . . ."
>
> "Because of course," Madame cut in suddenly, "your art will reveal your inner selves! That's it, isn't it? Because your art will display your *souls!*"[29]

The brutal truth is that there are no deferrals, for any reason: "Poor creatures. What did we do to you? With all our schemes and plans?" (254). This is where the novel draws together art, humanism, and institutional ideology. These "creatures" will always be so and nothing more, despite all the schemes and plans of the school which, it turns out, have given the children not only false hope, but useless capacity as well.

Confronted with this negation, Kathy asks the obvious questions, which echo precisely the questions Ishiguro poses above: "Why did we do all of that work in the first place? Why train us, encourage us, make us produce all of that? If we're just going to give donations anyway, then die, why all those lessons? Why all those books and discussions?" (254). The answer Ishiguro gives in the interview is that education and art soften the blow of mortality, and this answer is voiced by a teacher in the school as well. But before that happens, another, equally revealing answer is given. As it turns out, the careful cultivation of humanity in the children was done, if not to save their lives, then to "improve" them. It is here that the discourse of liberal sentimentality is laid bare, and it is done so against precisely the "narrow slot of technical possibilities" of which Nancy writes, one irrevocably tied to history. In a passage that raises many issues, Madame declares,

> You must try and see it *historically*. After the war, in the early fifties, when the great breakthroughs in science followed one after the other so rapidly, there wasn't time to take stock, to ask the sensible questions. Suddenly there were all these new *possibilities* laid before us, all these ways to cure so many previously incurable conditions. This was what the world noticed the most, wanted the most. And for a long time, people preferred to believe these organs appeared from nowhere, or at most that they grew in a kind of vacuum. Yes, there were arguments. But by the time people became concerned about . . . about . . . *students*, by the time they came to consider just how you were reared, whether you should have been brought into existence at all, well by then it was too late. There was no way to reverse the process. How can you ask a world that has come to regard cancer as curable, how can you ask a world to put away that cure, to go back to the dark days? There was no going back. However uncomfortable people were about your existence, their overwhelming concern was that their own children, their spouses, their parents, their friends, did not die from cancer, motor neuron disease, heart disease. So for a long time you were kept in the shadows, and people did their best not to think about you. And if they did, they tried to convince themselves you weren't really like us. That you were less than human, so it didn't matter. And that was how things stood until our little movement came along. But do you see what we were up against? We were virtually attempting to square the circle. Here was the world, requiring students to donate. While that remained the case, there would always be a barrier against seeing you as properly human. Well, we fought that battle for many years, and what we won for you, at least, were many improvements, though of course, you were only a select few. But then came the Morningdale scandal, then other things, and before we knew it, the climate had quite changed. No one wanted to be seen supporting us anymore. (263, emphases added)

There are thus two historical moments. In the postwar period, that of the "baby boom," new scientific discoveries complement the burgeoning of new life with technologies to enhance life and cure disease via another mode of life production—cloning. Like the people on the dock Marlow addresses in *The Heart of Darkness*, the citizens of the civilized world prefer not to know the origins of their sustenance and order. The threshold they in all cases do not want to cross is that which would argue the equivalence of the clones to human beings. As long as the clones can be regarded as subhuman, their otherness is indelible and fatal. Hailsham's effort, its decency, is to try to square the system by cultivating the students (as the clones are known, and as consistent with the original title of the novel) in another way—through education and the arts. The point is that by that time an overwhelming need, and the means to satisfy that need, was already instantiated, there was no going back. The Morningdale scandal just tipped the balance absolutely against the students.

Morningdale is a geneticist who wants to breed humans that are superior to normal human beings; this elicits unexpected scrutiny of the entire cloning enterprise, and especially Hailsham's efforts to produce evidence of the children's humanity. As long as the clones are regarded as subhuman, the status quo is fine, or if they are slightly improved, that does not seem to matter to the citizens at large, but "a generation of created children who'd take their place in society? Children demonstrably *superior* to the rest of us? Oh no. That frightened people. They recoiled from that" (264). Hence, the Hailsham project is caught precisely at the wrong moment. We should thus see it as performing an *in*decent act, as Ishiguro argues may be the case with an ethics out of sync with history. This notion that the clones could be equal to or better than humans is obviated by the fact that, according to the clones, their models, or what they call "possibles" (humans whom they are modeled after), likely come from the dregs of society: "We're modeled from *trash*. Junkies, prostitutes, winos, tramps. Convicts, maybe, just so long as they aren't psychos. That's what we come from" (166).

This does not differ in the least from the sites in which Scheper-Hughes did her fieldwork on transplants: "We have gone to many of the places where the economically and politically dispossessed—including refugees, the homeless, street children, undocumented workers, prisoners, AWOL soldiers, aging prostitutes, cigarette smugglers, petty thieves, and other marginalized people—are lured into selling their organs."[30] Nevertheless, it is precisely because of the abject status of the donors ("trash") that we have a paradox, it seems. To accept the organ from these "people," one must go to the bottom of society—either to those so desperate for funds that they will literally sell their lives, or, in Ishiguro's fictional construct, to artificial life. In both cases, radical otherness is required to make the deal (a) possible because of the financial differential and (b) possible because, absent financial compensation to square the ethics of the act, the donors are not even human anyway, so no obligation of compensation really applies. On the other hand, these abjected objects from abjected souls are purified as they are torn out of the host body and transplanted to the receiving body—their otherness is somehow leeched out. If not, we cannot help but think that some of that abject state must be absorbed into the host body.

It is here that we find the toggle point of liberal sentiment and economic neoliberalism: "Indeed, commercialized transplant exemplifies better than any other biomedical technology the reach of economic liberalism. Transplant technology trades comfortably in the domain of postmodern bioethics, with its values of disposability and free and transparent circulation. The uninhibited circulation of bought and sold kidneys exemplifies a neoliberal political discourse based on juridical concepts of the autonomous individual subject, equality (at least, equality of opportunity), radical freedom, accumulation, and universalism, expressed in the expansion of medical rights and medical citizenship."[31] In order for this to work, some adequate model of recompense and exclusion from that obligation must exist. Either we compensate along the axis of sameness (we can transfer benefits and cash to those who give their organs), or we don't have to provide compensation because the donors are beneath our obligation (for instance, the clones, but this scenario should not be read only in the realm of fiction; those who look and act sufficiently different from us, those mute or deaf or living in other hemispheres are just as likely to be invisible members of the "biosociety").

Rose points to exactly this kind of problematic—classical ethics are no longer adequate.

> What is clear, however, is that the classical distinction made in moral philosophy between that which is not human—ownable, tradeable, commodifiable—and that which is human—not legitimate material for

such commodification—can no longer do the work that is required to resolve this issue: that distinction is itself what is at stake in the politics of the contemporary bioeconomy. The tensions between the intensifying somatic ethics in the West, with the centrality it accords to the management of one's own health and body to contemporary self-fashioning, and the inequities and injustices of the local and global economic, technological, and biomedical infrastructure required to support such a somatic ethic, seems to me to be a constitutive feature of contemporary biopolitics.[32]

This is a key element in Ishiguro's text—history, and the ethical gaps that open up when things change in certain ways, leaving individuals clueless at best, catastrophically wrong at others. Responding to the children's incredulity at the randomness of their existence, their teacher again reiterates the "narrow slot" of time that has determined their particular degree of humanity: human enough to feel the absurdity and horror of their existence, but not human enough to be allowed to live.

> "I can see," Miss Emily said, "that it might look as though you were simply pawns in a game. It can certainly be looked at like that. But think of it. You were lucky pawns. There was a certain climate and now it's gone. You have to accept that sometimes that's how things happen in this world. People's opinions, their feelings, they go one way, then the other. It just so happens you grew up at a certain point in this process."
>
> "It might be just some trend that came and went," I said. "But for us, it's our life." (266)

It is here that the notions of historical possibility, conflicting institutional operativeness (the imperatives of technoscience and liberalism) come into play, and these considerations link up with Ishiguro's concern about good people thinking they are doing good things that turn out to be wrong. At a precise moment in time, Hailsham is a noble experiment in granting humanness, that is, sameness, to the clone children. That is what their artistic production is supposed to attest to. What are (any) beings to do? "Our" lives, each, are caught, it seems, in the jaws of history and contingency, and this drives our sense of how to act toward others. The overwhelming imperative is to live (as we saw in *L'intrus*), to stave off that great equalizer, death. Everything can be geared to this goal, including making art, and that has been its constant myth—immortality through art. But here, Ishiguro brings us into the not-so-brave world of operative art, that which is deployed not for the children's immortality, or even mortality, or even, as they imagine, to postpone their death sentences for three years. It is to instantiate some small degree of recognition, that they are not to be abjected and greeted with horror. The irony of course is that even the perpetrators of the system cannot squelch their aversion to the children. They may not have brought them into this world, but their acts of kindness toward them are blindered and self-centered. The institution is driven by a sentimentality, not an ethics.

In this case, art and those who would endow the children with artistic sensibilities stand on a par with the entire notion of being a "carer"— which is to be no more than a handmaiden to death. But again, this perception is exactly the opposite of that of the ministers of Hailsham, and of Ishiguro himself, who also expresses the idea that "bubbles," protections against the truth of death—art, in other words—help. We can almost hear Ishiguro's voice as well as one teacher declares, "I'm so *proud* to see you both. You built your lives on what we gave you. You wouldn't be who you are today if we'd not protected you. You wouldn't have become absorbed in your lessons, you wouldn't have lost yourselves in your art and your writing. Why should you have done, knowing what lay in store for each of you? You would have told us it was all pointless, and how could we have argued with you?'" (268). In the end, liberal sentimentalism meets economic neoliberalism. Yet moments after Scheper-Hughes offers that stinging indictment, she adds, "To give them their due, however, these new transplant transactions are a blend of altruism and commerce; consent and coercion; gifts and theft; science and sorcery; care and human sacrifice."[33] This just serves to confirm the doubleness, the ambivalence that I find in Ishiguro's text, despite his attempt to gloss over the "sadness" of the story. If we are to in any way recover Ishiguro's project, to take it from the jaws of contradiction (artistic transcendence and liberal sentimentalism versus historical contingency and ethical ambiguity), we need to invent another optics.

Inexact Exchange

To start to answer the question of whether or not "it" was all worth it, we need to return to the second part of the contradiction I have outlined. The first part is, again, the notion that art offers solace, that its "bubble" is benign, that the children of Hailsham are like us and need that protection. The second part is that they are emphatically *not* like "us," and that their difference abides not only in the manner in which they are born and die, but also in the system that mediates their lives and deaths with those of the human beings in the novel. Born into the bioeconomic system, the clones exist precisely in that liminal zone Scheper-Hughes describes as concomitant with the invention of transplants: "Transplantation demanded a radical redefinition of death, to allow the immediate harvesting of organs from bodies neither completely dead nor yet still living."[34] As such, there is not only a demand to redefine death, but with it comes an uncertainty as to the clones' actual "biovalue" until such issues can be resolved. This is a term Catherine Waldby initially proposed to "characterize the ways that bodies and tissues derived from the dead are redeployed for the preservation and enhancement of the health and vitality of the living."[35] This opacity, this liminal zone that the children occupy, of uncertain value and affective status, is well reflected in this meditation.

> Maybe from as early as when you're five or six, there's been a whisper going at the back of your head, saying: "One day, maybe not so long from now, you'll get to know how it feels." So you're waiting, even if you don't quite know it, waiting for the moment when you realize that you really are different from them; that there are people out there, like Madame, who don't hate you or wish you any harm, but who nonetheless shudder at the very thought of you—of how you were brought into this world and why—and who dread the idea of your hand brushing against theirs. The first time you glimpse yourself through the eyes of a person like that, it's a cold moment. It's like walking past a mirror you've walked past every day of your life, and suddenly it shows you something else, something troubling and strange. (36)

Otherness in this novel is empathic and clear at times, at others not. That is the problem. The very existence of some, like the speaker above, is borne of difference. The tragedy of this abjection by others is that the very reason behind the speaker's birth is to give life to others who "shudder" at the very thought of her, not because of her purpose, but precisely because her "delivery" into the world is via a very precisely different mechanism.

We can hark back to notion of seeing oneself through the eyes of others. In this instance, it is a deeply ambiguous phenomenon that produces a profound sense of alienation. It puts the speaker "in her place" and forces a re-recognition that will offer her a knowledge that is at once comforting and horrifying. She knows her destiny more clearly and more sharply than "others," and it is indeed hopeless and troubling. Still, what is perhaps even more disturbing is the relation between this self and that other—what accounts for this dread and horror? In *Never Let Me Go* it is the eerie mimetic proximity of the speaker, a "donor," to actual human beings, and the horrifying difference of their coming into the world.

These children's coming into self-knowledge takes place not by simply filling out a "coming of age" narrative, which Ishiguro insists is the backbone of the story, but also via a growing recognition of the nature of their institutional home. Ishiguro marks the acquisition of self-knowledge not only against the shifting historical circumstances of the narrative, but also within the specific institutional structures that deliver recognition. In the following passage he slips from an individual character's reflection on her past and present, her changing perceptions of herself and her classmates, to her reading of that perceptual change against the backdrop of the institution in which the clones have been placed, and their definition of self against those outside: "Thinking back now, I can see we were just at that age when we knew a few things about ourselves—about who we were, how we were different from our guardians, from the people outside—but hadn't yet understood what any of it meant" (36).

It is characteristic of this novel to continually slide back and forth between the narrator's reflections on her particular life and her appeal to the reader for some acknowledgment of common experience. Kathy wants to feel *some* convergence between her childhood and that of her reader—she constantly attempts to achieve a bond of recognition, attempting to place her life fully into a generic, that is to say, shared narrative of growing up. The passage continues, openly addressing the reader: "I'm sure somewhere in your childhood, you too had an experience like ours that day" (36). But even as she makes that appeal, the sentence next moves into a recognition of difference, only to finish with a movement back to an appeal to the common, and that common ground in this sequence is not in experience, but in feeling: "similar if not in the actual details, then inside, in the feelings" (36).

Yet, once again, as we come to expect, this moment is then swept back into the specific case of the institution that houses the children. Even as the narrator continues to use the second-person term of address, the "actual details" belie the intimacy of shared experience and shared feeling: "Because it doesn't really matter how well your guardians try to prepare you: all the talks, videos, discussions, warnings, none of that can really bring it home. Not when you're eight years old, and you're all together in a place like Hailsham; when you've got guardians like the ones we had; when the gardeners and the delivery men joke and laugh with you and call you 'sweetheart'" (ibid.). Even at this early point in the novel we have started to suspect what the term "guardian" means, and it is precisely not generic. The guardians' efforts to "prepare" the children are unlike anything one would expect at a typical boarding school. "None of it can bring it home" not only because you are young but because you are in a place "like Hailsham" and have qualitatively different sorts of guardians than other children at other schools. This sinister, or at least suspect, tone is closed off by a final evocation of the universal and everyday, but by then it is too late. A "place like Hailsham" is clearly distinct from other places, and the relationship between those who live there and those who live outside is defined by the nature of the institution itself—it is home to particularly "produced" beings. But what of the interactions between those beings on the inside?

Two discourses mediate this relationship. First, there is the discourse of exchange: people give things to other people. The issue of reciprocity here ranges from the complex to the nonexistent. Second, and attached to the first, is the discourse of recognition: when exchange takes place, it always does so as a gesture of recognition. The problem is, it is as often as not a moment of misrecognition. Just as the children are and are not human—exact enough to donate viable organs, inexact enough to kill by so demanding—things are and are not what they seem to be. Moments of exchange and recognition occur over and over again, but throughout the novel there is a sense of haunting, which troubles the supposedly clean exchanges and clear moments of recognition: "When you lift an arm, or when someone sits up in bed, you can feel this pale, shadowy movement all around you in the tiles" (18).

But there is one critical difference in terms of the idea of exchange: the children of Hailsham give, but what they receive in return is incommensurate with their donation. At one point in the novel, one teacher finally breaks down and, troubled by the veil of ignorance that never seems to lift for these children, she tells them of their fate. Critically, her description of their fate is drawn by contrasting it to normal human lives.

> "I know you don't mean any harm. But there's just too much talk like this. I hear it all the time, it's been allowed to go on, and it's not right." I could see more drops coming off the gutter and landing on her shoulder, but she didn't seem to notice. "If no one else will talk to you," she continued, "then I will. The problem, as I see it, is that you've been told and not told. You've been told, but none of you really understand, and I dare say, some people are quite happy to leave it that way. But I'm not. If you're going to have decent lives, then you've got to know and know properly. None of you will go to America, none of you will be film stars. And none of you will be working in supermarkets as I heard some of you planning the other day. Your lives are set out for you. You'll become adults, then before you're old, before you're even middle-aged, you'll start to donate your vital organs. That's what each of you was created to do. You're not like the actors you watch on your videos, you're not even like me. You were brought into this world for a purpose, and your futures, all of them, have been decided. So you're not to talk that way any more. You'll be leaving Hailsham before long, and it's not so far off, the day you'll be preparing for your first donations." (81)

The narrative momentum for this novel is thus largely taken up by the question of how these donors will be redeemed. If not by some thing, then at least by recognition as something less abject?

Art in this novel, art may be the key to human recognition, but it is an ambiguous token: " 'Even you, Ruth, you didn't dare boss Christy around. All because we thought she was great at poetry. But we didn't know a thing about poetry. We didn't care about it. It's strange' " (18). Christy is granted immunity from being "bossed around" because of her reputed skill at writing poetry, but this efficacious token of exchange, this product of energy spent, is not only misrecognized, but even the object of indifference. How is it that human energy can be expended and yet its value be unknown? How can things of value be at once acted on and unknown? And, finally, how does art partake of both these problematics?

The problem, of course, is, what is given in return? There are two answers. The children produce poems and artwork, and can either "sell" them for tokens or have them "taken" by the headmistress. In the first instance, tokens can then be traded for other items. But if one's work is appropriated by Madame, it bestows both great honor and nothing, for it is a mystery as to what happens to those works once they are appropriated. This leads to "the tokens controversy."

> The tokens controversy was, I suppose, all part of our getting more acquisitive as we grew older. For years—I think I've said already—we'd thought that having work chosen for the billiards room, never mind taken away by Madame, was a huge triumph. But by the time we were ten, we'd grown more ambivalent about it. The Exchanges, with their system of tokens as currency, had given us a keen eye for pricing up anything we produced. We'd become preoccupied with T-shirts, with decorating around our beds, with personalising our desks. And of course, we had our "collections" to think of. (38)

With this new acquisitiveness, rational economic behavior sets in, and the vague pride which is given in exchange for having Madame take away one's artwork no longer is salient: "By the time we were ten, this whole notion that it was a great honour to have something taken by Madame collided with a feeling that we were losing our most marketable stuff" (39). Art, then, is "stuff" to be converted to cash. When the children ask what happens to the expropriated works, they are told by a teacher that "it's for a good reason" (40). Hence, "reason" or causality is not for them to know at this point in their lives. The "conversion" of art to something else is mystified. This in itself may not appear significant, but coupled with all that we have discussed thus far, it becomes clear that human effort, the expenditure of energy, the deployment of bodies (and body parts) become transformed into an absented value that forms the lure of the text—where does all this art go, and for what? Until we can answer that, the "system" simply does not function; it always has an aporia, and a calculated one at that. This aporia is founded on the notion, again, of a scheme of recognition and identification that is skewed, corrupted, and mimetically false. Donors seem to be one thing but are not, and even though they give themselves entirely to others in the most sacrificial way possible, recognition of this breeds repulsion, not gratitude. A child can be good at poetry and earn the deference of her peers, but they have no idea what poetry actually is. Art can be made and praised, and then the highest compliment turns out to be privation and seeming exploitation. It is not just a faulty exchange system we are confronted with, but a flawed system of human recognition and reward. In other words, what is this all worth?

We seem thus to have come to an impasse. If we buy into the redemptive narrative Ishiguro offers—that "they" are "just like us" and that art and education are necessary to our relief from death, enjoyment of life, and ability to act well toward others—we are still nagged by the question, *are* they really like *us*? If we go to the second reading, that this narrative is inescapably linked to issues of contingency, slots of possibilities, and historical materialism, and that those issues affect strongly how we relate to others and act toward them, we are forced to acknowledge the inexactness of that formula (they are alike and not alike us), and that that reading goes in exactly the opposite direction than that the author insists on. If we are not satisfied with Ishiguro's answer—that art cushions us against the horrible knowledge of our death to come—then we either have to come up with something new or adapt his point of view to a new critical framework. I will do the latter.

My compromise, or perhaps evasive strategy, is to imagine that redemption nonetheless takes place, but only if we acquiesce to inexactness, incommensurate exchange, and near equivalence. In sum, there is a way that falseness is tied to misrecognition, and in this instance it is redemptive. I have raised the question, if art cannot be exchanged for a clear value, if it can't even be recognized as such, or name a fixed and certain thing, what good is it? The title of Ishiguro's novel comes from a song that the narrator hears and makes her own. She has no idea what the song is really about, or rather she doesn't care; its mimetic qualities are absent to her, and what we find instead is pure affect, and, most important, affect that is delivered via an imaginary narrative.

> What was so special about this song? Well, the thing was, I didn't used to listen properly to the words—I just waited for that bit that went, "Baby, baby, never let me go . . ." And what I'd imagine was a woman who'd been told she couldn't have babies, who'd really, really wanted them all her life. Then there's a sort of miracle and she has a baby, and she holds this baby very close to her and walks around singing: "Baby, never let me go . . ." partly because she's so happy, but also because she's so afraid something will happen, that the baby will get ill or be taken away from her. Even at the time, I realized this couldn't be right, that this interpreta-

tion didn't fit with the rest of the lyrics. But that wasn't an issue with me. The song was about what I said, and I used to listen to it again and again, on my own, whenever I got the chance. (70)

"Properly" here means the entire song; the integrity of the whole is set aside in favor of that fragment that is able to satisfy the narrative needs of the speaker. It serves as a prompt for her desired text. What she has made of it is a reflective text, for of course she cannot have a baby. But the romantic notion that one is granted a kind of immortality through one's children takes on another color here. For Kathy's entire existence is much more determinately about "passing on" her life to others than even "ordinary" human beings, who may of course choose to or not to pro- create. Her very coming-into-the-world is occasioned by the same no- tion of "operativeness" that we saw in Jean-Luc Nancy: the battle against death requires death. The horrible irony is that, unlike a mother who might likely live to see her child born and grow up, Kathy's fate is to slowly give too much of herself to remain alive. So it is rather the reverse—hers is not the voice of the mother asking that the child remain, but rather that of the child, whose existence, in this case, will indeed be set adrift, and whose existence has always already had that fate inscribed in its body. Only an act of charity on the part of Madame and the society she inevitably represents, despite liberal intentions, can save Kathy, and to save Kathy would be to destroy the operative community of Hailsham and other institutions like it. Something always has to be sacrificed into the terrible logic of incommensurate exchange. But sometimes, rarely and preciously, that inexactness is the source of beauty and love.

Kathy loses the tape of the song she loves so much; like everything in the novel it is taken from her. Letting go is not the question—it is the impossibility of hanging on. Yet in this scene, which takes place a little over a quarter of the way through the novel, we find perhaps its finest redemptive moment. Kathy's friend Ruth has looked all over for the tape Kathy has lost. She can't find it, but she gives Kathy another: " 'Kathy, it's not your one. The one you lost. I tried to find it for you, but it's really gone' " (75). Kathy accepts the tape.

> I saw how Ruth wasn't to know that [the music was quite unlike that of the song I loved], how to Ruth, who didn't know the first thing about music, this tape might easily make up for the one I'd lost. And suddenly I felt the disappointment ebbing away and being replaced by a real happi-

ness. We didn't do things like hug each other much at Hailsham. But I squeezed one of her hands in both mine when I thanked her. She said: "I found it at the last Sale. I just thought it's the sort of thing you'd like." And I said that, yes, it was exactly the sort of thing.

I still have it now. I don't play it much because the music has nothing to do with anything. It's an object, like a brooch or a ring, and especially now Ruth has gone, it's become one of my most precious possessions. (76)

The music is meaningless, the gesture is everything; the exchange is absolutely wrong, and perfectly right. But the gesture itself then yields to something even larger: it is the trace of love and loss—Ruth is gone. Ishiguro's phrasing strikes me as a little odd; it is a characteristic of his prose to sometimes miss the usual locution by a hair, and that simply calls attention to it. First of all, rather than refer to the tape as such, Kathy refers to it as "the music," but it is music that is not listened to "very much." The tape then becomes analogized as an object "like a brooch or a ring," a silent, mute thing, but one of greater value than a simple tape recording that wasn't the right music anyway. Its value resides doubly: in the gesture of pure giving without expectation of recompense, and in the fact of Ruth's ultimate sacrifice—her body for others. There is thus a chiasmatic movement, of exchange of recognized value and at least the gesture of repayment ("We didn't do things like hug each other much at Hailsham. But I squeezed one of her hands in both mine when I thanked her"), which militates against the unredeemed sacrifice of Ruth to some anonymous beneficiaries.

The End?

But I am not sure. Can we rest well with the "inexact exchange" theory I have mounted? If this were one sort of world, or perhaps at certain times during the day or night when one feels either particularly optimistic or fatalistic, one might latch onto that. But there is a strong part of me that says that if art is to matter as *more* than that (without, again, diminishing my respect for and even love of such a notion), if we are to not set aside materially produced and enacted otherness (no, "we" are not all alike in this great stream of life) quite so easily, and rather attend to and call out for criticism and remediation such violent acts of decidedly *un*social and *in*decent bioeconomics, then we should take our lesson from the other side of Ishiguro's novel, dwell, not sentimentally but with anger, on its sad side, and hope that we are not mere victims of bad timing, a slot of possibilities that does not include justice, or at least some recognition of it. In that weird way, we might actually see that the Hailsham project was not exactly wrongheaded—they, after all, wanted to recognize the children as somehow human *enough*. We might rather fashion other weapons than "only" art, such as art mobilized in a critical, not apologetic, manner. We might struggle to invent a critical literary art that takes into account our "slot of possibilities" and addresses art and history, culture and race, in all their contingency.

In Ruth Ozeki's *My Year of Meats*, we come full circle back to an examination of how others are delivered to us via a different sort of literary medium. Similar to Nancy's and Ishiguro's use of the body as a nexus of self with other, Ozeki puts this "common ground" at the core of her novel. But rather than seeing bodies meet through the transplantation of organs, she views the commonness created by the fact that distinctly different bodies occupying divergent geocultural spaces ingest, internalize, and assimilate the same materials into their respective bodies. While this can have positive effects, depending on the materials we are speaking about, it can also have catastrophically negative effects as well. It is in militating against the latter that Ozeki invents her poetics of trans-Pacific solidarity, which itself offers an entirely different way of being in common, across literary and other media.

4

Pacific Oceanic Feeling:
Affect, Otherness, Mediation

Freud begins *Civilization and Its Discontents* with a personal tale: a friend comes to his house and remarks on the book Freud has just written, *The Future of an Illusion*. Agreeing with its skeptical remarks about religion, the friend tells Freud that he has often experienced "an oceanic feeling" that, all on its own, unmediated by any religious doctrine, provided a sense of transcendence. Furthermore, he surmises that he is not alone in having this sort of feeling—perhaps, he says, "millions" have felt similarly. Freud writes,

> I had sent him my small book that treats religion as an illusion, and he answered that he entirely agreed with my judgment upon religion, but that he was sorry I had not properly appreciated the true source of religious *sentiments*. This, he says, consists in a peculiar *feeling*, which he himself is never without, which he finds confirmed by many others, and which he may suppose is present in millions of people. It is a feeling which he would like to call a *sensation* of "eternity," a feeling as of something limitless, unbounded—as it were, "oceanic." This *feeling*, he adds, is a purely subjective fact, not an article of faith.[1]

While Freud's friend could hardly be more emphatic that this was a "feeling," an *affect*, registering on his body, he also asserts that while it is "subjective," it is something millions of others feel as well, or so he thinks. Unfortunately, Freud quickly presents himself as a counter-example: "I cannot discover that this 'oceanic' feeling in myself. It is not easy to deal scientifically with feelings. One can attempt to describe their physiological signs. Where this is not possible—and I am afraid that the oceanic feeling too will defy this kind of characterization—nothing remains but to fall back on the ideational content which is most readily associated with the feeling."[2] From the empirical fact that he himself has never had that "oceanic feeling," Freud concludes that it cannot be a universal feeling, and that whether it exists at all demands scientific study. Yet even before *that* has been undertaken, Freud presumes its failure, and prescribes instead that the object of study switch from the feeling itself and its registering on the body to a psychoanalytic study of the "ideational content" that one might associate with that feeling.

Freud also makes the distinction between affect and ideational content in *The Interpretation of Dreams* in a way that highlights the way dreams are resistant to being segregated analytically from everyday mental processes precisely because affect can pass over borders that confound ideational content: "Dreams insist with greater energy upon their right to be included among our real mental experiences more in respect to their affective than in respect to their ideational content."[3] As André Green notes,

> On waking, it is impossible to reject the affect of dreams as absurd, as one might be tempted to do with their contents. Dreams allow us to make a strange discrepancy between the representative content and affective state that would correspond to it in a waking state. An examination of the relations between manifest content and latent content forces us to acknowledge that the affect is right: "Analysis shows us that the ideational material has undergone displacements and substitutions, whereas affects have remained unaltered."[4]

In contrast to ideational content, affects are something persistent *as themselves*. Undistorted by repressive mechanisms that affect ideational content, they stand outside the characteristic dreamwork and assume an indisputable place in the psyche—they simply are, and are so powerfully. The problem that haunts the endeavor to ascertain what, precisely, this "oceanic feeling" is—its nature, its sources, it transmittability, its scope—is the question of the gap between bodies which may or may not be experiencing the oceanic reach of affect. It is relatively easier to see if people share an idea, or the notion of an idea, but how in the world can one see if others are sharing a *feeling*, one that is murky, indistinct, but nonetheless real to oneself? Is everyone swimming in the same ocean? What does an *oceanic* feeling imply? To get to the point of this book: how is the otherness that abides between people overwhelmed by an otherness that touches all?

Let's take another example of an eerie feeling, this one emanating more perceptibly from the space around one's body. Teresa Brennan writes,

> Is there anyone who has not, at least once, walked into a room and "felt the atmosphere"? But as many have paused to wonder how they've received this impression, and why it seemed both attractive and certain, there is no record of their curiosity in the copious literature on group and crowd psychology, or in the psychological and psychoanalytic writing that claims that one person can feel another's feelings. . . . This is not especially surprising, as any inquiry into *how* one feels the other's affects, or the "atmosphere," has to take account of physiology as well as the *social, psychological* factors that generated the atmosphere in the first place. The transmission of affect, whether it is grief, anxiety, or danger, is social and psychological in origin. But the transmission is also responsible for bodily changes; some are brief changes, as in a whiff of the room's atmosphere, some longer-lasting. In other words the transmission of affect, if only for an instant, alters the biochemistry and neurology of the subject. The "atmosphere" or the environment really gets into the individual. Physically and biologically, something is present that was not there before, but it did not originate sui generis: it was not generated solely or sometimes even in part by the individual organism or its genes.[5]

No longer speaking in terms of an individual's sense of a vague and amorphous atmosphere that implicitly connects him to something greater than himself, out there, Brennan's case is based on actual physical proximity with the co-inhabitants of a spatially delimited affective world. In that, it is rigorously interactive with real things (be they other bodies, other things, or molecules of one sort or another). This interaction is more than physiological; it is eminently connected to others, physically, socially, and psychologically. Brennan declares, "My theory is an alternative to psychoanalytic theory or meta-psychology in that it postulates an origin for affects that is independent of the individual experiencing them. These affects come from the other, but we deny them. Or they come from us, but we pretend (habitually) that they come from the other. Envy, anger, aggressive behavior—these are the problems of the other. Over tolerance, over generosity, these are our problems."[6]

Here Brennan begins by taking the view commonly held (at least as far back as Benedict de Spinoza) that the affects are amorphous, at-mospheric things that easily pass from body to body. In terms of things like the sentiments, this is not only a good thing, but something neces-sary for ethical sensibilities when dealing in a social world filled with other individuals. We need to be able to empathize, to feel as if their experience were ours. However, this porousness means that we do not know where the cycle of affect originates. In Brennan's argument, this lack of knowledge is exploited by the ego bent on exculpating itself from the charge of being the source of bad affect. Nevertheless, while "bad" or negative affect can be attributed to others, there is also the chance that the origin of bad affect is actually within our psyches—it is simply that that source has been disavowed. And while one would surely attend to the ever-increasing contact with racial, national, cultural, and eth-nic otherness (and more) that contemporary history has brought into "our" world, that is, the actual physical coming into proximity that we now negotiate, it is this mechanism of disavowing responsibility for negative affect that I want to dwell on.

Brennan draws our attention to the coping mechanisms the psyche deploys to deal with adverse affect. For as much as one might celebrate the positive "good spirits" that flow lavishly among people, there is also the fear that bad affect can also travel like a bad virus: in that case it has to be contained. One's own body must have the intelligence to sense it and the psychic strength to convert it into something harmless. Indeed, throughout the various discourses that take the affects as their subjects, one element appearing in all seems to be control and conversion. The stability and energy of the body, of the psyche, have to be maintained, and able to both exploit positive affect and ward off negative affect. What is looked for is some kind of homeostatic mechanism to deal with affect. The literary imagination serves this purpose. It is the imagination that suggests a broad set of relations between the self and the other, and specifically the relation between these two entities and the collective system that delivers others to the self. In cycling through the various pos-sibilities of the origin of affect (where did that affect come from, why am I acting this way—in response to someone else's affect, or to mine?), the ego swims in a kind of affective ocean, something not dissimilar to Lacan's imaginary. In a way that echoes the idea of "stepping into the other person's shoes" that we saw at the start of this study, Terry Eagle-ton argues, "the importance of Lacan's lecture lay in its illustration of the imaginary—that strange realm of the human psyche in which subjects and objects (if we can even speak of such a division at this early point) appear constantly to exchange places and live each other's lives. In this play of projecting and reflecting, things seem to pass in and out of each other without mediation, feel one another from the inside with all the sensuous immediacy with which they experience their own interiors."[7]

We thus come back to the question of how much otherness is required to make sure the body is vital, engaged in a social world, responding to the human conditions therein, and how much otherness can reach deeply into the individual's mind and body and transform it in ways that change its identity and modes of behavior—mental and physical— beyond the pale. One way to avoid the "clash of affects" might be to postulate a common goal or interest. After all, one cannot tread water indefinitely. One has to act in the world, and acting means making choices. If we are not members of the oceanic swimming club, paying our dues to some God, or if we do not accept Freud's alternative— "civilization"—as that mechanism for balancing, directing, containing, suppressing, and rechanneling drives and emotions, in the eighteenth century something else arises to accept and house oceanic feeling. It is the market. The eighteenth century is known as a time when "senti- ment" flourished as a particular sign of humanity and civilization. It is also recognized that sentiment found its way into a number of different spheres, including the field of economics. Eagleton notes, "The cult of sentiment was the feel-good factor of a successful mercantile nation, but it was a social force as well as a state of mind. Feeling could oil the wheels of commerce, allowing the Irish-born poet and novelist Henry Brooke to write rhapsodically of how the merchant 'brings up the re- motest regions to converse . . . [a]nd just knits into one family, and weaves into one web, the affinity and brotherhood of all mankind.' "[8] And here let us not lose sight of what Brooke's rhetorical sweep now makes part of the promise: the global now extends to diverse popula- tions that he assumes will fall into economic kinship naturally. This of course has to do not only with economic sentiment, but also a way of mapping common behavior and interests in general. People feel certain ways and act on the basis of those feelings.

Variants of this coupling of economic behavior with human behavior in an organic form continue into the next century. Most germane for this study, Catherine Gallagher sees that both the discourses of political economy and of literary narrative share similar themes, rhetorics, and narrative strategies: "Before novelists like Charles Dickens and George Eliot incorporated them into extended narrative forms . . . political economy's organic premises were already structured as plots, as highly consequentialist, if extremely schematic, stories about the processes of life and death, pain and pleasure."⁹ These "consequentialist" plots disclose a specific kind of realism. Gallagher divides these narratives into two groups: " 'Bioeconomic' plots of political economy [are] the stories of how the economy circulates Life, with a capital L"; alongside such narratives are "somaeconomic" plots, whose accounts show "how pleasure and pain, happiness and unhappiness, desire and exhaustion, stimulate economic activity and are in turn modified by it." She continues: " 'Bioeconomic' plots trace the interconnections among human life, its sustenance, and modes of production and exchange; they track the reciprocal effects of economic activity and life forms generally. 'Somaeconomic' plots describe more intensively feelings that are the sensual and effective causes and consequences of economic extortion."¹⁰ In other words, both the issues of rational choice and of affect are presented respectively in Gallagher's analysis. They are distributed differentially, but essentially they tap into the same overall logic of embodiment. Ultimately, and essentially, the market becomes pretty much what Henry Brooke wants, although Gallagher's description is much less sanguine. Rather than a huge human family of sentimentally connected economic actors, we have a "megabeing": "Capital looks like a life form in another sense as well: it seemed to be the aggregate of numerous individual persons responding—as all living organisms do—to the stimuli in pain and pleasure. It was a megabeing whose telos was expanding wealth and whose motive was believed to be the promise of individual happiness."¹¹ Here then is the oceanic feeling of the bioeconomic sphere. Indeed, it is the argument of Albert O. Hirschman's classic study of "the passions and the interests" that the unruly passions of human beings were tamed into, converted into, economic "interests" precisely during this period.¹²

I will consider how the emotional and affective realms persist today as another set of indices to human commonality. In particular, I will look at how these things, supposedly shared by all, become mobilized to guide human economic (and other) behavior across cultures—the assumption being that certain affective chords can be struck and have resonance despite cultural and racial difference. These choices of be-havior have profound consequences for the mind and for the body. In fact, in the case of Ruth Ozeki's novel *My Year of Meats*, cultural, racial, and indeed national difference become leveraged in the attempt to instill in the Japanese housewife the appetite for American beef, the assumption being that American domestic norms can become more attractive to those on the other side of the Pacific because there is something still exceptional about the United States. One of the prob-lems is that those pushing American red meat do not understand that images of the American Heartland, no matter how well dressed, served up, and resonant in their own affective sphere, simply don't lead to the intended effects, not only for some Japanese, but also for some Ameri-cans. The key question thus becomes, is this attempt to transmit affect tapping into something innate in all humans, or is it creating a feeling in the Japanese audience? Looked at more broadly, how can affect spread across national, cultural, racial, and other borders? What different sorts of affect flow differently, and in what kinds of directions? Where is the wellspring of global affect? How does the self, particularly construed, absorb or fight off affect?

Indeed, since early on it is a well-established notion that affect is a virulently contagious thing that knows no boundaries. Thus, in this book's discussion of the threat that too much otherness presents, affect can be the prime delivery system of that crisis, or at least radical distur-bance. How can we keep it under control, once it has been let free to circulate in public? Eagleton's Irish merchant looks at the bright, and profitable, side: sentimental affinities can create a global family, perhaps dissolving the divide between *homo economicus* and *homo reciprocans*. In this sense, as attached to sentiment, "disinterestedness" meant the sus-pension of self-interest for the sake of participating ethically in a larger social sphere. Or, to use Gallagher's term, individuals must happily invest their affects in the "megabeing." In Adam Smith's imagery, the rise of capitalism would lift all boats, the success of individuals would posi-tively affect all. In this view of things, peoples remotely located would all be speaking the same language. But what happens when "nonharmo-nious" elements contribute their own disagreeable affect, or resist, or are unresponsive to, the good feelings we attempt to keep in circulation, investing and reinvesting in the socioeconomic sphere?

In Ozeki's novel, affect is deployed toward specific and determinedly nonspiritual ends. Indeed, the novel's advertising campaign is premised on the idea that by viewing families in the American Heartland, watching them as they prepare beef and talk about their marriages and children in positive terms, the Japanese will be infected with the same affect and mimic that behavior: they will want to have lives just like the Americans they see on the screen, and they will see the beef Americans eat as a necessary element of that affective world. Indeed, perhaps by ingesting the same material, integrating *that* otherness into their selves, they will indeed become "Americans" not only in gesture and habit, but also in essence. This scheme drives Ozeki's novel in its transit across the Pacific Ocean—this is the *trans-Pacific* oceanic feeling. In my reading of this novel I not only address the idea of affect and otherness, but also draw together the subjects of the previous chapters: rationality and realism, the human and nonhuman body, and art. Furthermore, I will ask how Ozeki's works probe into a very specific historical moment in U.S.-Japan trade, one which happens to coincide with a crisis in the proliferation of the use of hormonal additives in food, but it is also more than that. In terms of the "narrow slot of possibilities," this novel marks the historical coincidence of radical changes in pharmaceutical, genetic, and media technologies, Asia-Pacific trade relations, global economics and ecologies. *My Year of Meats* treats each of these issues within a careful and deliberate critique of literature and media—it is these instruments of the imagination that deliver affect and prompt imaginary identification with the other. Essential to this critique is a questioning of the relation between truth and fiction, fact and fabrication. Ultimately, these lines are blurred under the regime of affect. "Ideational content" is inseparable from feeling.

In *My Year of Meats* all these questions are subordinated to the novel's specific historical context: the historical past of the American Heartland is seen to be merely a simulacrum, one that needs heavy retooling to be at all effective trans-Pacifically. Its supposed purity and authenticity are exposed as barely there, as the real agents of farming—agribusiness and chemical corporations—are disclosed to have drastically distorted whatever nostalgic elements might remain. (This recalls the "slot" that Coetzee notes between traditional animal husbandry and the modern meat industry.) Affect now is as much driven by drugs that change the neurological, physiological, and reproductive systems of the animal and human bodies they enter as it might be by contact with others. Put another way, the room Brennan enters might well carry the feeling of a chemical buzz, oozing out the pores of the other people in the room. If the accoutrement of the "oceanic" religious world was incense, the perfume of trans-Pacific affect here is a sizzling steak, if the dreams of the novel's fictional multinational corporation, BEEF-EX, are to be realized.

The body and its registering of emotion, affect, and the materials it takes into itself is thematized consistently in Ruth Ozeki's work in the 1990s. In fact, *My Year of Meats* (1998) was preceded by her two important films: *Body of Correspondence* (1994, co-written and co-directed by Marina Zurkow) and *Halving the Bones* (1995). The former aired on PBS and won the New Visions Award; the latter screened at Sundance, the Museum of Modern Art, and the Montreal World Film Festival. Meat, bodies, and bones work both figuratively and literally in each of these works and across all sorts of boundaries: in *Body of Correspondence* two dead lesbian lovers come back to life and take material form via a third party's discovery and reading of their love letters, written over the span of a lifetime; in *Halving the Bones* Ozeki documents her trip to Japan to retrieve the bones of her grandmother and her trip back to New Haven, Connecticut, to share them with her mother, along the way narrating her mother's memories of her mother and even giving voice to Ozeki's grandmother via some grainy home movies Ozeki's grandfather supposedly took of her. In *My Year of Meats*, Ozeki draws together several elements that are found in the films: the issues of media, representation, and reception; of writing and reading; of bodies both "human" and "animal," and the food and drugs they ingest; of race, gender, nation and culture, and, throughout, history. And, of course, affect. If in *Halving the Bones* we see the ways the materiality of a few remnants of bone set off a series of meditations in Ozeki and her mother, meditations that are built on a series of affective moments and loop into each other, sometimes harmoniously and sometimes not; and if in *Body of Correspondence* we find the written word itself not only conveying affect between the white lover and her Eurasian counterpart, but also to and through the white male third party, in *My Year of Meats* we find affect circulating via media, bodies, food and drugs, between East and West, male and female, animal and human, in a narrative text that effectively uses that phenomenon to blur the categorical boundaries between each.

The first-person narrator of *My Year of Meats* is a young Japanese American filmmaker recruited to shoot a series of "sociological commercials" in the heartland of the United States, to be broadcast across the Pacific and into the homes of Japanese housewives, instantiating identification, desire, and appetite at once, not to mention purchasing habits. The meat born and bred in the United States will thus be prepared and consumed, processed, and assimilated into Japanese bodies, or so the story goes. Add to this Ozeki's prominent subtext of DES (diethylstilbestrol), bovine growth hormones, "mad cow disease," and animal and human reproduction, and you can see why I regard this novel as "remarkable" in its fit into this study: we have in one form or another precisely an address to issues of reason and rationality (the marketing logic of the transnational beef corporation mobilizes "rationality" in the form of consumption, "inveigling" Japanese consumers to make certain choices); to the issue of bodies (the global effects of food and drug production, the effects of those on the animal and human reproductive body, the ways alien materials are commonly ingested by diverse human bodies globally); and, most especially here, the issue of the affective power of the other. Furthermore, the novel's dual focus on media and ethics throughout helps us likewise to hone in on the abiding concern of this study: how is it, today, that we can best understand the nature of how the other is delivered to us, and we to "them," and how does literary narrative offer a particular mode of deliverance, of imagining the affective connections among others, different from the delivery systems we have investigated and their assumptions of human sameness? Most specifically, how can literary texts capture the phenomenon of system overload—how can we imagine otherness outside and beyond the "delivery systems" that run on common units? What kind of alternative *critical* delivery system might literature be?

To set the framework for my analysis of *My Year of Meats*, I will first move through some key ideas on otherness and affect, emphasizing how the notion of affect historically has had at its core the idea of equilibrium. Spinoza and others will convert unruly and destabilizing affect into controllable substances so as to preserve the self. Looking back at my initial discussion of rationality, I will take up Spinoza's notion of the affects as it engages the idea of reason and control and equilibrium. In ways that echo the problematic I have outlined in this study, Spinoza is concerned with the question of too much otherness, specifically, too much affect produced by others. I then touch on the transformation that occurs at the turn of the eighteenth century, as the emotions are no longer regarded as invaders from the outside world, but rather as something inherent in human nature. Nevertheless, in terms of the constitution of the self, this highlights the question of how much of "us" is constituted from within, as we enliven and realize our inner natures, and how much comes from without, through the integration of the affect of others. It is precisely in the late twentieth century and in our contemporary age that increased and intensified globalization produces the historical situation wherein affect is of such volume and mass that it threatens to overflow the boundaries of acceptable and manageable otherness, and the question of who "we" are becomes especially vexed. With so much affective "data" flowing through the Ethernet, permeating our senses through not only radio and television but also the handheld devices, laptops, tablets, and whatever new and "better" devices are invented, we have the constitution of a new sort of ultrapermeable human being. I end my introductory section with a discussion of Teresa Brennan's work on the transmission of affect as it engages with the other in the present day. In the end, this book is not so involved in championing the unbridled bursting forth of otherness, nor in adjudicating the proper balance between self and other—I do not wish to draw some line or standard. Rather, I see this as an emblematic problem of globalization, and see contemporary literature as profoundly engaged in puzzling out how the delivery systems that convey others as the same function, or not.

Affect, Others, Behavior, Equilibrium

These are the keywords for my consideration of the role affect plays in managing the flow and stasis of affect within the body and psyche. Affect here is a delivery system that is both the common ground of sensation and reaction, and a mediating space for the circulation of feelings, emotions, and the registering of otherness. The goal always is to remain both active and vital, and to maintain at the same time a sense of equilibrium. For one of the earliest analysts of affect, Spinoza, this dynamic and imperative is felt at the core of the human being; affect is both a necessary part of human life, and yet it may threaten to overwhelm us with its energy and force, leading us to act in ways that go against our self-interest. Affect in itself for Spinoza is not necessarily bad—it's all a matter of how we invest it.

> Whatever so disposes the human body that it can be affected in a great
> many ways, or renders it capable of affecting external bodies in a great
> many ways, is useful to man; the more it renders the body capable of
> being affected in a great many ways, or of affecting other bodies, the
> more useful it is; on the other hand, what renders the body less capable
> of these things is harmful. Those things are good which bring about the
> preservation of the proportion of motion and rest the human body's
> parts have to one another; on the other hand, those things are evil which
> bring it about that the parts of the human body have a different propor-
> tion of motion and rest to one another.[13]

The essential thing to keep vital at all times, despite the buffeting of
affect emanating from the world and more specifically the world of
others, is our true nature. The affects that draw on our energies in bad
ways depress us, or take our eyes away from our forward-moving progress. Spinoza asserts, "We call good, or evil, what is useful to, or harmful
to, preserving our being, that is, what increases or diminishes, aids or
restrains, our power of acting. Therefore, insofar as we perceive that a
thing affects us with joy or sadness, we call it good over evil."[14] But here
Spinoza makes his essential move. These "whats," these bodiless affects,
are managed precisely as they are brought into the realm of knowledge,
drawn away from being powerful things to which we stand as *passive*
beings. Our passivity before the passions can be reversed if we reify
these vital forces into conceptual knowledge and integrate them rationally and purposefully into our active being.

Take the example of pity, one of the key emotions we noted with
Aristotle. Are we not to be moved by it, seeing ourselves "in the other
person's shoes"? Is this not what the imagination is for, to present us
with the grounds for identification and sympathy? In Spinoza's view,
pity is an evil thing, for it takes us away from ourselves and can indeed
harm us, turning us into its passive victims. It preys on us, disarming our
rational power and our ability to convert affect wisely.

> Pity, in a man who lives according to the guidance of reason, is both evil
> of itself and useless. For pity is a sadness, and therefore, of itself, evil. To
> this we may add that he who is easily touched by the affect of pity, and
> moved by another's suffering or tears, often does something he later
> repents—both because, from an affect, we do nothing which we certainly
> know to be good, and because we are easily deceived by false tears.[15]

In the following passage, Spinoza draws all these elements together: self-good, affect and its conversion under reason's dominance, and a transition from passively receiving affect to rationalizing it and deploying it in ways that actively promote the body (and this would of course include jettisoning negative affect altogether).

> An affect which is a passion is a confused idea. Therefore, if we should form a clear and distinct idea of the affect itself, this idea will only be distinguished by reason from the affect itself in so far as it is related only to the mind. Therefore the affect will cease to be a passion. For the more an affect is known to us, then the more it is in our power, and the less the mind is acted upon by it.[16]

In sum, harking back to Freud, this is the move from affect to ideational content, a way of disarming affect's ability to insist on its presence as such in our lives. This tames affect, reining it in and transforming it into an idea, an object of the rational mind that can be held at a distance and abstracted.

Not only is this important in and of itself, but it is also the necessary first step to building and nurturing something of even greater importance to the perpetuation of our "true natures"—a *community* of people like ourselves: "Nothing can agree more with the nature of any thing than other individuals of the same species. And so nothing is more useful to man in preserving his being and enjoying a rational life than the man who is guided by reason."[17] We can see thus that in Spinoza the affects act as the medium between individuals; it is their point of psychic contact, and they act kinesthetically. People can be "moved" by them. Thus, learning to deal with affect becomes a primary way to regulate both oneself and one's relation to others. Ethics in this sense is geared toward the "good" of stability, and the positive, active, rational use of energy. For the individual, it means that she will not be tossed about by random stimuli; for humankind, it means the maintenance and growth of a community likewise informed, and controlled, by reason. In the eighteenth century, although the passions are turned into more benign internal sentiments, the view that the affects are indices to sociality and a key element in guiding behavior toward others does not change.

Amélie Oksenberg Rorty notes that during this period,

> instead of being reactions to invasions from something external to the self, passions became the very activities of the mind, its own motions. So

transformed they become."proper motives, and along with desires, the beginnings of actions. During this period, emotions also ceased to be merely turbulent commotions: among them appear sentiments, ways of feeling pleasures and pains as evaluations, and so as the proper guides to action. Some of these sentiments, those that are social in origin as well in direction—calm passions and sentiments that we acquire from others—make morality possible.[18]

In this new scheme of things, the imagination takes on a different, and critical role, for it facilitates the new, socially required ability to trace the sympathetic links between people, and thus suggests a moral sentiment. *Pace* Spinoza, Rorty asserts, "The imagination remains closely allied with the sentiments even after it has become an active power; but now instead of being a threat to justice and virtues, it provides the condition for the possibility of sympathetic morality."[19] Thus, the imagination, too, becomes enlisted to map out an "oceanic feeling" between bodies mingling in social space, but here it exerts its power on affect, bringing the affective body and the registering mind into proper contact, and, furthermore, connecting bodies of a similar disposition together. The imagination would bring into the mind "a train of thoughts that are useful to the *union* of the soul and body, and they are useful to the *body* as a member of that union."[20]

The reasonableness of this plan of action is matched only by its import. For the passions are not just over there, they are present in the atmosphere the moment we enter into social space. And even though the emotions were no longer seen as "invaders," at this point in history David Hume seems to continue at least one strand of Spinoza's thought: he, too, remarks on the ability of the emotions to pass easily, promiscuously, among bodies and to affect others, striking similar chords and, critically for our study, producing similar behavior. "The passions," Hume comments, "are so contagious that they pass with the greatest facility from one person to another, and produce correspondent movements in all human breasts."[21] Commenting on this passage, Eagleton captures some of the strangeness of this characterization of the passions: "There is something magical about this affect of contagion, as though your fright or jealousy might literally infect my own innards, pass like some emotional virus from your body to mine."[22] Thus, despite the fact that the emotions were no longer thought to be external to us and instigators of dangerous, irrational behavior, we still find the notion that their influence on us, whether it be to introduce something new into our natures or to tap into something preexisting, requires the deployment of both reason and the imagination to maintain the proper balance in the affective economy of things. It is here that Adela Pinch brings out an important paradox that will deeply inform our discussion of otherness: "On the one hand, [Hume's *Treatise*] asserts that feelings are individual, and that philosophy itself as well as social and aesthetic experience depends on individuals who can rely on the individual authenticity of their own emotional responsiveness. On the other hand, it also contends that feelings are transsubjective entities that pass between persons; that our feelings are always really someone else's; that it is passion that allows us to be persons, rather than the other way around."[23] The cycle of affect thus engages a similar doubleness in terms of who we are and how we got to be that; "human nature" is both individually manifested and produced from without, circulating in social space. It is clearer than ever that this regulatory body has always to deal with the amount of otherness that it can handle without being drawn out of its healthful nature.

Up to this point, we have charted the transition from Spinoza's conceptualization of the affects as things to be mastered by conversion into ideas. Reason is called on to do this. If we accept that one strong source of affect is the other, then we can see that mastering its affective power is key to self-preservation, the key "good" to be had. Later on, this notion changes to one in which affect, as part of the sentimental and emotional world, is accepted as part of human nature, but nonetheless remains something that can be counterproductive, if not destructive, if left to its own devices.[24] Here, it is up to the imagination to rein in the equilibrium-threatening power of the sentiments. Thus, both conceptually and figuratively, we have a pair of powers to tame and enlist the affects. It is not hard to imagine that literature might be precisely that thing that can trace the pathways of affect in the formation of self and other. The affects are a measure of not only the individual subject, but also her relation to her social world, and furthermore, the production of ever-expanding social worlds. The ways people *affect* each other, reaching into the bodies and psyches of others and motivating them to act similarly, for better or worse, is a constant element in all discussions of affect, and this carries over to our discussion of the literary as a particular way of delivering affect.

Modern Times: Ego, Affect, Imagination, Otherness

Affective responses seem to the individual to be aroused easily by factors over which he has little control, with difficulty by factors which he can control and to endure for periods of time which he controls only with great difficulty if at all. They are in these respects somewhat alien to the individual. They are the primitive gods within the individual.
—SILVAN TOMKINS

I want to draw together the main concerns I have about affect and otherness. If in Spinoza affect posed a threat to the maintenance of the self, and in Hume and others it was contagious in ways that could either facilitate sociability or threaten it, and in Freud it was an obdurate, murky thing that lingered in the shadows of consciousness, in the contemporary age it has been read as similarly threatening the equilibrium of the self but managed by particular psychic displacements. In this vein I want to consider one key aspect of the work of Teresa Brennan on affect. She ventures into similar territory as Silvan Tomkins in that she is interested in both the "alien" nature of affect and its shifting and complex environment, especially as it stands in relation to the system of the drives. Tomkins notes, "The drive system with its relatively primitive signal and feedback mechanisms will work well enough because of this predictable and small variability of the internal environment. The affect system of man operates, however, within a much more uncertain and variable environment."[25]

There are three things I want to draw out from Teresa Brennan's provocative study of affect. First is the notion that the ego is above all a self-preserving mechanism, and furthermore one that uses all sorts of sometimes devious mechanisms to do so. This is particularly so with its regard of the other and the potential effect it can have on the ego. In performing its acts of self-preservation, the ego draws on both real and imagined memories of the other, mingling them together to adjust and balance itself.

> The ego, originally the arbiter of conflicts between one's own good and that of the other, is less able to discern this when the ego itself becomes a distorted arbiter, an arbiter that judges in order to arbitrate. Each of the affective constellations known to us as desires related to lack or sins is a state of the ego in which its self-protective function has been distorted

by imaginary factors. Thus, envy can result from an imaginary belittle-ment, anger can result from imaginary insults, and so forth. The ego, in other words, is not only a perceptive preservative function but also a constellation of memories and desires associated with imaginary threats to its prestige as well as its existence.[26]

What is most striking here is that we find an inventory of relations to the other not necessarily based on any real encounter, but often on a par-ticularly imagined one, one based on the preservation and "prestige" of the ego. Furthermore, it takes the form of not only a constellation of memories and desires, but, I would add, a *serial* set of memories and desires that become narrated ("she did that to me and therefore I . . ."). One should also look at the obverse side of this scenario, where we would be discussing not supposed insults, envy, and so on, but rather ego-building imaginaries—one's superior strength or intelligence fed by flattering affect imagined to emanate from the other. In short, we have a repertoire of narratives that support and enhance the ego's sense of well-being by imagining and regulating a certain affective relation to the other.

A second point that I draw from Brennan is that the responsibility for one's negative affect often becomes projected on the other. Here I would venture that this projection is in part made possible by an imagi-nary invention of the other and one's memory of one's relation to it, an invention that allows one to disavow the responsibility for negative affect and instead attribute its source to the other. Guilt, shame, anger, are all made the responsibility of the other in an effort to preserve the ego's positive self-image. This happens especially when one has gath-ered into oneself a critical mass of negative affect: "The need to project intensifies as the affects, and the drives promoting it, accumulate. The person projecting the judgment is freed from its depressing effects on him or herself. However, he or she is dependent on the other carrying that projected affect, just as the master depends on the slave."[27] Criti-cally for the present study, this equilibrium-making displacement pro-duces as well a zero-sum economy of affect: the more I free myself up from negative affect by projecting it on you, the more you are weighed down by it, and vice versa, in essence producing an economy of psychic health and illness, or, in Spinoza's terms, good and evil. Brennan de-clares, "If I take your aggression on board and turn it back against myself as depression I have less energy and you have more, because you are not inhibited by a drive that limits you when it is turned inward. In this case, the affect appears as the passive manifestation of the other's active drive. . . . This is true for narcissism, envy, inverted aggression or depression and anxiety, and the inertia accompanying all of them."[28] Finally, Brennan asserts, "If the general thesis of this book is right, that evidence also shows that the prevalence of these disorders is relationally and socially exacerbated. We construct our own attractors, but the force of what we attract varies according to affective circumstance."[29]

This last comment is critical for my study in that it introduces the relational aspect of the transmission of affect, along with the social dimension, and this is the third point I want to bring forward from Brennan. She posits a hypothesis about the *historical* "affective circumstance" of the late twentieth century. She argues that the relation between self and other changed, and in fact became more intense.

> In the 1990s, depression was the most rapidly growing disorder in Europe and the United States, while concern with boundaries was also proliferating. Could these things be related? Have boundaries come to matter because self-definition by projection is less available than it was during the last few sexist and colonial centuries—there are now too few willing receptacles—or because of an accumulation of environmental-inflected affects? Either way, boundaries may matter now because there is too much affective stuff to dispose of, too much that is directed away from the self with no place to go. . . . But this increase of affects is also a real thing, historically produced. The reality of the increase makes the Western individual especially more concerned with securing a private fortress, personal boundaries, against the unsolicited emotional intrusions of the other. The fear of being "taken over" is certainly in the air, although the transmission of negative affect generally is not recognized for what it is. Boundaries, paradoxically, are an issue in a period where the transmission of affect is denied.[30]

If Brennan is correct in her fundamental theorization of affect and its transmittability, then the customary way that white, Eurocentric, masculinist, and hetereonormative societies have construed their inner "bad" affect as emanating from the place of the other (raced, non-European, feminine, non-hetero-normed) reached a point of tension in the 1990s because the other pushed back, no longer accepting the narrative of being the source of evil (here I employ Spinoza's vocabulary:

"evil" is that which impinges on the health of the self). Bad affect now has no place to go except back into the self. According to Brennan's hypothesis, the Euroamerican subject, unable to recognize its *own* pathologies, must resort to psychoanalysis to trace the roots of affective damage, or to drugs to numb and dull the power of affect. I am not at all sure I accept this conjecture—there are simply too many assumptions built into it, most especially the notion that the resistance of the other, its border-enforcing powers, were or are that great. Nonetheless, Brennan raises an interesting point: how much of the affective relation between self and other is colored by this dynamic, this act of projection that relies on an *imagined* relation to the other? How much of our self-preservation is based on the affective economy sketched out here by Brennan? And how does this mechanism include a complementary dynamic—while we project on the other the responsibility for our negative affect, we protect ourselves from the invasion of the other's affect into our own psyches? And finally, how does this play out in terms of the particular affective relationships that exist at particular historical moments? How do certain "slots of possibilities" open up when specific "delivery systems" come into effect?

I will argue here, via my reading of Ozeki's novel, that the contagious spread of affect lives on today not only because of its supposedly supreme survival powers, but also and importantly because new global markets and the media that advertise them to the world tap into an assumed base of common emotional and affective registers, and affect and global media enhance one another in ever-increasing efficiencies. We are now more and more opened up to, exposed to, and saturated by media in multifarious forms, via a proliferation of devices that interface with our lives and bodies nearly continually. And let us not ignore the fact that these are paired with somatic and physiological appetites and needs. A global economy relies in no small measure on the idea of a global consumer society that registers the same affects (or at least seems to). If they do not exist, then they must be instantiated. Here let me say that I am under no illusion that there is or even can be an exact replication of need and desire, emotion and affect across borders of any kind. But that does not really matter. What counts is the end result in the behavior of people and the material conditions that enable them to make certain choices—who will buy and consume these things, repeatedly, and who is able to? Therefore, we must account for both the material historical conditions of affect and the role the imagination plays in the reception and projection of affect. In fact, I want us to note the centrality of the imagination, and the imaginary, in dealing with not only affect, but also with mapping one's position or location in "oceanic feeling," one's neighborliness with the other, and one's position in the flow of feeling. For it becomes increasingly difficult to see where affect comes from, especially when the "rational" and the "real" are blended into the fantastic.

Before I get to *My Year of Meats*, however, I want to delve into Ruth Ozeki's and Marina Zurkow's short film, *Body of Correspondence*. I use this film to introduce Ozeki's ways of thinking about bodies and affect, reading and writing. This schematic reading will both frame my reading of the novel and also help us understand how Ozeki elaborates these main issues in a complex and sometimes baffling fashion in her novel.

Body of Correspondence

There are three characters in the film: "O" is an elegant Eurasian woman in her late fifties who teaches comparative literature in Japan; "N" is a blond Jewish woman slightly younger than O who works at the Museum of Natural History in New York; finally, there is a paunchy, balding man called "the Archivist," who works in an unnamed museum in upstate New York.

The Archivist has been asked by a colleague to help sort through a box of items that the museum has been storing for many years, to see if there is anything worth keeping. He takes the materials, which include a number of letters between N and O, and goes through them, touching the objects, reading the texts, and in the process slowly becoming drawn to them.

> Archivist: Inside the large box were two smaller boxes labeled N. and O. Each contained a collection of papers. Careful to note original order, which in this case was seemingly random, I began reading the documents. . . . But then, one night, as I was finishing up the catalogue of ephemera, I happened to lay out several items on the desktop. Something about the grouping appealed to me, as did the way the light from the gooseneck lamp struck the arrangement. I often make photographic records, but the impulse I had at this moment was different somehow. I

felt compelled to photograph these objects, not as evidence, but . . . as illustration.

An illustration of what? I . . . don't know. . . . Something . . . not evident. Entirely narrative. I emptied the shoe boxes onto the bed and started to interfile and reorder the documents. To violate the two fundamental principles of my profession. I had to keep reminding myself that no one cared. That everybody was dead. These things were meaningless . . . unless I interfered. . . . I was aware, too, of a concurrent sense of power.[31]

Here, the perceived "order" of the papers is disorder. Perhaps it is that very randomness that yields a particular affect when illuminated by the lamp. The Archivist is drawn to create something "entirely narrative"; the haphazard arrangement of things demands that they be made into "something." He is given not only the right to do this ("everybody was dead"), but also apparently the imperative to make meaning out of meaninglessness. The issue of course is that these "meaningless" artifacts created by these dead figures are open to violation (a key theme in the film). As in Brennan's theory, the other is without a boundary to protect itself from such violation, such projection of affect, at least not at this point in the film's diegesis.

What follows is a set of flashbacks and projections forward that tap into the fantasies and stories within stories that the letters contain. It slowly becomes evident that the Archivist's own actions and the events that occur in his story are mimicking elements from the letters he is reading; the violation now becomes doubled over, as the stories and commentaries of the animated other impose themselves back on the Archivist, and elements from their stories begin to replicate themselves in his life. But this affective phenomenon works in reverse as well—as their letters move forward in time, the authors begin to disclose events from their past that shed new light on their relationship. Yet these disclosures are often not presented entirely as "real," but as narratives that contain a mixture of real and made-up elements. Crucially, they evince not only the psychic displacements and fantasies of the young girls, but also those of the Archivist, whose shadowy presence works its way into the girls' past, just as their stories begin to insinuate themselves into his life.

The Archivist's gaze makes its way back in time, but what is more, his presence is felt retroactively in events that in real time preceded his reading. It is precisely as these events become narrated that the presence of

1. *Body of Correspondence*, 1994. Courtesy of Ruth Ozeki
and Marina Zurkow.

the Archivist is felt not only as an animating figure who is reading the
texts in the future, but also as an actual actor in the past. The affect the
letters produce in him is thereby thrown into a dystemporal circuit of
affect and animation, reading, seeing, and performing. N writes to O,

> Anyway, a weird thing has been happening for two weeks. I've noticed a
> guy on the fourth floor of the building across the street is looking out his
> window with binoculars. One night I saw him standing there. At first I
> was going to pull down the shade, but then guess what? I didn't. I started
> to get undressed for bed instead. I turned on the radio and did a little
> dance. I got really sweaty and after a few minutes I thought I was going
> to throw-up. I'm sure he was watching. If my mother knew she'd proba-
> bly get jealous. Don't tell anyone, or they'll probably think your pen pal
> is a perv. Does anyone see into your window?

One central event in N's life is her rape at the hands of a traveling
encyclopedia salesman, "Will DeForest," who is staying at the hotel
where she is working. N's letter contains this narrative, whose status in

the real world is uncertain: "Will DeForest comes rolling into a small dust bowl of a town. He is a traveling salesman with a trunk-full of encyclopedias. But his specialty is arson, setting brushfires in the hearts of young girls well-versed in the art of Harlequin Romance." Now was he actually a traveling salesman, or someone else in another situation? What sorts of "young girls" are aroused by Harlequin romances?

Then the Archivist's own life starts to follow suit; during his reading and imaginative reconstruction of the letters, their mixture of fantasy and sometimes brutal realism carries over into his world. As he reads each letter, its affective qualities reach into his mind and his body. Seeming to mimic Will DeForest, he has sex with the young girl who is working at the motel where he is staying. Similarly, O's sexual encounter with "the Shingon Monk" many years later in Japan is narrated in her letter fantastically—the "monk" is dressed in loud golf outfit—and these fantasies find affective and mimetic force in the world of the Archivist. During his reading of this letter, the Archivist, seeming to borrow garb from O's Japanese story, sheds a kimono and immerses himself in a filthy bathtub.

The Archivist's scene combines two elements from O's letter—one in which she tells how the Monk takes her to a bath, and one in which the Monk tells his own story of building a fire in the woods:

> It grew dark. He spoke in a low voice about the austerity of meditative practices at the temple. How, in the hottest month of the summer, he would strip to his loincloth and go into the forest to collect wood—hard wood because it burns long and hot. He would build a huge fire and when the coals were bright, he'd spread them on the ground in a burning carpet. Then he would walk barefoot across them. He took hold of my foot and raked his long nails across the sole.

By scratching his nails across O's foot, the Monk attempts to reproduce for her the sensation of the coals on his foot. Just as the Monk approximates the affect of his experience through this gesture, the Archivist's affective reaction to the bath's heat is his particular adaptation of the Monk's sensing of the fire's heat to his own steamy environment. In brief, the "realism" of the letters is compromised not only within the letters themselves, warped by the distance between individual experience, reshaped by different media, distorted or displaced by the authors' own workings out of their psychic conflicts, but also, affect flows in all directions, emanating from both self and other.

2. and (below) 3. Both from *Body of Correspondence,* 1994. Courtesy of Rut Ozeki and Marina Zurkow.

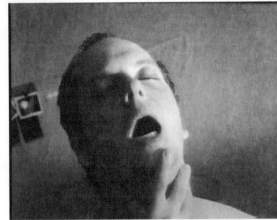

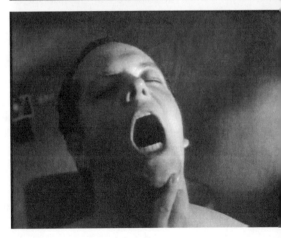

We and the Archivist are put in the same position as N; we hear O's voice telling this tale, and each of us—viewer, N, Archivist—feel the influx of affect. Not unlike Hume's pronouncement about the contagious properties of affect, we find that a narrative such as this can kick off psychic responses, wherein each figure in the narrative becomes affected, with emotion and affect not only brought into their lives, but coloring their actions and thoughts as well in real ways. This, after all, is how the Archivist begins this path off proper archival procedure. As we are ourselves swept up in the diegesis, we need to remind ourselves that while the textual elements are assumedly static (the voiceover conveys the text to us aurally), the visualization is perhaps that of the letter-writer, or perhaps the Archivist's own. In that respect, as well as in others, just as much as we do not know how much "truth" of whatever kind abides in the tales that the girls tell each other, we do not know how much of himself the Archivist is putting in. Here we find precisely the dynamic Brennan mentions: how much positive affect is falsely claimed as one's own when it really originates in the other, or is said to come from the other, when it is a matter of distancing oneself from the bad affect in one's own psyche?

This all results in reassessing the text, but be filmic or literary: in this state of things, affect is not only worked out within the individual ego, but played out dynamically with projections onto the other and introjections into self. We find again and again the uneasy relation literature has always had to "the real." We can reconsider the old adage "All literature is autobiography" with a keener sense of how the workings out of the self engage the other in very specific ways. Critically, in contemporary literature there is a qualitative difference. Today's "global" literature is especially attuned to the massive and intensive ways that affect circulates globally, driven by all sorts of motives and goals, and comes into different kinds of contact with distant others and their own senses of affect.

This phenomenon is emblematized in the final scenes of "Body of Correspondence." If at the start we discover that the Archivist's act of reading has, in a super-phenomenological manner, *actually* "animated" the text—or, to be more accurate, conjured up and given flesh to the dead—as the film proceeds, the narrative power is gradually placed in the hands of the dead: they *demand* to be made flesh, not to encounter him, but to be fully realized before each other.

O: My dearest N., You've changed. I've changed. I'm afraid I wasn't able to explain why a meeting in the flesh seems so vital to me now.

N: What? You think we can be lovers, after all these years . . . ?!

/ . . . /

O: I don't know. Call it intuition but, please, accept it with grace. This is and is not about sex. This is about our corporeal selves. I do want. I am sorely wanting. I want to see you. I want you to see me. I need to reassure myself that I do exist, now, in the flesh, embodied. Eyes are important. This is what I think. I think eyes are mirrors, and I am reborn into the world through so many blinks and squints, as daughter, as mother, as teacher. . . . My longest gaze belongs to you. And I need your eyes, because I'm growing older and without them, I am as insubstantial as vellum. So, call it double reflex, but like a photograph, I need a good shot of you.

This need for a "good shot," for the actual bodily presence of her lover, is a direct repudiation of the opening lines of the film, which narrate a story of solitariness and death.

O: "An old lady lived alone and died . . ."

N: Now that's an approximate truth if there ever was one. . . . Here is how that story would go: "An old lady lived alone and died. People came to look for her, and they found: stacks of newspapers, carefully sorted out by date; cardboard containers and Kleenex boxes and egg cartons re-used to organize the refuse of a lifetime."

Instead, O and N plot their resurrection, and reunion. O says, "Of course, we both hoped this excavation would come, and now that I have access to my boxes again, I am triumphant at the stubbornness of my acquisition."

Their "excavation" is initially in the hands of a person who might find and open the box. Nevertheless, once opened, that individual is susceptible and bendable to the affective power contained within. The Archivist's own loneliness, his solitariness, makes him especially vulnerable to affective contagion: "I still, to this day, do not know what drew me to the box. . . . I thought I understood her feelings. . . . I had no human ties. . . . We had something in common."

The newly resurrected women enter the Archivist's motel room while he is in the woods, burning their letters. They steal their "ephemera" back from him, then go to the museum and steal what remains of their

4.

5.

Both from *Body of Correspondence*, 1994.
Courtesy of Ruth Ozeki and Marina Zurkow.

objects. In a neatly symmetrical way, as the Archivist destroys the items that have entered too strongly into his life, N and O have preserved those very things by taking them back into their world.

How does affect come to flow in this narrative space between minds and bodies? While the contagion between individual selves is clearly emphasized in this film, so too is the representative system: how do stories themselves become archived, filed away and fit into a system of preservation? How do we assume they will stay there, then emerge intact and perfectly reiterable as they are exhumed each time by new readers? The Archivist speaks the last lines of *Body of Correspondence*.

> In regards and with respect. . . . This is where I started, and I come back now . . . to those words . . . to explain my actions. As an archivist I have an . . . abiding . . . respect for materials that manage to survive. It was my intention only to breathe life into this correspondence.
>
> It was precisely this regard that led me to . . . stare harder.

The gap to be closed is exactly that which exists between mere survival and life. However, the intensification of his stare both animates the materials and unleashes a reciprocal, if not greater, effect on him. Thus, he ends up destroying the materials (or so he thinks). The final words bespeak thus an utterly misplaced sense of control, of equilibrium-making: "Its contents have been . . . properly assessed and . . . appropriately stored. And I am satisfied with the small role I have played in this undertaking." These last lines are uttered precisely as the two authors, the now revivified ghosts, are stealing their objects back from the museum.

The contagious power of affect, its tremendous ability to attract us and yet also its ability to overflow the boundaries of self and other, archivist and artifact, author and reader, is thus put before us in *Body of Correspondence*. At the same time, in a commensurate fashion, the issue of truth and fiction, authenticity and illusion, are insinuated into the very delivery system of affect. To parse these out would seem to be the imperative for any effort to mobilize affect's suasive powers for ethical good. And these intimately bound issues are indeed at the heart of *My Year of Meats*.

My Year of Meats

Ruth Ozeki's novel attempts to ascertain the function of literature in a world of globally networked corporate mediazation. She is especially interested in the different ways in which people might be affected both by literary texts and by media images so as to act ethically and with a sense of being together. *My Year of Meats* tells the story of Jane Tagaki Little, a documentary filmmaker barely scraping by, who is willingly recruited by a multinational corporation, BEEF-EX, to create a "documentary series" that is actually an extended series of commercials designed to hook Japanese consumers on American beef. The show will send the crew out into the American Heartland to find "typical" American housewives, interview them about their lives, and meanwhile have them prepare their favorite beef recipes to share with their Japanese counterparts. Theirs is not only a pedagogical relationship, but also an economic one—the company is anxious to "find" the "authentic" America, because its exoticism sells well. Jane ruefully confesses, "Although my heart was set on being a documentarian, it seems I was more useful as a go-between, a cultural pimp, selling off the cast illusion of America to a cramped population on that small string of Pacific islands."[32] Asian American relations are thus intensely and insistently mediated by both national and transnational economics, playing off affect and sentimentality at all levels: "Locating our subjects felt like a confidence game, really. I'd inveigle a nice woman with her civic duty to promote American meat abroad and thereby help rectify the trade imbalance with Japan" (35). Ozeki is interested in how advertising and media merge together to produce hybrid genres wherein fiction and reality mix, how "illusions" of national cultures are used to instill trans-Pacific affect and consumer behavior, and to do so at a specific juncture ("slot of possibility") in Asian American history.

The depiction of Asia Pacific, and Japan in particular, as a central market in the global economy was set forward in the mid-1980s, perhaps most vividly in Ken'ichi Ōmae's notion of "triad power." Ōmae, a Japanese employee of the American research company McKinsey, put forward the idea of a tripolar world reality consisting of Europe, North America, and Japan and the "four dragons" of East Asia. While the first two "poles" had long been major trade partners, the inclusion of Japan was attributed to, among other things, the flourishing of a new kind of modern subjectivity. According to J. R. Goodyear, "The Japanese, for so long eschewing foreign goods in favor of Japanese products, [were] embracing a new sub-group individualism (or, viewed globally, convergence) and responding increasingly to the allure of foreign brands."[33] That is to say, the postwar era had yielded a Japanese consumer driven by Western "individual" desires and geared toward "foreign" goods.

Two decades later, the centrality of Japan seemed just as strong, as revealed in the title of the book *Leveraging Japan* (2000). The publisher's blurb reads,

> Japan's current shift from a manufacturing to a consumer economy is creating unprecedented opportunities for any company with the savvy to exploit this, the world's second largest market. Certainly, as the Japanese economy continues to rebound, more and more companies will continue to stake and build their presence there and use it as a springboard to enter other growing Asian markets. In *Leveraging Japan*, three leading authorities on market strategy and Japan present the new rules of Japanese marketing and discuss the evolution of other emerging Asian markets. These experts then share the same strategies that they've used to help American Express, Avon, Levi Strauss, and KFC, among other multinational companies, successfully establish a presence in Japan and leverage that presence to enter other Asian markets.[34]

The "strategies" include one of the core elements in Ozeki's novel: advertising. Armand Mattelart describes a transformation of that field as well during this same period.

> Advertising has become a central actor within the public space. It has overflowed the cramped frame of the commercial break in order to constitute itself as a mode of communication. From the isolated and isolable product, it has become a diffuse environment, pregnant and present in the every day. Yesterday a simple instrument, today a central feature. Its field of competence is so diversified and branching that it forms a social network which enervates media, economies, cultures, political and civil society, international relations. Network of networks, these systems of connection regulate the relations between individuals and groups. The so-called communications society chases the so-called consumer society.[35]

Mattelart's point here—that the generic and practical boundaries between advertising and heretofore separate realms of public discourse (media, economics, culture) have broken down, as has the boundary between public and private, such that a globalized system of affect draws on multiple sources, stimuli, and media at once to generate the desired consumer behavior, nestled within this brand of "everyday world"—is one of the main features of both Mattelart's study and Ozeki's novel: this is the present-day form of affective contagion. Instilling need or desire for a commodity or service draws on both preexisting habits and newly invented and imagined ones, which then are disseminated in forms that include not only the customary "sound bite," but also less clearly defined media forms such as the infomercial, a "tweet," or a Facebook post. This very hybridity means that the usual ways of filtering and processing information, heretofore relatively compartmentalized into discrete spaces and habits of reading and viewing, are disarmed. "Information" flows through in many guises and enters into our decision-making in myriad, sometimes invisible, ways. (This is the argument of the Vance Packard's classic study, *The Hidden Persuaders*, now celebrating its fiftieth anniversary, but of course without today's sophisticated global delivery systems in place.) An upshot of this is that our processes for decoding discrete kinds of information are now outmoded, as generic distinctions have lapsed and public and private spaces interpenetrate. New regimes of sense-making have taken hold of us as our affective world seems to have become more and more oceanic and borderless.[36]

Nevertheless, the "newness" of the market did not mean that only contemporary images were to be deployed. The particular East-West historical context of the eighties created a strange anachronism. Jane receives this directive from BEEF-EX.

> *Note on All-American values*—our ideal American wife must have enough in common with the average Japanese housewife so as not to appear either threatening or contemptible. *My American Wife!* of the 90s must be a modern role model, just as her mother was a model to Japanese wives after World War II. However, nowadays a spanking-new refrigerator or automatic can opener is not a "must." In recent years, due to Japan's "economic miracle," the Japanese housewife is more accustomed to these amenities even than her American counterpart. The agency thinks we must replace this emphasis on old-fashioned consumerism with contemporary wholesome values, represented not by gadgets for the wife's sole convenience but by good, nourishing food for her entire family. And that means meat. (13)

The standard accoutrements of the modern kitchen are indeed more likely to be produced in Japan than in America, and the latest models more likely to be found in the Japanese kitchen than in the American one. If the design and manufacturing of modern appliances, electronics, and automobiles are now the purview of Asia, what can America offer? The one thing Japan's environment cannot produce en masse: beef. And this resort to red meat as an essential and unique (albeit outdated) ingredient of American history jibes well with what were considered to be the most potent global advertising images. Recognizing the contemporary material history of East-West trade relations, and the futility of selling to the Japanese products that they already possess, Jane's "documentary" reaches back to a glorious past of the American Heartland, in a gesture following precisely this campaign advice found in the 1985 annual report of the global advertising giant Saatchi and Saatchi: "Capitalize on universally recognized cultural symbols and references. . . . [W]ithout TV and motion picture education about the virile, rugged character of the American West, the worldwide proliferation of the Marlboro brand would not been possible. . . . This cultural convergence is manifest too in the worldwide popularity of films like Rambo or Ghostbusters, pop music idols like Madonna, and books, both fiction and nonfiction."[37]

The irony, of course, is that by that time the mode of meat production found in the American West was gone, superseded by new technological and chemically enhanced modes of production, which have created a qualitatively as well as quantitatively different product. Furthermore, not only has a mode of beef production been eclipsed by new technologies and agribusiness, but also the general program of "Americanization" on the global stage has had its day. We have, in short, the weird juxtaposition of a set of cultural icons rooted in an outmoded history that still has global affect. It is as if the world of media and the world of history have been delinked. Mattelart comments, "If the doctrine of globalization is constructed on the ruins of the doctrines of Americanization, it reveals no less a fascination for the products of the U.S. culture industries, those 'natural supports of universality,' as a member of the agency puts it."[38] That is to say, where the political potency of "Americanization" has flagged, the affective potency of its imagery has not. If anything, it has remained insistently in the global consciousness as a "present" thing: "authenticity" is thus detemporalized, separated into two components—the historical referent of the image set against its affective power.

The point of all this is of course not to amplify the admiration and perhaps even envy of the Japanese for things American, or even simply to get them to "buy American." It is to change their habits of food consumption, not just their media intake. And this in turn converts sentimental affect into economic behavior and physiological change. Affect is linked critically to bodies, as well as to psyches. How do patterns of consumption move from images and values to purchasing behavior and then to actually bringing those products into our bodies, incorporating "them" into us? Here the full impact of "otherness" is felt in all levels of being, in a network that reaches from the individual body to collective material history, to global relations of production and consumption and back again. This topic had already been the focus of studies in the 1980s, especially in Mexico. The following passage tells of the effect of food marketing not only on the consumer habits and bodies of Mexicans, but also on its national agricultural economy:

> The evolution of the food industry . . . leads to the conclusion that there is a tendency to produce sumptuary foods. We speak of sumptuary consumption not only because these products are consumed preferentially by the rich but also because they form a market alongside the middle and low sectors and are unnecessary for a good diet. On the contrary, their acquisition indicates that the lower classes are sacrificing consumption of the necessary basic foodstuffs. . . . Those who suffer most are the poorest classes, whose diet is composed of maize, beans, fats and oils. The consumption of fizzy drinks and desserts has increased the intake of pure sugar with detrimental effect. In other words these calories are ever more expensive.[39]

This transformation of the Mexican diet is thus not only more expensive in terms of money, but also in terms of health, and ultimately it imposes a change in the national agricultural economy: "This model of consumption is also a model of production. The cradle of the civilization of maize has been converted into an importer, at ever-increasing prices, of what was previously exported."[40] The case of Mexico is not unique, of course. Similar transformations of consumption and production were found throughout the Indian subcontinent and Central and South America during what was called the "Green Revolution," which involved not only the high-density use of powerful and costly fertilizers and pesticides, but also the tailoring of agricultural production to the specific needs of First World countries, such that often the environment was ruined for native products.[41]

Let us return now to the issue of the hybridization of genre, for it is in a powerful mix of fact and fiction, of documentary and of commercial, that we find a potent blending of the affective market imaginary that instills these new appetites and preferences. Mattelart draws our attention to "the 'fictionalization' of advertising and the increasing presence of the advertising mode in the production of fiction: two processes which give each other mutual support and consecrate modern advertising as the paragon of mediatized modernity."[42] He notes the proliferation of neologisms that evince this phenomenon: "*Infomercials, Advertorials, Pubbligiornalismo, Publireportage.*" Such mixed genres "erase the lines between news and commercials, advertising and editorial, publicity and journalism, publicity and reportage, between promotional surface and editorial content, advertising and the program."[43] Of course, the situation today, decades later, has proven that this phenomenon has only become more entrenched, facilitated by the easy dissemination globally of both actual information and contrived "reports," by the blurring of the border between journalism and opinion pieces, and by the production of social media platforms available to millions on their cell phones. But this genre-crossing also disarms the ability to distinguish cleanly truth from fiction, or fiction from truth. Indeed, Ozeki's novel demonstrates how our habits of processing information no longer dwell on such distinctions, if affect is the dominant key (how many "followers" do you have on Twitter? How many Facebook "friends" do you boast?).

Critically, this isn't merely a fanciful invention of new forms of communication. Such devices are all geared to confuse the consumer, blending excitement, interest, "information" with either thinly veiled lies or outright deceptions. The most infamous early case of this was when Nestlé, between 1974 and 1976, sent personnel into Third World hospitals to promote the use of its powdered baby formula. Salespeople were dressed up as nurses, exuding the virtues of Western hygienic practices, modern health and well-being, set against the "backwards" Third World habit of nursing one's own child. The company conveniently ignored significant cultural and material realities. They distributed free samples of the product to new mothers, who mixed the powder with unsanitized water, causing infants to become ill and even to die. Many of those who survived were unable to be breastfed, since their mothers had stopped lactating: "[Nestlé] was reproached with failing to consider the environment in which the products were offered for consumption: a cultural tradition of prolonged lactation, closely linked to the natural spacing of births, defective hygienic conditions, lack of drinking water."[44] Only a worldwide protest halted this marketing campaign.

It is a similar attempt to revise the Japanese diet, to infiltrate "culture" via food consumption, that introduces Ozeki's indictment not only of the beef industry, but also of an entire range of interlinked corporate interests that show no reluctance to contaminate our bodies as well as our spirits. It is not simply a matter of eating meat; more important, it involves consuming materials laced with additives and hormones undisclosed to us. Alongside of her indictment of the meat industry, Ozeki pays equal attention to the historical use of the drug DES, which was widely prescribed in the postwar period to prevent miscarriages. Between 1938 and 1971, 10 to 15 million women and babies were exposed to this synthetic estrogen. It was later discovered that the drug actually created birth defects in babies. The Centers for Disease Control notes,

> In 1953, published research showed that DES did not prevent miscarriages or premature births. However, DES continued to be prescribed until 1971. In that year, the Food and Drug Administration (FDA) issued a Drug Bulletin advising physicians to stop prescribing DES to pregnant women. The FDA warning was based on a study published in 1971 that identified DES as a cause of a rare vaginal cancer in girls and young women who had been exposed to DES before birth (in the womb).[45]

In its own progressive version of an "infonovel," *My Year of Meats* contains an appendix with full information, research materials, and articles on both the meat industry and DES. In an interview included in the book, Ozeki seems to echo Mattelart as she notes, "I see our lives as being part of an enormous web of interconnected spheres, where the workings of the larger social, political, and corporate machinery impact something as private and intimate as the descent of an egg through a woman's fallopian tube. This is the resonance I want to conjecture in my books."[46]

This network draws on particular delivery systems, and Ozeki's novel focuses on the complex one of affect production. Indeed, one of the key themes of the novel has to do precisely with the blurring boundaries between the real and the contrived, authenticity and art, the documentary and the commercial, private and public. Breaking down these distinctions enables the flow of commodities. As Jane declares, in the melding of the two we find the most potent forms of persuasion: "The strategy was to develop a powerful synergy between the commercials and the documentary vehicles in order to stimulate consumer purchase motivation" (41). Critically, this motivation is built on the general affective system. No area of the Japanese "body" should be impermeable.

Ozeki registers the effect of Jane's "product" not only on the general forms of producing and perceiving images of difference, but also on the microcosmic sensory perceptions of it as registered on the body itself. In a fascinating passage we move the distance from the phonic to the ideology of consumption: "She [Akiko] liked the sounds of the parallel Japanese r's, with their delicate flick of the tongue across the palate, and the plosive *pu* like a kiss or a fart in the middle of a big American dinner. She liked the size of things American. Convenient. Economical. Big and simple" (19). In a similar fashion, the aesthetic of difference prompts an attempt at mimicry: "What a beautiful name, thought Akiko. Suzie Flowers [a person represented in one of the commercials] laughed easily, but Akiko was practicing how to do this too" (21). Another example is found in a country-and-western song that Akiko particularly likes, even though she cannot understand the lyrics: "It felt like Bobby Joe [Creely] was telling her a story and if only she could understand the words she would be able to identify with it perfectly. Unfortunately, there was no Japanese translation on the lyric sheet" (77). Both these examples resemble nothing so much as what Teresa Brennan here describes.

> Nervous entrainment may also depend on body movements and gestures, particularly through the imitation of rhythms (effected by sight, touch, and hearing). In understanding the aural rhythmic component evident in the vocal interactions of a parent and child, Richard Restak suggests we attend to the study of prosody—"the melody, pitch, and stress of human speech"—where auditory cues clearly have priority over visual ones. Rhythm is a tool and expression of agency, just as words are. They can literally convey tone of an utterance, and, in this sense, it does unite word and affect.[47]

Crucially, the efficacy of this contagious affect is borne out precisely in Akiko's subsequent behavior.

> She'd heard the song on the *My American Wife!* program about the Korean children in Louisiana. It was a good show, and she'd given it a 9 in Authenticity. She especially liked the music. She'd written down the names of Bobbie Jo and also Rockin' Dopsie at the bottom of the paper where she copied the week's recipe. The next day she took the bullet train to town and found the CDs at Tower Records in Shibuya. It took her most of the day, but it was worth the trip. When she got home to her apartment she put on the Rockin' Dopsie CD and cooked the Cajun-style Baby Back Ribs. They turned out exceptionally well and she gave it a 9 in Delicious. (77–78)

As the novel progresses, we see a slow detachment from the obsession with literal translation, and a greater indulgence in and sympathy for the incomplete, and sometimes incommensurate. This has everything to do with what we discover about affect and how the loosening of the demands for "truth" (for lack of a better word) feed into affect's particular relation to dreams and the imaginary, as we saw in Freud, as well as its ability to channel itself into a number of directions and forms: "His songs made her feel reckless and even a little dangerous. . . . She'd never seen heat rising before, or met a woman like the one in the song who carried a straight razor. Akiko didn't know what a straight razor was, but suddenly she wished she could have one too" (79).[48] Thus the songs create not only affective behavior, but also purchasing behavior. .

In this highly commercialized environment, where art, truth, and affect are put into the service of profit, all geared to integrating the formerly other into new habits and behaviors, Jane tries to salve her conscience: how can she accept complacency in "inveigling"? She rationalizes: "I had spent so many years, in both Japan and America, floundering in a miasma of misinformation about culture and race, I was determined to use this window into mainstream network television to *educate*. Perhaps it was naïve, but I believed, honestly, that I could use wives to sell meat in the service of a Larger Truth" (27). Advertising is thus the means to an end of her own invention; the commercials will be her Trojan horse, delivering the truth. Nevertheless, how can truth coexist with falsity? Are the very narrative strategies that deliver affect incompatible with truth? That is to say, does affect, in its multiformal, multidispositional nature, submerge epistemology beneath the sentimental "hook"? Is there a way to install and maintain a boundary between "bad" media and "good" content?

One of the first shows Jane tapes is of a Mexican family. If we look to this segment in hopes that we will find some example of the "truth" Jane wishes to convey, we seem to have just such material.

> The boy, whose name was Bobby, lived there with his parents, Alberto and Catalina Martinez. Alberto, or Bert, as he now preferred to be called, was a farm worker. He'd lost his left hand to a hay baler in Abilene seven years earlier, a few months after he and Catalina (Cathy) had emigrated from Mexico, just in time for Bobby to be born an American citizen. That had been Cathy's dream, to have an American son, and Bert had paid for her dream with his hand. (58)

While the story conspicuously attributes the cost of the American Dream to one of the chief targets of Ozeki's indictment—agribusiness—what is actually foregrounded is the "immigrant story." Alberto's preference for an Anglo name and the absence of any remark on his or anyone else's part about his accident remove any explicit critique; this "truth" disappears before the dominant narrative of the American immigrant's dream. The power of *that* story is what cements the affective bond between West and East, as imaginatively triangulated through the Mexican boy: "Bobby smiled at the camera, a little Mexican boy shyly offering his American Supper to the nation of Japan. Everything was in slow motion. It was a surreal and exquisite moment" (61). And, indeed, this image and narrative produces the intended effect thousands of miles away: "Toes tucked neatly beneath her, she [Akiko] watched the screen, where a young Mexican child stood in the middle of a waving field of wheat. . . . Akiko felt the tears well up in her eyes as, pen in hand, she smoothed out the sheet of paper, ready to take down the day's recipe" (63).

On hearing the favorable "reviews" of this segment, Jane writes to her employers: "I was very happy to hear about the high ratings for the Martinez show. . . . I will do my best to increase the Authenticity and General Interest of the program" (64). She has successfully exploited the mixed form of the "top seller," invented in the mid-'80s.

> The reader of the "top seller" has two expectations: the expectation of pleasure and the expectation for enrichment. . . . How then to resolve the

contradiction between expectations of enrichment and pleasure, the tension between "serious" and "entertaining"? In short, how to legitimize pleasure? Answers: at the level of form, through what advertising people call "indicators of authenticity"; as for background, through "true references, consensual values, symbolic exchange"; so that enrichment occurs in counterpoint with pleasure.[49]

Advertising is thus most successful when "simple pleasures" are complemented and legitimized by some sense of social value or ethical purpose. Here, at the nexus of national cultures, "authenticity" yields understanding; a sad story, empathy; a hopeful one, optimism about the world. The question then becomes, how we are seduced by such authenticity? What kinds of otherness do we let overwhelm and pacify us, and what others do we reject and ward off? How are we predisposed toward certain kinds of authenticity and not others? And finally, how can one appropriate those instruments to deliver "truth" rather than "authenticity"? That is, can Jane's scheme really work, or will its very delivery system obviate that chance?

Two kinds of cynicism emerge. The first has to do with the fact that no matter how profound and even uplifting the affective delivery system, the ultimate issue for some will always be the bottom line. This is nowhere more apparent than in the segment Jane shoots at a Southern church, filled with African American worshippers. Being present in the church meeting seems to produce another transformative moment, not only for Jane and her crew, but even for John Ueno, Jane's misogynistic, wife-abusing Japanese boss who has recently attempted to rape Jane.

> The ladies on either side responded, grabbing Ueno and me and wrapping us in their arms, then passing us off to another neighbor, to be similarly embraced. Catharsis was close at hand. I dimly understood it, felt it gathering all around me. And the miracle was, so did Ueno. . . . All around him, people were dancing and writhing and singing and shaking and speaking in tongues, and others were caring for them, laying on their hands, supporting their frenzy. Sweat was pouring down Ueno's face, pure distilled alcohol by the smell of it, and he was sobbing. (112–13)

Yet this affective "transformation" in "oceanic feeling" is quickly shown to be only transitory, for Ueno ends up disallowing broadcast of the show: "How could a Japanese housewife relate to a poor black family with nine children?" (130). Ueno's dip in oceanic feeling does nothing to change him. The personal does not *have* to segue the political; private "enlightenment" does not necessarily result in public betterment. To get at the question of the effectiveness of affect in instilling ethical behavior we need to delve deeper.

If we see this moment of cynicism as both a critique of capitalism and Jane's naïveté, it still does not seem to amount to much. Yet a second kind of cynicism that comes into play in the course of the novel is sharper and more devastating than this first, for it shows how even the reputed victims of capital and the profit motive can be turned into its agents. We find this in the story of the Bukowsky family, whose daughter Christina is paralyzed, indeed comatose, having been hit by a Walmart truck. As the company has refused to assume any responsibility, it falls to the family to care for their daughter alone. But soon the townspeople take an interest. They in fact begin a collective ritual of empathy and transference: "Each person brought something that he or she loved" (134). These visits and the talismans that are brought for the girl to touch create a communal affective ritual that gradually works a miracle: Christina emerges from her coma.

Yet it does not end there, for Jane then tells us, "The media got hold of the story and pumped it for all it was worth from every angle, including the exploitation of small-town America by the corporate retail giants" (135). It is here that we begin to ask if this exploitation is at all different from what Jane has been doing, complete with the reliance on stock narrative devices that peddle certain models of affective "reality"—even, or mostly, mythologized ones.

> The town of Quarry had discovered a new natural resource—compassion—and they were mining it and marketing it to America. Quarry became Hope, and Mr. Bukowsky was elected mayor. . . . The townspeople found jobs with the Center or started their own businesses as affiliated service providers. . . . The Mayor and Mrs. Bukowsky starred in a promotional videotape, "Welcome to Our Living Room: The Bukowsky Method of Compassion and Renewal," and published a best-selling book by the same name. (136)

The "affect," and what is mimed, has nothing anymore to do with compassion or sympathy, and everything to do with commercialism. Are we to take this positively, is this some sort of poetic justice, has the family finally received its due? Not exactly, although, because of the media attention, Walmart does take responsibility. All this is rather a matter of profiting beyond justice, and commodifying what was originally an "authentic" act of compassion. Indeed, it seems that the sentimental world has here been infected by the contagion of capitalistic behavior. Yet Jane offers no comment on this turn of events; instead she focuses on the efficacy of her docudrama and her own perspicacity: "I felt the warm smugness that comes over me when I know that there is another heart-wrenching documentary moment at hand, being exquisitely recorded" (175).

Ultimately, Jane recognizes not only the necessity to "manipulate" sentiment, but also precisely the need to be fictive: "I wanted to make programs with documentary integrity and at first I believed in a truth that existed—singular empirical absolute. But slowly, as my skills improved and I learned about editing and camera angles and the effect that music can have on meaning, I realized that truth was like race and could be measured only in ever-diminishing approximations" (176). Until the very end of the novel, Jane persists in rationalizing the need to deploy the rhetorical strategies of storytelling within the frame of televisual media, and in the process, the "real" becomes simply one ingredient among others: "The program was a good one, really solid, moving, the best I'd made. It could even effect social change. And so I continued, taking out the stutters and catches from the women's voices, creating a seamless flow in a reality that was no longer theirs and not quite so real anymore" (179). Here it seems we have the most explicit capitulation to the "hybrid form" of media as seen in Mattelart.

We have thus far spoken about Jane's gradual admission that creating an effective story is a particular blend of myth and reality, affect and aesthetics. But what is to be effected by this mix? I'd like to return to these questions: how do stories do their work? Once affect has been installed, how is it supposed to be harnessed to an ethical action? Critically, for this study, how is the ratio of otherness adjusted, amplified, or "smoothed out"? First, Ozeki makes the argument that stories can shift perspective and provide the opportunity for one to see oneself and one's world differently. In a key episode, we find Bunny Dunn, the mother of a girl poisoned by hormones in cattle-feed, describing first her own complacency and then the transformative work the film has done. On seeing Jane's film of her daughter, Bunny Dunn is transformed from a silent victim to a witness: "You just get used to it. Until something happens, that wakes you up and makes you see different. That's what happened when you all showed up. I saw her with your eyes, and everything looked different. Wrong. . . . [I]t was like I finally made a choice, talkin' for the camera, it felt good. Like I was takin' a stand" (294–95). And when she shows her husband the tape, it is "like finally he understood" (357). This reconfiguration of subjectivity comes about because the mediated narrative has allowed the subject to achieve an exterior point of view of itself. This in turn allows the individual to distance herself from her immediate "interest" (in this case, one invested in denial), and to take part in an ethical community, one that is constituted precisely by a common experience of viewing both events and mediated images.

Thus, once her purely commercial skills at producing and controlling affect at will are honed, Jane finds an ethical purpose for them. She embarks on a project of finding historical facts, suppressed information, and miscellaneous data, and then forging stories that transcend "mere" facticity, that dwell in the seam between information and affective fiction. Jane's final disquisition attempts to answer the question of form and truth, that is, what formal properties are needed to make truth attractive, persuasive, and affective. At this point, she has succeeded in exposing the dangers of hormone-laced feed and the chemically infested environment of the slaughterhouse. This takes place not through the direct action she imagines, but, in a twist that is in keeping with the nature of the narrative, via information leaked to the press. Jane works backward from the "success" of her enterprise to a diagnosis of the pathologies of the media and the public.

> I had succeeded: I got a small but critical piece of information about the corruption of meats in America out to the world, and possibly even saved a little girl's life in the process. And maybe that is the important part of the story, but the truth is so much more complex. . . . Like all the parts of the Gulf War that were never reported. That war was certainly a Thing That Gained by Being Painted. And like Suzie's tale, a small but Outstandingly Splendid Thing. I mean, I take a Japanese television crew to Iowa to film a documentary about this American wife, and we make total fiction of the facts of her life, and now, a year later she tells me that those facts have turned right around and aligned themselves with our fiction. So go figure. . . . In the Year of Meats, truth wasn't stranger than fiction; it was fiction. Ma says I'm neither here nor there, and if that's the

case, so be it. Half documentarian, half fabulist. . . . Maybe sometimes you have to make things up, to tell truths that alter outcomes. (360)

Armed with such perceptions of and conclusions about both audience reception and the requisite rhetorical tools of the media, Jane's question about "who would want to see it" is transparently disingenuous. In fact, as we have seen before, Jane possesses a sharp awareness of what kinds of stories people not only want to see, but seem *compelled* to see. Furthermore, she not only knows which buttons to push, but also has a fairly good sense of what will happen when they are pushed. Jane's "documentaries" are primarily geared toward eliciting interest and sympathy from a broad moderate and liberal audience already primed for an authentic multicultural moment that itself taps into a more traditional American narrative of self-improvement.

Nevertheless, the episode in question, the one that actually might have saved at least one life, the one that is the most graphic and disturbing indictment of the meat industry, relies not on that multicultural ideology, but on a weird mixture of horror and voyeurism. The young girl's body is proffered as evidence, and that evidence is compelling not (only) because of the deformity of the body, but because of the particularly sexual and erotic nature of those deformities and the way they are framed by her half-brother's actions.

It is here that we need finally to address the multiple layers of narrative point of view and authorial voice. We should not rush to assume that Jane and Ozeki take on exactly the same point of view. For the noted slippages should be evidence enough that Ozeki has set up a sympathetic, but not perfect, protagonist. There are telling contradictions between what Jane says and thinks about any one issue and her actions and assessments at other points. If we can accept that point of difference, then the book is at once more complicated and more interesting. For it now appears that Jane cannot stand outside her own critique of the media. To be sure, she makes critical remarks about the media and even incriminates herself from time to time, but these instances of explicit confession again run the risk of sounding both sanctimonious and ironic. It is the unselfconscious contradictions that strike me as most meaningful, as in Jane's disingenuous question. And it is in those moments that we might perceive an intelligence outside Jane's. It is this doubling that gives the book its true critical edge, a critical edge that allows us to return to our basic questions with a different sense of how the novel works to problematize notions of literary form, the media, ethics, and affect. It is a creative and critical perspective on its own *literary* delivery system.

Ozeki claims: "By having Jane discuss the shortcomings of happy endings right smack in the middle of one, I was hoping to invite the reader into a more complex relationship with the ending. In essence, I point an authorial finger at the very thing that I am writing, and poke a hole in the seamlessness of the happy ending by making it self-referential and reflexive. Ironic."[50] However, that is itself only half the story. For while here she endows Jane with this self-reflexivity, at other points she disallows Jane that capacity, and the "authorial finger" is pointed not at the "thing being written," but at the point of view that guides it—that is, Jane's own interior point of view. The novel thus unabashedly raises the question of modern mediatized storytelling and the ethical application of stories from a number of angles. It is in inventing and deploying this metacritique of the media that *My Year of Meats* shows the promise of a critical mode of reading and writing in our contemporary age.

The final drawing together of these issues is staged in a juxtaposition of Jane's book and Sei Shonagon's tenth-century text, *The Pillow Book*. Throughout the novel, all three main women's voices quote *The Pillow Book*; Ozeki includes quotations from Shonagon, and both Akiko and Jane respond to and play off these quotations. Adele Pinch makes this observation regarding quotations:

> Quotations, in other words, can be topographical features of the space of the mind as well as of the space of a sonnet. Locating feelings elsewhere, shifting between textual practice and the mental or social practice, quotation can serve as a name for the problems of this book as a whole: the tendency of affective life to get located *among rather than within people*, or in the interests to seize between different explanations and stories of their origins, arising as much from rhetorical or fictional situations as from the mind's own motions.[51]

What is of interest to me here is Pinch's attention, both in this passage and in her remarks on Hume, to the dialectic between affect as originating in the self and affect as originating in and circulating textually among others. In Ozeki, this public circulation of affect is echoed in the circulation of mass media, and partakes in the problematic of modernity. One problem with affect and ethical thinking again is this—where does affect start? Who brings it into social space? This question goes directly to that of the precise constitution of the individual as an ethical being and social actor. But the other question is, why and how does this matter, this search for origin? From Levinas to Nancy, and others, an ethical self is "always already" "accountable" to an other, already constituted in relation to an other or its trace. In this sense, ethics is not and cannot be the sole property of one, but is inescapably that of "us."

At the end, after all the communal acts of reading and writing have taken place, Jane finally decides that her stance toward her narrative will be different from Shonagon's—while Sei Shonagon hid her book, Jane will bring hers forward into the *public* realm. As opposed to Shonagon, who writes, "Whatever people may think of my book, I still regret that it ever came to light" (354), Jane asserts, "Whatever people may think of my book, I will make it public, bring it to light unflinchingly. That is the modern thing to do" (361). Here we need to underscore the historical, ethical, and aesthetic difference that this remark draws in order to delineate Jane's project. As opposed to what she sees as Shonagon's private text of the eleventh century, Jane insists on the obligations the modern age places on her. It is modern to be public, revelatory of the private. In particular, it is a specific kind of private knowledge that is to be brought into the light of public scrutiny. Crucially, this information and knowledge is to be conveyed in a particular affective form. In this manner, in its own hybrid narrative form, which blends all manner of communication and affect, *My Year of Meats* poses itself as an antidote to the kind of melding of private and public, fact (or its appearance) and fiction, perpetrated by global advertising that Mattelart decries. And yet it is an uneasy and slippery remedy, always open to being converted into what it is fighting against, precisely because affect is murky, untamable, prone to be diverted or converted by the ego's need to protect and privilege itself. And it is here that we can broaden this notion to incorporate the general topic of this study: contemporary literature and its deliverance of others. What Ozeki has made us consider, "unflinchingly," is the border between literature and other media.

In a wonderful blurb for *My Year of Meats*, the director John Sayles (self-identified, first, as "former member, Amalgamated Meat Packers and Butcher Workers of North America" and, second, as "director of 'Matewan' and 'Men with Guns'") writes, "This is a very cool book, satirical but never mean, funny, peopled by fully inhabited characters who are both blind and self-aware. Ruth Ozeki's *My Year of Meats* reassures us that media and culture, though bound inextricably, will never become one."[52] The question of course is where Sayles would place "literature" within this ostensibly separate (now and forever) dyad? I would venture that it resides in both media and culture, if by *media* we mean delivery systems that bring others into contact with each other, and by *culture* we mean organic common-places that regenerate themselves. Literature brings us into imaginative contact with others, embedded in media, and as an expressive form of "culture." At least that is a starting hypothesis. In the conclusion to this study, I want to see how literature is challenged these days precisely to mean something in a *particular* way that lets it reside in the space in between, and therefore in a critical position that might yield ethical results.

Conclusion

In the course of this book, while I have focused in each chapter on, respectively, rationality and realism as they confront new forms of otherness in a new historical, technological, and political landscape; the issue of the body and the possibility of its regeneration or preservation via the implantation of or consumption of the other's organs; and the issue of affect as it manages the "oceanic" pool of affect shared among those like and unlike ourselves, I have stressed that each one of these moments, each one of these "slots," partakes of a set of key issues. In chapter 1 we asked, what is human? How do I behave toward others that I now recognize, given the critique of the underpinnings of rationality that dissolving the human-nonhuman dyad discloses? And as we find ourselves pressed to question what kinds of affect overcome us as well, given this new opening, we review the ways our bodies exist at the expense of other bodies now not so different from our own. How to represent that new connection, or the decomposition of the delivery system of rationality and realism? In chapter 2 we see what happens when the political contingency of "the interregnum" creates the need and the imperative to rethink bonds of kinship, race, ethnicity, gender. This brings us in touch with chapter 1's question about literary form: how do these newly cohered stories come to be told? What is the new "delivery system" that can adequately manage to narrate this historical moment, and who can take ownership of it, who can claim rights to it? Here, too, the affective realm is deeply involved, as loyalties, loves, and appeals to ideals all push bodies into acts of suicide, betrayal, illicit passion. Chapter 3 takes up all these concerns, most obviously Coetzee's attention to how biotechnologies have changed the way meat is produced on a mass scale, and how it is we determine what is human. How do we breed creatures only to have them give their lives for us, unacknowledged and unrecompensed? How in Ishiguro's novel is the "children's" lack of affect assumed, and how is art, the one testament to humanness, so easily ignored? What kind of rationality is applied to produce these nonhuman bodies for the sustenance of the "human," and how does that distinction begin to crumble, once we let in the issue of ethics? Finally, in chapter 4, we again find the issues of biotechnology, the production of a particularly construed "other" for the service solely of our bodies (whether it be the otherness of a drug, a hormone, or the flesh and body of a "nonhuman animal" that itself is laced with drugs, hormones, and other "nonorganic" feed), and the systems of rationalization that deliver them to us—media, technology, advertising—which each manipulate and redirect the currents of affect that flow not only across the Pacific, but also between mother and fetus, between women, and between races. The same question comes back with intensity in Ozeki's novel: how to tell not only a story, but an ethically affective and humane story, in the midst of a world where all boundaries seem blurred purposefully? Here, in my conclusion, I will venture a broader frame for this idea of "delivery systems" and end with an address to the notion of reading literature in our contemporary age—an age marked, in its own "slot," as one impacted on by new forms of communication—and to the notion of decoding information.

In his seminal work, *Fallible Man*, Paul Ricoeur draws together the issues of affect, self, the self's manner of connecting to others. He schematizes this process within a triad comprising economics, politics, and culture in a way that is not dissimilar to what I have been calling "delivery systems." By that I have meant the media and discourses through which others are delivered to us as like "us." In order for others to move through those mediating systems, I have argued that a degree of sameness has to be assumed. We assume that people think and act in ways that display a certain degree of rationality that is within our normative definitions of reason; that people have human bodies that are composed and function in basically similar ways; and that people register affect in common manners. And yet the fact of the matter is that these assumptions are often proven to be only partly true—otherness and difference continue to abide in lesser or greater ways. What are the consequences of this for these systems, and for our understanding of what actually binds us?

I also have argued that in terms of our modern notions of literature, a degree of otherness is *required* in order that the ethical, self-bettering, imagination-enhancing function of literature, instantiated in the eighteenth century and still with us in at least a residual form, is realized. We need to have some impetus to be more than what we were coming into our encounter with the text. And yet at the same time I have emphasized the fact that *too much* otherness can defeat those ambitions. Throughout this study I have shown how literature—these days in particular—has dramatized that problematic and thus is positioned in a critical tension with the sameness that is supposed to inform and enable global "delivery systems." The consequences of this tension are most visible perhaps in the area of affect: we want to feel connected to something larger than individual selves, we are instructed to engage in an ethical relation to others that do not resemble us, yet we withdraw when we are affected too much by unpleasurable, bad, affect. How to maintain that equilibrium or growth without danger? Above all, I have insisted on paying attention to the material practices of deliverance—the ways rationality, choice, the disposition and distribution of the body and its affects are made manifest in our relations with "others."

Ricoeur similarly draws our attention to the ways that intersubjective (self-other) relations are mediated by economics, politics, and culture, but only insofar as "shapeless" affect is given objective form in and through them. He sees people as inhabiting a shared pool of affect, not unlike the "oceanic" feeling. The problem he sees here is not all that different from the one we noted—the murky, unanchored character of affect and its uncertain relationship to both self and other. Affect can either join people together, as it is objectified in those three spheres of human interaction, or retreat back into the self.

> These are feelings which are essentially formless, moods, *Stimmungen,* or, as someone has termed them, atmospheric feelings. . . . Through their formless character they denote the fundamental feeling of which the determined feelings are the schemata, namely, man's very *openness to being.* . . . All feelings are capable of acquiring form or of returning to a formless state; this is a consequence of the intentional structure of feeling in general: in turn, it takes on form in accordance with the objects of knowledge to which fastens its felt epithets, or returns to the formless in accordance with the law of interiorization, of introception, of the plunging-back into the ground of life from which intentional acts emerge.[1]

Here, then, is the problematic of "openness to being," of letting oneself be open to otherness: feelings can remain formless (in which case they flow back into the self, retaining their murky shapeless quality) or acquire form through contact with the objective world of others. Crucially, the latter is possible only insofar as feelings attach themselves to and take form in "objects of knowledge," that is, in ways of *knowing* the world that already exists—again, Ricoeur selects economics, politics, and culture as specific objective and objectifying discourses.

It is not enough to simply "see" an other; it is critical to see the other as present in an objective, human-made, intersubjective world in which we appear as subjects also inflected by that encounter.

> A reflection that would end the intersubjective constitution of the thing at the level of the mutuality of seeing would remain abstract. We must add the economic, political, and cultural dimensions to objectivity; *they make a human world out of the mere nature they start with.* The investigation of authentic human affectivity, therefore, must be guided by the progress of objectivity. If feeling reveals my adherence to and my inheritance in aspects of the world that I no longer set over against myself as objects, it is necessary to show the new aspects of objectivity that are interiorized in the feelings of having, power, and worth.[2]

That is to say, rather than having affect fall *back* into oneself and maintaining a stance toward the objective world (in which others reside) as outside oneself, one sees that the objective world of others is actually interiorized *as such* into one's own self as well, making oneself available to others according to the same system of objectification. Rather than ward off that "other" affect, one incorporates it into oneself, but as part of an objective (that is, no longer shapeless) world.

Ricoeur describes in further detail this process of objectification and mutual regard.

> The truly human quests establish new relations with other persons at the same time as a new relation to things. Strictly speaking, the mutuality of seeing is a very poor intersubjective relation. The "difference" of a Self from others is constituted only in connection with things that themselves belong to the economic, political and cultural dimensions. Consequently, we must specify and articulate the relationship of the Self to another Self by means of the objectivity that is built on the themes of having, power, and worth.[3]

In other words, we come into an understanding of and mutual affective relation to others via a basic dyad of having or not having (the economic relation)—this is how we see and feel their relation to us. In turn, the economic relation is related to a political relationship—having things that others don't means having a dominant relation over them: "The objectification of man's power over man in an institution is the new '*object*' that can serve us as a guide in an immense world of feelings that manifest affectively the diverse modalities of human power according to which it is exercised, opposed, courted, or undergone. All the social roles the man may exercise initiate situations that political institutions consolidate into an object."[4]

But what about "culture," and how does it connect with "worth"? Well, it is here that the very idea of humanity resides. What is crucial for my study is that this cultural realm of worth-endowing remains objective, no less than the other two members of Ricoeur's trio (economics and politics). Culture does not remain at the level of the formless; it is not something interiorized subjectively, unrelatable to others, that is, as totally private and unexchangable "feeling." Culture, in other words, does not remain akin to the Lacanian imaginary. Ricoeur insists that art is an objective thing, but, crucially, a thing of the world shared with others, and works of art, no less than economic or political objects, convey a sense of worth, this time a worth measured not by having or by holding power, but precisely by being human.

> It is necessary to add to this wholly "formal" objectivity of the *idea* of humanity the "material" objectivity of the cultural works that express this humanity. If the economic sphere is objectified in the goods and forms of having, and the political sphere in institutions and all the forms of power, then hyper-economic and hyper-political humanity is expressed in monuments that bear witness to the search for recognition. "Works" of art and literature, and, in general, works of the mind, insofar as they not merely mirror an environment and an epoch but search out man's possibilities, are the true "objects" that manifest the abstract universality of the idea of humanity through their concrete universality. . . . Cultural objectivity is the very relation of man to man represented in the idea of humanity; only cultural testimonies endow it with the destiny of things, in the form of monuments existing in the world: but these things are "works." It is this formal and material objectivity of the idea of man that engenders an affectivity to its measure: the cycle of feelings of esteem.[5]

It is precisely in the active (that is, not passive) character of art that we find something close to what I have been calling the delivery system of *literature*, which is able to reside as "hyper-economic" and "hyper-political" humanity. Culture—and literature, as an objective form of culture—exists both in contact with economic and political objectifications of humanity, and beyond them. It is a delivery system that is characterized via its ability to be a metasystem reflecting back on the ways "the human," negotiated precisely in the rationing of self and other, same and different, can be imagined as is, and otherwise.

To follow the attention Ricoeur appears to give the precise nature of objective and objectifying forms (economics, politics, culture), it would seem critical at this point to attend to the objective status of literature, most particularly, how it coheres and delivers stories of others, and, most crucially, how it is read. In this respect it is worth quoting at length Mark Poster's catalog of questions about today's global media.

> Increasing global relations catalyze the question of culture: are the basic conditions of culture changed, diminished, or supplemented as a result of intensified exchanges across national, ethnic, and territorial borders? What are the major discursive regimes that have emerged in connection with the phenomenon of global culture? What models of analysis are best suited to examine these exchanges—translation, transcoding, mixing, hybridity, homogenization? Do they appear to pose the most productive questions in the present context? Do these concepts articulate the challenges and opportunities posed for culture by the rapid intensification of global exchanges? One might inquire as well, at another level, about the epistemological conditions for framing the problems of global culture. What discursive positions enable asking the question in the first place? What are the conditions of writing/speech/word processing that open a critical stance on the question of global culture? Is the subject, the "I think" of the Western philosophical tradition, an appropriate position of discourse in order to initialize questions about global culture? Does the fact that a large proportion of global exchanges occur only with the mediation of information machines incite a need to redefine the notion of the other?[6]

We have ourselves already raised several of these questions, directly, and indirectly. In concluding this study, I want to narrow this highly useful set of interests down to two: one regards the objective forms that texts which carry information take; the other is the way that those texts are decoded or read. These issues press on the very act of making sense and, in my study, specifically on the act of making sense of self and other. Jerome McGann asks these questions: "Must we regard the physical channels of communications as part of the message of the texts we study? Or are the channels to be treated as purely vehicular forms whose ideal condition is to be transparent to the texts they deliver? How important, for the reader of a novel or any other text, are the work's various materials, means, and modes of production?"[7] In asking these questions, he taps into exactly the dilemma of reading literature today. Not only literature is itself, as "it" is, already inflected internally in its language by a new language of the Web and the social forms it connects and produces, and the very materiality of the text is now variously distributed across paper and screen (and multiple types of screens and devices that have their own operating systems, formats, rhythms, lives, and morphologies), but also, and critically for me, the *modes of reading* through and in which we put together data, text, and aesthetic forms have changed.

For many, the explosion of multiple forms, venues, and delivery systems, for both worldwide input and output, is a liberating and democratizing possibility. Speaking specifically to the issue of writing literary history, but also, I would say, to the issue of teaching literature in the academy, Amy J. Elias asks, "might not the high seriousness currently demanded of literary history blind us to the aristocratic coterie we form to protect decorum—and to how decorum and seriousness are linked to form in ways that protect disciplinary history from encroachment by amateurs, the unapprenticed, the lumpen professoriat?"[8] According to her, the rise of affordable Internet technology has created a new despecialized zone for the dissemination of information, images, sound, opinion: "Rather than merely the enclave of programmers or hackers (though these are privileged netizens and may yet control this space in the end), the Web is, in fact, evolving spaces filled with content produced by intelligent and socially engaged amateurs and experts in numerous fields."[9]

If we accept this idea, then it is no wonder that in the following passage Elias's appropriation and update of Wolfgang Iser takes on a "radical" dimension as she leaves the cloister of the academy: "Dialogism between text and reader and movement itself constitute the virtual reality created by reading. In writing that this convergence between text and reader creates a virtual space somehow beyond both, a space emerging from interactivity, Iser situates the 'virtuality' of the text in the space of dialogic movement itself, in the space of interaction rather than the space of identity."[10] Within this brave new world of infinite modes of connection, there is less and less constraint, since "decorum and seriousness" have been made optional. Elias cites approvingly Mark Poster's assertion that "technology . . . puts cultural acts, symbolizations in all forms, in the hands of all participants; it radically decentralizes the positions of speech, publishing, film-making, radio and television broadcasting, in short the apparatuses of cultural production."[11]

But let us pause for a moment before we log on. What is striking for me is how quickly and vastly Elias sweeps us past the "space of identity" and into "a space of interaction," and seems to value interaction for its own sake. Poster's quote is only slightly less rapturous and naïve—he at least cites the obvious "apparatuses of cultural production," if only to send them spinning off-center fairly quickly. He does, however, rightfully draw our attention to the key question of symbolization. What I want to emphasize is that not every person's symbolic is everyone, or anyone, else's. I want to insist that the symbolic realm is not so easily up for grabs. There is no level playing field, and it is a huge mistake to imagine that sufficient "quantity"—herein merely the potential of a "multitude" coming together sometime, someday, to "de-center" the world system in politically efficient ways—can or will ever come about merely because there is the technological possibility of it happening as people "interact."

Rather than fetishizing difference, otherness, or, identity, my book has tried to linger a bit with the question of the *production* of sameness and otherness, and the ethical and political choices that go into that. I have no clear argument with any of the above, and even hold open the possibility that, yes, as many of their staunchest advocates argue, such conceptualizations of the here and now might lead to a real increase in democratic, self-empowering movements. But ultimately it does not at all do away with two basic problems I have tried to wrestle with in these pages. First, that all networks, open as they are, have an endpoint.

Elias notes, "Danah Boyd and Nicole Ellison define a social network site as 'web-based services that allow individuals to (1) construct a public or semi-public profile within a bounded system, (2) articulate a list of other users with whom they share a connection, and (3) view and traverse their list of connections and those made by others within the systems. The nature and nomenclature of these connections may vary from site to site.' "[12] Here we see that each network has a set of preferences, or criteria for selection, for opting-in. What *exactly* this "connection" is that is shared (number 2) is irrelevant in terms of detail, but important in essence. That people can be connected in any way in any given social network is pretty true, yet to me it is a trivial point. What I am interested in are the ways that the delivery systems I have treated in this study aspire to (if not assume) universality and yet at the same time reaggregate difference. And when we add in the issue of the presentation of other people's lives and stories in literature, I want to see what various modes of *reading* can yield that is different from decoding data and information about others and their lives.

The issue for me is that, given the hybrid forms Mattelart alerted us to a long time ago, and the ways that the lines between information, data, propaganda, advertisement, art have been blurred, how can we imagine that we can still apply our usual ways of reading onto texts that now sit only partially within what we used to call "literary" form? Or, better yet, how flexible are both literary form and modes of reading literature? In terms of the readings put forward here, there is no doubt that they are influenced by my own rootedness in the literary criticism of the late twentieth century. But I've also tried to consistently infuse my reading practice with the recognition of how the form and content of contemporary literature is imbricated with other delivery systems that present their own representations of self and other, either directly or by implication. I want finally to return to Ozeki's *My Year of Meats*, then consider briefly Gary Shteyngart's *Super Sad True Love Story*, as examples of precisely my concerns with form and reading, affect and ethics in the contemporary world.

In *My Year of Meats*, the actual nature of Jane's "book" seems to belie her claim to its "being modern"—the novel seems rather an eminently postmodern text. This can be seen, for example, in her repeated meditations on the notion that fiction and truth are at one with each other, that facts are randomly extracted from a mass of possible data. And yet the novel ends up focusing on that alignment between the world of fiction created in the ersatz documentary and the reality it seeks to expose, that is, on a modern resolution. While one might dwell on the postmodern world of the novel—the crisis of connection in an age of simulacra and fragmentation, media imaging and just-in-time production of affect—in this last statement Ozeki opens a historical question: is it only in the modern, with all its baggage, that we can locate ethics? Is the postmodern world of late capital actually unable to anchor a sense of belonging and obligation? Can the fragmentation and loss of grounding associated with the postmodern actually be exploited by and recuperated by the "modern"?

In fact, Ozeki's novel can easily be read as a calculated and persistent rebuttal of the postmodern. We find the constant activities of piecing together, which deploys a multiplicity of communication devices: the novel is peppered with trans-Pacific faxes, telephone calls, answering-machine recordings, cell-phone calls from jet airliners, video tapes, office memos. The printed page of the novel itself replicates that of faxes, memos, and so on, but gathers those heterogeneous, objective forms back into its dominant narrative space. What we end up with seems therefore an eminently modern project. However, how is this "modern" project actually given form? It is not as simple as it may appear. Ozeki constantly balances between Jane's film and her novel, and her novel and the texts and information that encase it.

Thus, when Jane says, "Whatever people may think of my *book*," it is here that Ozeki's voice emerges most clearly as distinct from Jane's— after all, Jane has not written a book, she has made a film. As this is the case, we can better understand at once Ozeki's authorial distance (which varies from moment to moment) from Jane's point of view, and the project of the novel itself. The very material form of the narrative that delivers this important ethical message to us is decidedly not the media represented in the narrative. And yet, the novel itself is embedded within another set of documents—we are provided with information sources on the meat industry, documentation on DES, women's health resources, as well as sample study questions for the novel. If Ozeki mocks the BEEF-EX series for attempting to blunt its sheer commercialism by couching the programs as "documentaries" which purport to present cross-cultural understanding (the segments include interviews with the families about their lives and habits; there is a "sociological survey" that asks the Japanese audience to respond to the programs), her own text parallels these strategies. That is, it is "packaged" in a similar fashion. There is a novel, but the "book" is *not only* a novel, not *only* "literature."

Ozeki's text is linked both by the logic and symbolic structure of its diegesis and also through its surrounding texts, to the material history of the contemporary. This complementarity can be appreciated as Ozeki appropriating what Walter Benjamin called "technique" or "tendency," that is, the particular mode of cultural production within a specific social formation.[13] It may also be seen as suggesting that in this historical age, neither of the two elements—what used to be called the "literary" and the "nonliterary"—can efficiently stand alone to deliver an ethically effective text. And we should be explicit here: the tension we have been speaking of all this time is between the particular imaginative function of literature and the global codifications and disseminations of *information*. Ozeki's literary narrative discloses her attempt to exploit our current registering of globalization as information and literature's modernist ability to lend new forms of information an affective and ethical content. This, then, would be a way to start accounting for the objective and objectifying status of "culture," through which, according to Ricoeur, we come to see one another in ways other than the inward-turning, shapeless form of affect.

But I'd like to press the question further, given the specific literary texts we have treated in these pages. We need to ask, do these different forms and their accompanying phenomenologies disable, or rather revise, our capacity to imagine others? How is otherness available to us, and what does it look like once it gets here? And how might the very technologies that bring us into some sort of contact allow for any sort of consolidated ethical action? Ozeki's text is hardly a revolutionary one in any formal sense. And yet its formal presentation raises critical questions about the persisting role of a literary genre, or, indeed, *all* cultural forms in an age of increasingly extensive and intensive media.[14] But as crucial as the objective form of literature is today, both the authors whose work I address in this conclusion place equal attention to the intimately related phenomenon of reading. How do readers today *put together* information? How does this decoding stand in relation to reading literature?

Shteyngart's *Super Sad True Love Story* is aptly titled. The surplus of affect, its authenticity as an event and as a felt thing, its questioning of the capacity of·people so connected by both "conventional" forms of narrative and new forms of media (emails, texts, etc.) to love, and, finally, the status of "story" are all in center place. Similar to the ways Ozeki's novel delves into the new, hybrid forms of communication—the things Mattelart drew our attention to: "*Infomercials, Advertorials, Pub-bligiornalismo, Publireportage*" which, as noted in the previous chapter, "erase the lines between news and commercials, advertising and editorial, publicity and journalism, publicity and reportage, between promotional surface and editorial content, advertising and the program"—Shteyngart is concerned with the ways different media not only appear to us in texts, but how these texts and information permeate our world, therein creating a hybrid form of daily life wherein the private and public are no longer separate.[15] In his novel, for example, "credit poles" adorn the sidewalks, flashing the credit scores of passersby. One's cholesterol scores, index of "sexiness," income, employment, relationships, and personal history—what used to be private pieces of information—are broadcast publicly with abandon.

Despite the common concerns of Shteyngart and Ozeki, the structure of Shteyngart's novel is much less ambitious and complex than that of Ozeki's. While Ozeki fuses a number of media, and in their interaction on multiple levels creates a way to critique each separately and also together, Shteyngart's novel is basically structured bilaterally, with the split between two narrative forms: a journal kept by the male protagonist; and a series of text messages and emails mostly written by the female protagonist, along with her friends' and relatives' responses. Shteyngart's chapters alternate between these two formats: on one hand, a traditional, easily read, conventional form of self-narration; on the other, a piecemeal assortment of comments, observations, asides. Nevertheless, within this basic structure lie a number of important distinctions. The journal, of course, is ostensibly addressed to the book itself as a kind of proxy ("dear journal"), while the second set of narratives are actual communications between people. On the surface, given the extremely thin content of the texts and emails, we are inclined to see them, rather than the self-reflective diary, as shallow. In fact, at the end of the novel, we see that posterity has been kinder to the latter rather than the former, which is read as self-indulgent and narcissistic. We thus need to ask the question, is it a matter of form or of reading? Are conventional, "respected" aesthetic forms of self-presentation guaranteed better value against forms of communication that aspire to no more than casual, barely reflective thoughts or half-thoughts? The issues of form, and process, go hand in hand: how do we *see* others, these days?

In *Super Sad True Love Story* the character Eunice Park describes (via email) her boyfriend's attachment to books (which are regarded as anything but aesthetic objects—they are thought to exude a disagreeable odor): "Anyway, what kind of freaked me out was that I saw Len reading a book. (No, it didn't SMELL. He uses Pine-Sol on them.) And I don't mean scanning a text like we did in Euro Classics with that Chatterhouse of Parma, I mean seriously READING. He had this ruler out and he was moving it down the page very slowly and just like whispering little things to himself, like trying to understand every little part of it."[16] Well at least she recognizes this strange activity as reading. She herself has not acquired that skill: " 'I've never really learned how to read texts,' she said. 'Just to scan them for info' " (277).

If Eunice has not learned to read texts, conversely Len has learned to love the digital display of his "äppärät," a kind of PDA that is worn around the neck: "I'm learning to worship my äppärät's screen, the colorful pulsating mosaic of it, the fact that it knows every last stinking detail about the world, whereas my books only know the minds of their authors" (78). Counterposed to the revelation of an other's "mind," that standard deliverance of otherness that literature takes as its task, the characters in *Super Sad True Love Story* are drawn to detail, particles of information that float about, drawn into significance in random and transient manners. The question then becomes, what to do with it? Compared to Len's sustained reflections, Eunice's texts seem only very loosely connected. A tension thus lies between how one reads the two, what kinds of mental operations to place on them. In the passage below, we find Len trying to figure out what kind of story to weave out of bits of information he has acquired about Eunice's family. The progression of information and his reflections on it insert the data into different literary genres, from a private-eye story to an immigrant story to a love story. As each of these genres comes into sight, it is in turn integrated into a master narrative that conveys the desire and the need Len feels for Eunice, and his deployment of his own immigrant story against the one he has made up for them, out of these data.

> My retro äppärät churned slowly with data, which told me that the father's business was failing. A chart appeared, giving the income for the last eighteen months; the *yuan* amounts were in steady decline since they had mistakenly left California for New Jersey—July's income after expenses was eight thousand *yuan*, about half of my own, and I do not have a family of four to support.

The mother did not have any data, she belonged solely to the home, but Sally, as the youngest of the Parks, was awash in it. From her profile I learned that she was a heavier girl than Eunice, the weight plunged into her round cheeks and the slow curvature of her arms and breasts. Still, her LDL cholesterol was way beneath the norm, while the HDL surged ahead to form an unheard-of ratio. Even with her weight, she could live to be 120 if she maintained her present diet and did her morning stretches. After checking her health, I examined her purchases and felt Eunice's as well. The Park sisters favored extra-small shirts in strict business patterns, austere grey sweaters distinguished only by their provenance and price, pearly earrings, $100 children's socks (their feet were that small), panties shaped like gift bows, bars of Swiss chocolate at random delis, footwear, footwear, footwear. I watched their Allied-WasteCVSCitigroup account rise and fall like the chest of a living, and breathing animal. . . . I beheld the numerical totality of the Park family and I wanted to save them from themselves, from the idiotic consumer culture that was bleeding them softly. I wanted to give them counsel and to prove to them that—as the son of immigrants myself—I could be trusted. (38)

Taking up the issue of affect, we see how this data is seen to both disclose what the Parks are affected by—their desire for certain objects and foodstuffs—and the way that in turn affects Len as he steps into their shoes, so to speak, to imagine what kind of composite creatures they are, that he is going to attach himself to. Not only objects and food, but the very registry of their holdings, their Allied-WasteCVSCitigroup account, is anthropomorphized, seeming to give off affect and receive it as well. In the midst of this sea of affect, "awash" with data, we find humans are read as behaving along the same systems of behavior— Retail and Images (this is the often-referred-to essential dyad in the novel). It almost seems as if these bits of data are struggling to be made into something, or, more correctly, as if Len's mind is relentlessly trying to make sense of them, of how they can be put together variously to yield different results. This, of course, is not terribly revolutionary— narratology has variously formulated models that all show that fictions are made up of information and ways of decoding it. What is different here, and in Ozeki's text, is that "narrative information" is presented precisely *as* "information," not aestheticized or symbolically coded, as it is in sorting out how different media present information to us that these two novels emblematize the crosshatching of private-public, literary system–information system, and many other formerly distinct (or perhaps less indistinct) spheres.

For Len, a traditionalist if nothing else, two things most conspicuously bind data together: love and death. Eros and Thanatos are the big, sad drivers of affect; it is they that cohere information. In fact, he is, like all of us, fixated on acquiring and prolonging the first, and evading and delaying the latter. The question becomes how they cohere data into stories. Len hopes, in a process of "dechronification," to postpone death. But his attempt to qualify for this procedure seems doomed to failure: "My first stab at dechronification—gone. My hair would continue to turn gray, and then one day it would fall out entirely, and then, on a day meaninglessly close to the present one, meaninglessly *like* the present one, I would disappear from the earth. And all these emotions, all these yearnings, all these *data*, if that helps to clinch the enormity of what I'm talking about, would be gone" (70). The trajectory of that catalog is of course important here: emotions, yearnings, data. Affect, passion, is declared, then intensified and made active, only to bow in expressive and indeed affective power before that which is truly significant—data. The question, once again, is how to put data together. If it is the thing that draws attention and meaning, then what kinds of meaning come out of its decoding? Similarly, as we puzzle out that question, we are compelled to ask, how do we (still) read literature? Can literature work outside data, and yield something different in its being *read*?

Len gets to find out the answers to these questions because the same thing happens in *Super Sad True Love Story* as happens in *My Year of Meats*: information is leaked, the private is launched into the public, without acknowledgment or control: "When I wrote these diary entries so many decades ago, it never occurred to me that *any* text would *ever* find a new generation of readers. I had no idea that some unknown individual or group would breach my privacy and Eunice's to pillage our GlobalTeens accounts and put together the text you see on your screen" (327). And, as in *My Year of Meats*, this leaking of information proves to have positive effects. Where Jane's "story" draws attention to the meat industry's dubious practices and the harmful effects of growth hormones, Len's "story" finds a new generation of readers. Nonetheless, whereas Jane's story ends relatively well, Len's story ends, for him, as one of loss, sorrow, alienation, without—to my mind—any particular redemption.

But as the Stateside critics have unanimously agreed, the gems in the text are Eunice Park's GlobalTeens entries. They "present a welcome relief from Lenny's relentless navelgazing," to quote Jeffrey Schott-Liu in his *whorefuckrevu*. "She is not a born writer, as befits a generation reared on Images and Retail, but her writing is more interesting and more alive than anything else I have read from that illiterate period. She can be bitchy, to be sure, and there's a patina of upper-middle-class entitlement, but what comes through is a real interest in the world around her—an attempt to negotiate her way through the precarious legacy of her family and to form her own opinions about love and physical attraction and commerce and friendship, all set in a world whose cruelties gradually begin to mirror those of her own childhood." I would add that, whatever one may say about my former love, and whatever terrible things she's written about me, unlike her friends, unlike Joshie, unlike myself, unlike so many Americans at the time of our country's collapse, Eunice Park did not possess the false idea that she was special. (327–28)

This means, it appears, that whatever value this text has is to be found primarily not in the old-style, self-reflective, psychologically and spiritually "deep" narration of Len's life (addressed to itself), but rather in the pieced-together prose-like data of Eunice. According to the character Schott-Liu, it is in Eunice's set of texts that "writing" is to be found. It is writing, nonetheless, that follows the same old thematics; it is, when put all together, "an attempt to negotiate her way through the precarious legacy of her family and to form her own opinions about love and physical attraction and commerce and friendship, all set in a world whose cruelties gradually begin to mirror those of her own childhood" —in other words, exactly the same themes as we find in Len's journal entries, but without the narcissism and self-absorption. Indeed, if we are going to carve out any space for political hope here, it would certainly not be with Len, but with Eunice and her sister, who, of all the characters, form political and human sympathies with the ragtag bunch of revolutionaries camping out in Central Park.

Nevertheless, when all is done, the hopeful, and positive, aspects of *Super Sad True Love Story* therefore reside not in an abiding value in old forms, or in the glitz and innovation of scintillating "data points," nor even in a faith that people can, *pace* Eunice herself, still *read*, and still want to read for the same things. Affect, politics, economic behavior all deliver others to us, and, crucially, the mediating mechanisms of the

Web and äppäräti do not meld everything into one simple grid. Shteyngart gives neither new nor old forms of information necessary value—
it's rather all in how we read. But how does he guide us toward that
reading? We abide Len's narcissism and Eunice's own not because of
their narratives, but, as in Ozeki's text, because of the englobing narrative. Like Ozeki, who shuttles back and forth between and among narrative and non-narrative forms, between Akiko and Jane as her stand-in
narrators, Shteyngart does the same, with Len and Eunice. What we
emerge with *is* a "modern" text, but one whose modernity is pinned on,
Ricoeur has made us aware, different forms of objectification. We are
"delivered" as "human" via this particular delivery system, one in which
we stand open to and saturated by information, yet our sense-making
appetites are still forming that information—about others, about ourselves—in terms of narratives that do not (yet) look radically different
from the pre-information age. And yet the persistence of narrative form
alone is no guarantee of meaning or affect. What I want to draw our
attention to, as signaled both in the subtitle to this study and to the
critical acts I have undertaken throughout, is the essential and necessary
act of reading, and specifically, for me, reading with an attention to the
issues of otherness that I have made the centerpiece of this book.

It is precisely because of this that these novels carry their existential
weight impressively. The fact of the matter is that even in its compromised, hybridized form, the "put together" text of *Super Sad True Love
Story*, cobbled together, still stands for something that outlasts death. In
this sense Shteyngart's "text," no less than Ozeki's "story," delivers us a
picture of reading that captures the reasoning, bodies, and affect of
others even as the overflow of each threatens to destablize the "system."
Literature, and a particular way of reading it for precisely this negotiation of otherness, can (still) help us, through this particular animation
of the imagination, weigh out the ratios of rationality and action, and, to
take a page from Len, of bodies and affect, life and death, even if what
we read is about super sad love (or maybe especially because of that
fact). The sadness in Len's life parallels the sadness in Eunice's: the
former looks into his own mortality, wishing it could be otherwise; the
latter looks to connect with the world, still as young as she is. These are
age-old themes. What is critical here, as with all the novels we have read
for this study, is that we exercise our capacity and moral willingness to
see others not "as they are," reduced to some standard data-point cali-

bration of weight, age, wealth, or power so as to move through the system efficiently, but framed within precisely those mediating and objective structures that are exposed for what they are—non-natural, human-made systems (or, as Ricoeur says, "works") that convey others to us in ways that reveal our assumptions, beliefs, values, and politics. That is to say, reading as I have suggested will be a self-reflective act that puts the question of ethics before that of epistemology.

Notes

Preface

1. See Jim Vallette, "Larry Summers' War against the Earth," 15 June 1999, *counterpunch*, http://www.counterpunch.org/.

2. Ibid.

3. Ibid.

4. For a rebuttal to this rationale, see Joseph E. Stiglitz, "Terrorism: There's No Futures in It," *Los Angeles Times*, 31 July 2003, B13.

5. *San Francisco Chronicle*, 30 August 2003.

6. "Terrorism Futures Market Plan Canceled," 29 July 2003, Fox News, http://www.foxnews.com/.

7. These events led me to organize a conference on rational choice theory and the humanities, the papers of which are collected in "States of Welfare," ed. Lauren M. E. Goodlad, Bruce Robbins, and Michael Rothberg, special issue of *Occasion* 2 (20 December 2010), which is available online at http://arcade.stanford.edu/. For more on the imagination, war, and terror, see my "Preemption, Perpetual War, and the Future of the Imagination."

Introduction

1. Huntington, "The United States," 76–77.

2. Ibid., 64.

3. Ibid., 112

4. Ibid., 115.

5. Sorensen, "Self-Strengthening Empathy," 75.

6. Wimsatt and Brooks, *Literary Criticism*, 59.

7. Ibid., 25.

8. Ibid., 27.

9. Smith, Theory of Moral Sentiments, 3–4.

10. Ibid., 7.

11. Ibid., 24.

12. Ibid., 23.

13. Ibid., 25.

14. Santayana, *Three Philosophical Poets*, 5. Quoted in Booth, *The Company We Keep*, 257.

15. Eliot, *Impressions of Theophrastus Such*, 276–77.

16. In the next chapter I'll show how Smith's notion of moral sentiment is not conventional in the sense of a simple interest in reproducing norms of sentiment. Smith also considers the imaginative leap outside the actual that can be found after one has sensed commonality.

17. Nussbaum, *Poetic Justice*, 5.

18. Ibid.

19. Booth, *The Company We Keep*, 223.

20. Nussbaum, *Poetic Justice*, 111.

21. Booth, *The Company We Keep*, 70.

22. Ibid., 488.

23. Sennett, *Respect in a World of Inequality*, 52.

24. Ibid., 52–53.

25. Boltanski, *Distant Suffering*, 7.

26. Ibid., 33.

27. Ibid., 24.

28. Ibid., 38.

29. Here he refers to Smith, *Theory of Moral Sentiments* (Oxford: Clarendon, 1982), 31.

30. See Piper, "Impartiality, Compassion, and Modal Imagination."

31. Boltanski, *Distant Suffering*, 50–51.

32. Nancy, *L'intrus*, 14. My translation.

Chapter 1: When Otherness Overcomes Reason

1. Gary Becker, *The Economic Approach to Human Behavior*, 8.

2. Abell, "Sociological Theory and Rational Choice Theory," 252.

3. Elster, "The Nature and Scope of Rational-Choice Explanation," 71.

4. Ibid.

5. Barthes, "The Reality Effect," 142. In the course of his essay Barthes argues for the importance of precisely these digressions, delays, changes of direction, surprises, and incidental details.

6. Hastie and Dawes, *Rational Choice in an Uncertain World*, 91, emphasis added.

7. Ibid., 134.

8. Ibid., 111.

9. Ibid., 112.

10. Ibid., emphasis added.

11. Elster, *Explaining Social Behavior*, 19.

12. Ibid.

13. Elster, *Nuts and Bolts for the Social Sciences*, 7–8.

14. Ibid., 8.

15. Ibid., 64.

16. Becker, *Realism in Modern Literature*, 5.

17. Ibid., 14.

18. Ibid. "This movement was one of the major political interests of romanticism, one that was given theoretical impetus by the French Revolution and practical impact by the repressive subjugation of such groups by Napoleon and later by the settlement at Vienna. The first successful self-assertion occurred during the Spanish colonies in the New World as a result of the Napoleonic wars' weakening of Spain. Even more important was the effective loosening of traditional imperial ties in Europe. Greece became an independent nation in 1827, Belgium in 1830, Serbia in 1843, Montenegro in 1851. Italy and Germany, for centuries congeries of associated feudal states, reached effective national identity in 1860 and 1871 respectively. Hungary achieved a degree of independence within the Austro-Hungarian Empire in 1867, and Norway, after a century-long troubled union with Sweden, became independent in 1905. The principle of self-determination, proclaimed by Woodrow Wilson at Versailles, was both a political and cultural force which had gathered impetus from the abortive revolutions of 1848 and the post-World War I settlement. It has continued to be a major current of this entry also, as succession states to the Russian, Austrian, and Turkish empires have won (and lost) independent existence and as colonial empires in Asia and Africa have been almost completely solved" (ibid., 14–15).

19. Galdós, "Obervaciones sobre la novela contemporánea en España," quoted in Becker, *Documents in Modern Literary Realism*, 13.

20. Galdós, "Contemporary Society in Novelistic Materials," quoted in Becker, *Documents of Modern Literary Realism*, 149.

21. Auerbach, *Mimesis*, 536.

22. Ibid., 549–50.

23. Ibid., 552, emphasis added.

24. Ibid., 552–53.

25. Thomas, *American Literary Realism and the Failed Promise of Contract*, 9.

26. Ibid., 8.

27. Jakobson, "Two Aspects of Language and Two Types of Aphasic Disturbances," 72.

28. "Results of a Conference of Anthropologists and Linguists," *Indiana University Publications in Anthropology and Linguistics* 8 (1953), 15, cited in Jakobson, "Two Aspects of Language and Two Types of Aphasic Disturbances," 82n.

29. See Lodge, *Modes of Modern Writing*.

30. Jakobson, "Two Aspects of Language and Two Types of Aphasic Disturbances," 77.

31. Ibid., 83.

32. Ibid., 82.

33. Schehr, *Figures of Alterity*, 13. I make a similar point in my essay "Universalisms and Minority Culture."

34. Ibid., 16.

35. Ibid., 22.

36. Ibid., 24.

37. I will have more to say about this subject in chapter 4.

38. Davidson, "The Interpersonal Comparison of Values," 73–74.

39. Morris, *Realism*, 147.

40. Shapere, "Evolution and Continuity in Social Change," 422.

41. Habermas, *The Philosophical Discourse of Modernity*, 312.

42. Ibid., 314. This is obvious from the large number of critiques of Habermas from feminists, as well as others.

43. Coetzee, *Elisabeth Costello*, 1. For further references to this novel in this discussion, I indicate only page numbers in the text.

44. See Attridge, *J. M. Coetzee and the Ethics of Reading*, 192–205, for a useful discussion of the role of realism in this novel, as well as for a fascinating account of Coetzee's use of Costello's speeches in his own lecturing.

45. Van Den Braembussche, "Sensus communis," 18. For more on the subject of the imagination and community, see my essay "Preemption, Perpetual War, and the Future of the Imagination."

46. I thank Regenia Gagnier for discussions on the Sublime and Beautiful.

47. See de Man, *Allegories of Reading*.

48. Levinas, "Enigma and Phenomenon," 67.

49. Coetzee, "Voiceless," n.p.

50. Ibid.

51. See Abrams, *The Mirror and the Lamp*. See also the work of Jon Elster and of Paisley Livingston (for example, Livingston's "Intentionalism in Aesthetics") on the idea of authorial choice and intentionality.

52. Coetzee, *Disgrace*, 112. For further references to this novel in this discussion, I indicate only page numbers in the text.

53. And we should recall the name of the organization that published Coetzee's remarks on animal rights: Voiceless.org.

Chapter 2: Whose Story Is It?

1. Gordimer, *My Son's Story*, 108. For further references to this novel in this discussion, I indicate only page numbers in the text.

2. Gordimer, *Selected Stories*, 12.

3. Ibid., 11.

4. Gordimer, *The Essential Gesture*, 276–77.

5. Gordimer, *Selected Stories*, 11–13.

6. Gordimer, *The Essential Gesture*, 134.

7. Ibid., 133–35.

8. Ibid., 265. She goes on to specify, "This vast difference will be evident even if capitalism survives, since South Africa's capitalism, like South Africa's whites-only democracy, has been unlike anyone else's. For example, free enterprise among us is for whites only, since black capitalists may trade only, and with many limitations on their 'free' enterprise, in black ghettos. In cities the kind of stores and services offered will change when the life-style of the majority—black, working-class—establishes the authority of the enfranchised demand in place of the dictated demand. At present the consumer gets what the producer's racially-estimated idea of his place in life decrees to be his needs" (ibid.).

9. Ibid., 138. Here Gordimer is quoting Dora Taylor, *The Role of Missionaries in Conquest*, 26.

10. Gordimer, *The Essential Gesture*, 32.

11. Ibid., 34–35.

12. Cooper-Clarke, "The Clash," 54.

13. A slightly different translation appears in Gramsci, *Selections from the Prison Notebooks of Antonio Gramsci*, 276.

14. Bazin, "An Interview with Nadine Gordimer," 576.

15. Gordimer, *The Essential Gesture*, 265.

16. Bazin, "An Interview with Nadine Gordimer," 576.

Chapter 3: Art: A Foreign Exchange

1. U.S. biotech data from Rose, *The Politics of Life Itself*, 35. Nelkin quoted in Rose, 39. Original is in Andrews and Nelkin, *Body Bazaar*, 5.

2. Rose, *The Politics of Life Itself*, 38.

3. Quoted in Nuland, *Doctors*, 465.

4. Ibid.

5. Winslade and Ross, *Choosing Life or Death*, quoted in Keyes and Wiest, *New Harvest*, 9.

6. Nancy, *L'intrus*, 14, my translation.

7. For this discussion, I cite Nancy's works by title in the text.

8. Again, "It is not a question of an *aliud* or an *alius*, or an *alienus*, or an other in general as the essential stranger who is opposed to what is proper, but of an *alter*, that is, 'one of the two.' The 'other,' this 'lowercase other,' is 'one' insofar as they are many; it is *each one*, and it is *each time* one, one *among* them, one among all and one *among* is all. In the same way, and reciprocally, 'we' is always inevitably 'us all,' where no one of us can be 'all' and each one of us is, in turn

(where all our turns are simultaneous as well as successive, in every sense), the other origin of the same world" (*Being Singular Plural*, 11).

9. I hesitate even to use words like *interstitial*, since in Nancy's lexicon, such terms rely on presumptions that he insists on putting into question, and reformulating, often quite radically. I hope this chapter's focus and particular argument can avoid as much as possible inadvertently creating misimpressions regarding the application of these terms.

10. "Presence itself is dis-position, the spacing of singularities" (*Being Singular Plural*, 14).

11. Consider also: "Our understanding (of the meaning of Being) is an understanding *that* we share understanding between us and, at the same time, *because* we share understanding between us: between us all, simultaneously— all the dead and the living, and all beings" (*Being Singular Plural*, 99).

12. Rose, *The Politics of Life Itself*, 23; Rabinow, *Artificiality and Enlightenment*, 102.

13. Scheper-Hughes, "The Last Commodity," 150.

14. Also: "Economic ties, technological operations, and political fusion (into a *body* or under a *leader*) represent to rather present, expose, and realize this essence necessarily in themselves. Essence is set to work in them; through them, it becomes its own work. This is what we have called 'totalitarianism,' but it might be better named 'immanentism,' as long as we do not restrict the term to designating certain types of societies or regimes but rather to see in it the general horizon of our time, encompassing both democracies and their fragile juridical parapets" (*The Inoperative Community*, 3).

15. Scheper-Hughes, "The Last Commodity," 145–46.

16. Titmuss, *The Gift Relationship*, 314, cited in Scheper-Hughes, "The Last Commodity," 164.

17. In terms of its plot, it is not hard to compare *Never Let Me Go* with Jodi Picoult's novel *My Sister's Keeper* (2004). In it, a young girl, Anna, brings a lawsuit to gain "medical emancipation" from her parents, who conceived her in order that she might donate tissue and organ to her older sister, Sara, who is dying of leukemia. The first line of the novel is Anna's: "When I was little, the great mystery to me wasn't *how* babies were made, but *why*" (7). As she grows, she becomes more and more troubled by the constant demands placed on her to give more of herself, emotionally and physically, to her sister: "If my parents were going to go to all that trouble, you'd think they'd have made sure to implant the genes for obedience, humility, and gratitude" (220).

Anna eventually wins her case, but is soon after fatally injured in an auto accident. Her "emancipation" revoked, her parents make the decision to remove her life support, and she, unwillingly and unwittingly, ends up donating the life-saving kidney to her sister. While Picoult's "delivery systems" include biomedicine and the legal system, what finally closes the case is cosmic karma. For Ishiguro, it is a collective historical fate that creates that slot of possibilities, and, most important, art, which fails to redeem as it should.

18. Ishiguro, *Conversations with Kazuo Ishiguro*, 202.

19. Ibid., 214.

20. Ibid.

21. Ibid., 197.

22. Ibid.

23. Ibid., 199.

24. Ibid., 215.

25. Ibid. In this regard, see Robbins, "Cruelty Is Bad."

26. Ishiguro, *Conversations with Kazuo Ishiguro*, 215.

27. Ibid., 213.

28. Ibid., 20.

29. Ishiguro, *Never Let Me Go*, 254. For further references to this text in this discussion, I indicate only page numbers in the text.

30. Scheper-Hughes, "The Last Commodity," 147.

31. Ibid., 148.

32. Rose, *The Politics of Life Itself*, 39.

33. Scheper-Hughes, "The Last Commodity," 150.

34. Ibid., 146.

35. Rose, *The Politics of Life Itself*, 32. See Waldby, *The Visible Human Project*. See also Waldby and Mitchell, *Tissue Economies*.

Chapter 4: Pacific Oceanic Feeling

1. Freud, *Civilization and Its Discontents*, 1, emphasis added.

2. Ibid., 11.

3. Cited in Green, *The Fabric of Affect in the Psychoanalytic Discourse*, 31.

4. Ibid.

5. Brennan, *The Transmission of Affect*, 1, emphasis added.

6. Ibid., 13.

7. Eagleton, *Trouble with Strangers*, 2.

8. Ibid., 18, citing Henry Brooke, *The Fool of Quality* (London, 1765), 1:41, emphasis added.

9. Gallagher, *The Body Economic*, 35.

10. Ibid.

11. Ibid., 50.

12. See Hirschman, *The Passions and the Interests*.

13. Spinoza, *Ethics*, 137.

14. Ibid., 120.

15. Ibid., 142.

16. Ibid., 163.

17. Ibid., 156.

18. Rorty, "From Passions to Emotions and Sentiments," 159.

19. Ibid., 160.

20. Ibid., 165.

21. Hume, *Treatise on Human Nature*, 655.

22. Eagleton, *Trouble with Strangers*, 47.

23. Pinch, *Strange Fits of Passion*, 19

24. See Eagleton, *Trouble with Strangers*, for a good discussion of this double-edged quality.

25. In Sedgwick and Frank, *Shame and Its Sisters*, 47.

26. Brennan, *The Transmission of Affect*, 111.

27. Ibid.

28. Ibid.

29. Ibid., 112.

30. Ibid., 15.

31. All quotations from film come from its working script, unpaginated, made available to me by Ozeki and Zurkow.

32. Ozeki, *My Year of Meats*, 9. For further references to this text in this discussion, I indicate only page numbers in the text.

33. Goodyear, "The Future Development of International Research," cited in Mattelart, *Advertising International*, 63.

34. See Fields, Hotaka, Wind, and Gunther, *Leveraging Japan*.

35. Mattelart, *Advertising International*, ix.

36. For two very interesting pieces on affect, race, and consumerism, see "Affect-Identity" and "Commodity, Race and Emotion," both by Jeffrey Santa Ana. In the former Santa Ana treats Ozeki's novel and specifically the issue of race and postmodernism.

37. In Mattelart, *Advertising International*, 53.

38. Ibid.

39. Ibid., 66, citing an unpublished paper by F. Rello et al., "La industria agroalimentaria" (Mexico: 1980).

40. Ibid.

41. For an excellent study of the "green revolution" in Mexico, see Cotter, *Troubled Harvest*.

42. Mattelart, *Advertising International*, 131.

43. Ibid., 130.

44. Ibid., 65.

45. "DES History," Centers for Disease Control and Prevention, http://www.cdc.gov/des/consumers/about/history.html/.

46. "A Conversation with Ruth Ozeki," appendix to *My Year of Meats*, 8.

47. Brennan, *The Transmission of Affect*, 70.

48. One of the few realms in which affect and mimicry do not lead to consumerism is in the realm of sexuality and pleasure. Here is Akiko looking at a soft-porn magazine: "The girl stared boldly at her. Akiko stared back, moving her finger around a little. She liked looking at the pictures. Even though they weren't so authentic, she found them sexy—but she was not sure whether she wanted to make love to the girl or simply to be her" (188).

49. Mattelart, *Advertising International*, 135.

50. In "A Conversation with Ruth Ozeki," appendix to *My Year of Meats*, 13.

51. Pinch, *Strange Fits of Passion*, 166, emphasis added.

52. In front matter of Ozeki, *My Year of Meats*.

Conclusion

1. Ricoeur, *Fallible Man*, 105, emphasis added.

2. Ibid., 112.

3. Ibid., 112–13.

4. Ibid., 118.

5. Ibid., 123–24, emphasis added.

6. Poster, "Global Media and Culture," 685–86.

7. McGann, "Literature, Meaning, and the Discontinuity of Fact," 47.

8. Elias, "Interactive Cosmopolitanism and Collaborative Technologies," 710.

9. Ibid., 713.

10. Ibid., 712.

11. Poster, "Cyberdemocracy," 267.

12. Elias, "Interactive Cosmopolitanism and Collaborative Technologies," 714, quoting Boyd and Ellison, "Social Network Sites," 211.

13. See Benjamin, "The Author as Producer."

14. As Alan Liu puts it, "The vital task for literary study in the age of advanced creative destruction, I believe, is to inquire into the aesthetic value— let us simply call it the literary—once managed by 'creative' literature but now busily seeking new management amid the ceaseless creation and recreation of the forms, styles, media, and institutions of postindustrial knowledge work" ("The Future Literary," 63).

15. Mattelart, *Advertising International*, 130.

16. Shteyngart, *Super Sad True Love Story*, 144. For further references to this text in this discussion, I indicate only page numbers in the text.

Bibliography

Abell, Peter. "Sociological Theory and Rational Choice Theory." *Social Theory*, ed. Bryan Turner, 252–77. Oxford: Blackwell, 1996.

Abrams, M. H. *The Mirror and the Lamp: Romantic Theory and the Critical Tradition.* New York: Oxford University Press, 1953.

Andrews, Lori B., and Dorothy Nelkin. *Body Bazaar: The Market for Human Tissue in a Biotechnology Age.* New York: Crown, 2001.

Aristotle. *The Rhetoric and the Poetics.* Translated by Rhys Roberts. New York: Modern Library, 1954.

Armstrong, Isobel. *The Radical Aesthetic.* Oxford: Blackwell, 2000.

Attridge, Derek. *J. M. Coetzee and the Ethics of Reading: Literature in the Event.* 1st edn. Chicago: University of Chicago Press, 2005.

Auerbach, Erich. *Mimesis: The Representation of Reality in Western Literature.* 50th anniversary edn. Princeton: Princeton University Press, 2003.

Barthes, Roland. "The Reality Effect." *The Rustle of Language*, 141–48. Translated by Richard Howard. Oxford: Blackwell, 1986.

Bazin, Nancy. "An Interview with Nadine Gordimer." *Contemporary Literature* 34.4 (winter 1995): 571–87.

Becker, Gary. *The Economic Approach to Human Behavior.* Chicago: University of Chicago Press, 1976.

Becker, George Joseph. *Documents in Modern Literary Realism.* Princeton: Princeton University Press, 1963.

——. *Realism in Modern Literature.* New York: Ungar, 1980.

Benjamin, Walter. "The Author as Producer." *Reflections: Essays, Aphorisms, Autobiographical Writings*, 220–38. Edited by Peter Demetz. New York: Schocken, 1987.

Boltanski, Luc. *Distant Suffering: Morality, Media and Politics.* Cambridge: Cambridge University Press, 1999.

Booth, Wayne C. *The Company We Keep: An Ethics of Fiction.* Berkeley: University of California Press, 1989.

Boyd, Danah M., and Nicole B. Ellison. "Social Network Sites: Definition, History, and Scholarship." *Journal of Computer-Mediated Communication* 13.1 (2007): Article 11.

Brecht, Bertolt. "On the Formalistic Character of the Theory of Realism." *Aesthetics and Politics*, ed. Ernst Bloch, 70–76. London: Verso, 1977.

Brennan, Teresa. *The Transmission of Affect*. Ithaca: Cornell University Press, 2004.

Cadet, Jean-Robert. *Restavec: From Haitian Slave Child to Middle Class American*. Austin: University of Texas Press, 1998.

Coetzee, J. M. *Disgrace*. New York: Viking, 1999.

——. *Elizabeth Costello*. 2nd edn. New York: Viking, 2003.

——. "Voiceless: I Feel Therefore I Am," 22 February 2007, http://www.voiceless.org.au/.

Cohen, Margaret, and Christopher Prendergast. *Spectacles of Realism: Body, Gender, Genre*. Minneapolis: University of Minnesota Press, 1995.

Cooper-Clarke, Diana. "The Clash: An Interview with Nadine Gordimer." *London Magazine*, February 1983, 45–59.

Cotter, Joseph. *Troubled Harvest: Agronomy and Revolution in Mexico, 1880–2003*. Westport, Conn.: Praeger, 2003.

Davidson, Donald. "The Interpersonal Comparison of Values." *Problems of Rationality*, 59–74. New York: Oxford University Press, 2004.

Davis, Todd F., ed. *Mapping the Ethical Turn: A Reader in Ethics, Culture, and Literary Theory*. Charlottesville: University of Virginia Press, 2001.

de Man, Paul. *Allegories of Reading*. New Haven: Yale University Press, 1979.

Eagleton, Terry. *Trouble with Strangers: A Study of Ethics*. London: Wiley-Blackwell, 2008.

Elias, Amy J. "Interactive Cosmopolitanism and Collaborative Technologies: New Foundations for Global Literary History." *New Literary History* 39.3 (summer 2008): 705–25.

Eliot, George. *Impressions of Theophrastus Such: Miscellaneous Essays*. Rosehill limited edn. Boston: Estes and Lauriat, 1894.

Elster, Jon. *Explaining Social Behavior: More Nuts and Bolts for the Social Sciences*, Cambridge: Cambridge University Press, 2007.

——. "The Nature and Scope of Rational-Choice Explanation." *Perspectives on the Philosophy of Donald Davidson*, ed. Ernest LePore and Brian McLaughlin, 60–72. Oxford: Blackwell, 1985.

——. *Nuts and Bolts for the Social Sciences*. Cambridge: Cambridge University Press, 1989.

Fields, George, Hotaka Katahira, Jerry Wind, and Robert E. Gunther. *Leveraging Japan: Marketing to the New Asia*. Hoboken, N.J.: Jossey-Bass, 1999.

Fluck, Winfried. "Fiction and Justice." *New Literary History* 34 (2003): 19–42.

Freud, Sigmund. *Civilization and Its Discontents (Standard Edition)*. New York: W. W. Norton, 1989.

Friedman, Thomas. *The World Is Flat 3.0*. New York: Picador, 2007.

Galdós, Benito Pérez. "Contemporary Society in Novelistic Material." *Discursos leídos ante la real academia en la recepión pública del Sr. D. Benito Pérez Galdós*, 5–16. Madrid: Est. Tip. De la Viuda é Hijos de Tello, 1897.

——. "Observaciones sobre la novela contemporánea en España." *Discursos leídos ante la real academia en la recepión pública del Sr. D. Benito Pérez Galdós,* 115–32. Madrid: Est. Tip. De la Viuda é Hijos de Tello 1897. Translated in George Joseph Becker, *Realism in Modern Literature.* New York: Ungar, 1980.

Gallagher, Catherine. *The Body Economic: Life, Death, and Sensation in Political Economy and the Victorian Novel.* Princeton: Princeton University Press, 2008.

Goodyear, J. R. "The Future Development of International Research: The Multilingual, Multinational, Multivariable." European Society for Opinion and Marketing Research seminar on international marketing research, Englefield Green, U.K., 16–18 November 1988.

Gordimer, Nadine. *Conversations with Nadine Gordimer.* Jackson: University of Mississippi Press, 1990.

——. *The Essential Gesture: Writing, Politics and Places.* New York: Knopf, 1988.

——. *My Son's Story.* New York: Penguin, 1991.

——. *Selected Stories.* New York: Viking, 1976.

Gramsci, Antonio. *Selections from the Prison Notebooks of Antonio Gramsci.* Edited and translated by Quintin Hoare and Geoffrey Nowell Smith. London: Lawrence and Wishart, 1971.

Green, Andre. *The Fabric of Affect in the Psychoanalytic Discourse.* 1st edn. New York: Routledge, 1999.

Habermas, Jürgen. *The Philosophical Discourse of Modernity.* Translated by Fredrick Lawrence. Cambridge: Massachusetts Institute of Technology Press, 1987.

Hastie, Reid, and Robyn M. Dawes. *Rational Choice in an Uncertain World: The Psychology of Judgment and Decision Making.* 2nd edn. Los Angeles: Sage, 2010.

Hirschman, Albert O. *The Passions and the Interests.* 20th anniversary edn. Princeton: Princeton University Press, 1997.

Hume, David. *Treatise on Human Nature.* London: Penguin, 1969.

Huntington, Samuel. "The United States." *The Crisis of Democracy: Report on the Governability of Democracies to the Trilateral Commission,* ed. Michel Crozier, Samuel Huntington, and Joji Watanuki, 59–118. New York: New York University Press, 1975.

Husserl, Edmund. *Cartesian Meditations: An Introduction to Phenomenology.* The Hague: M. Nijhoff, 1960.

International Commission for the Study of Communication Problems. *Many Voices, One World: Communication and Society, Today and Tomorrow: Towards a New, More Just and More Efficient World Information and Communication Order.* London: K. Page / Unipub, 1980.

Ishiguro, Kazuo. *Conversations with Kazuo Ishiguro.* Edited by Brian W. Shaffer and Cynthia F. Wong. 1st edn. Jackson: University Press of Mississippi, 2008.

——. *Never Let Me Go.* New York: Vintage, 2006.

Jakobson, Roman. "Two Aspects of Language and Two Types of Aphasic

Disturbances." Part 2 of *Fundamentals of Language,* by Roman Jakobson and Morris Halle, 2nd edn., 67–96. The Hague: Mouton, 1971.

Jakobson, Roman, and Morris Halle. *Fundamentals of Language.* 2nd edn. The Hague: Mouton, 1971.

Kant, Immanuel. *The Critique of Judgment.* Translated by James Creed Meredith. Oxford: Oxford University Press, 1978.

Keyes, C. Don, and Walter E. Wiest. *New Harvest: Transplanting Body Parts and Reaping the Benefits.* Clifton, N.J.: Humana Press, 1991.

Levinas, Emmanuel. "Enigma and Phenomenon." *Basic Philosophical Writings,* ed. Adriaan T. Peperzak, Simon Critchley, and Robert Bernasconi, 65–78. Bloomington: Indiana University Press, 1996.

Levitt, Theodore. "The Globalization of Markets." *Harvard Business Review* (June 1983): 92–102.

Liu, Alan. "The Future Literary: Literature and the Culture of Information." *Time and the Literary,* ed. Karen Newman, Jay Clayton, and Marianne Hirsch, 61–100. New York: Routledge, 2002.

Livingston, Paisley. "Intentionalism in Aesthetics." *New Literary History* 29.4 (1989): 831–46.

Lodge, David. *Modes of Modern Writing.* Ithaca: Cornell University Press, 1977.

Massumi, Brian. *Parables for the Virtual: Movement, Affect, Sensation.* Durham: Duke University Press, 2002.

Mattelart, Armand. *Advertising International: The Privatization of Public Space.* Revised edn. New York: Routledge, 1991.

McGann, Jerome. "Literature, Meaning, and the Discontinuity of Fact." *The Uses of Literary History,* ed. Marshall Brown, 45–51. Durham: Duke University Press, 1995.

Miller, J. Hillis. *Others.* Princeton: Princeton University Press, 2001.

Morris, Pam. *Realism.* London: Routledge, 2003.

Nancy, Jean-Luc. *Being Singular Plural.* Stanford: Stanford University Press, 2000.

——. *The Birth to Presence.* Stanford: Stanford University Press, 1993.

——. *Être Singulier Pluriel.* Paris: Editions Galilée, 1996.

——. *The Inoperative Community.* Minnesota: University of Minnesota Press, 1991.

——. *L'intrus.* Paris: Editions Galilée, 2000.

Nuland, Sherwin B. *Doctors: The Biography of Medicine.* 1st edn. New York: Knopf, 1988.

Nussbaum, Martha C. *Cultivating Humanity: A Classical Defense of Reform in Liberal Education.* Cambridge: Harvard University Press, 1998.

——. "Exactly and Responsibly: A Defense of Ethical Criticism." *Mapping the Ethical Turn: A Reader in Ethics, Culture, and Literary Theory,* ed. Todd F. Davis, 59–82. Charlottesville: University of Virginia Press, 2001.

——. *Poetic Justice: The Literary Imagination and Public Life.* Boston: Beacon, 1997.

Ōmae, Kenichi. *Triad Power: The Coming Shape of Global Competition.* New York: Free Press, 1985.

Ong, Aihwa, and Stephen J. Collier, eds. *Global Assemblages: Technology, Politics, and Ethics as Anthropological Problems.* Malden, Mass.: Wiley-Blackwell, 2005.

Ozeki, Ruth. *My Year of Meats.* New York: Penguin, 1998.

Ozeki, Ruth, and Marina Zurkow, writers and directors. *Body of Correspondence.* 1994.

——. Working script of *Body of Correspondence,* n.d.

Packard, Vance. *The Hidden Persuaders.* Boston: Ig Publishing, 2007.

Palumbo-Liu, David. "Preemption, Perpetual War, and the Future of the Imagination." *boundary 2* 33.1 (spring 2006): 151–70.

——. "Universalisms and Minority Culture." *differences* 7.1 (1995): 188–208.

Picoult, Jodi. *My Sister's Keeper.* New York: Washington Square Books, 2005.

Pinch, Adela. *Strange Fits of Passion: Epistemologies of Emotion, Hume to Austen.* 1st edn. Stanford: Stanford University Press, 1999.

Piper, Adrian. "Impartiality, Compassion, and Modal Imagination." *Ethics* 101 (July 1991): 726–57.

Poster, Mark. "Cyberdemocracy: The Internet and the Public Sphere." *Reading Digital Culture,* ed. David Trend, 259–69. Malden: Blackwell, 2001.

——. "Global Media and Culture." *New Literary History* 39.3 (summer 2008): 685–703.

Prendergast, Christopher. "Realism, 'God's Secret,' and the Body." *Spectacles of Realism: Body, Gender, Genre,* ed. Margaret Cohen and Christopher Prendergast, 1–10. Minneapolis: University of Minnesota Press, 1995.

Rabinow, Paul. *Artificiality and Enlightenment: From Sociobiology to Biosociality: Essays on the Anthropology of Reason.* Princeton: Princeton University Press, 1996.

Ricoeur, Paul. *Fallible Man.* Rev. edn. New York: Fordham University Press, 1986.

——. *Oneself as Another.* Chicago: University of Chicago Press, 1995.

Robbins, Bruce. "Cruelty Is Bad: Banality and Proximity in *Never Let Me Go.*" *Novel* 40.3 (summer 2007): 289–302.

Rorty, Amelie Oskenberg. "From Passions to Emotions and Sentiments." *Philosophy* 57.222 (April 1982): 159–72.

Rose, Nikolas. *The Politics of Life Itself: Biomedicine, Power, and Subjectivity in the Twenty-First Century.* Annotated edn. Princeton: Princeton University Press, 2006.

Rothschild, Emma. *Economic Sentiments: Adam Smith, Condorcet, and the Enlightenment.* Cambridge: Harvard University Press, 2001.

Santa Ana, Jeffrey. "Affect-Identity: The Emotions of Assimilation, Multiraciality, and Asian-American Subjectivity." *Asian North American Identities: Beyond the Hyphen,* ed. Eleanor Ty and Donald Goellnicht, 15–42. Bloomington: Indiana University Press, 2004.

———. "Commodity, Race and Emotion: The Commercialization of Human Feeling in Corporate Consumerism." *Studies in Symbolic Interaction* 33 (2009): 109–28.

Santayana, Georges. *Three Philosophical Poets*. New York: Doubleday, 1938.

Schehr, Lawrence R. *Figures of Alterity: French Realism and Its Others*. Stanford: Stanford University Press, 2003.

Scheper-Hughes, Nancy. "The Last Commodity: Post-Human Ethics and the Global Traffic in 'Fresh' Organs." *Global Assemblages: Technology, Politics, and Ethics as Anthropological Problems*, ed. Aihwa Ong and Stephen J. Collier, 145–68. Malden, Mass.: Wiley-Blackwell, 2005.

Schor, Naomi. *Reading in Detail: Aesthetics and the Feminine*. New York: Methuen, 1987.

Schutz, Alfred. *Collected Papers*. 4th edn. The Hague: M. Nijhoff, 1973.

Sedgwick, Eve Kosofsky, and Adam Frank. "Shame in the Cybernetic Fold: Reading Silvan Tomkins." *Shame and Its Sisters: A Silvan Tomkins Reader*, ed. Eve Kosofsky Sedgwick and Adam Frank, 1–28. Durham: Duke University Press, 1995.

———, eds. *Shame and Its Sisters: A Silvan Tomkins Reader*. Durham: Duke University Press, 1995.

Sennett, Richard. *Respect in a World of Inequality*. New York: W. W. Norton, 2004.

Shapere, Dudley. "Evolution and Continuity in Social Change." *Philosophy of Science* 56.3 (September 1989): 419–37.

Shteyngart, Gary. *Super Sad True Love Story: A Novel*. 1st edn. New York: Random House, 2010.

Smith, Adam. 1759. *Theory of Moral Sentiments*. Amherst, N.Y.: Prometheus, 2000.

Sorensen, Ray. "Self-Strengthening Empathy." *Philosophy and Phenomenological Research* 58.1 (1998): 75–98.

Spinoza, Benedict de. *Ethics*. New York: Penguin Classics, 2005.

Taylor, Dora (pseudo. Majeke). *The Role of Missionaries in Conquest*. Johannesburg: Society of Young Africa, 1952.

Thomas, Brook. *American Literary Realism and the Failed Promise of Contract*. Berkeley: University of California Press, 1997.

Titmuss, Richard Morris. *The Gift Relationship: From Human Blood to Social Policy*. 1st edn. New York: Pantheon, 1970.

Tomkins, Silvan S. "Affect and Cognition: 'Reasons' as Coincidental Causes of Affect Evocation." In Silvan S. Tomkins, *Affect Imagery Consciousness: The Complete Edition*. New York: Springer, 2008, 639–63.

Ty, Eleanor, and Donald Goellnicht, eds. *Asian North American Identities: Beyond the Hyphen*. Bloomington: Indiana University Press, 2004.

Van Den Braembussche, Antoon. "Sensus communis: Clarifications of a Kantian Concept on the Way to an Intercultural Dialogue between Western and

Indian Thought." *Sensus communis in a Multi- and Intercultural Perspective,* ed. Heinz Kimmerle and Herk Oosterling, 17–30. Wurzberg: Verlag Königshausen and Neumann, 2000.

Waldby, Cathy. *The Visible Human Project: Informatic Bodies and Posthuman Medicine.* London: Routledge, 2000.

Waldby, Catherine, and Robert Mitchell, eds. *Tissue Economies: Blood, Organs, and Cell Lines in Late Capitalism.* Durham: Duke University Press, 2006.

Watt, Ian P. *The Rise of the Novel: Studies in Defoe, Richardson, and Fielding.* 1st edn. Berkeley: University of California Press, 1957.

West, Paul. *The Very Rich Hours of Count von Stauffenberg.* Woodstock, N.Y.: Overlook Press, 1991.

Wimsatt, William K., and Cleanth Brooks. *Literary Criticism: A Short History.* 1st edn. New York: Knopf, 1957.

Winslade, William J., and Judith Wilson Ross. *Choosing Life or Death: A Guide for Patients, Families, and Professionals.* New York: Macmillan, 1986.

Index

David Palumbo-Liu is professor of Comparative Literature and, by courtesy, English at Stanford University. He is the author of *Asian/American: Historical Crossings of a Racial Frontier* (1999) and the editor, with Bruce Robbins and Nirvana Tanoukhi, of *Immanuel Wallerstein and the Problem of the World* (2011).